WINNIPEG
WITHDRAWN
MAR 2009
LIBRARY

D1246724

THE GREATEST MANITOBANS

MANITOBANS

THEY MADE A BETTER PROVINCE AND A BETTER WORLD

Winnipeg Free Press

THE GREATEST MANITOBANS
THEY MADE A BETTER PROVINCE AND A BETTER WORLD

(c) Copyright 2008 Winnipeg Free Press
All rights reserved

ISBN 978-0-9682575-4-8
Printed in Canada

LIBRARY AND ARCHIVES CANADA CATALOGUING IN PUBLICATION

Main entry under title:
THE GREATEST MANITOBANS

Includes bibliographical references
ISBN 978-0-9682575-4-8
1. Manitoba — Biography
2. Successful people — Manitoba — Biography

FC3355.G74 2008   971.27009'9   C2008-906245-0

WRITTEN BY

Buzz Currie, Gerald Flood, Gabrielle Giroday, Margo Goodhand, Darren Gudmundson, Meghan Hurley, Geoff Kirbyson, Bartley Kives, Larry Kusch, Dan Lett, Nick Martin, Alison Mayes, Bruce Owen, Alexandra Paul, Mia Rabson, Bill Redekop, Lindor Reynolds, Kevin Rollason, Paul Samyn, Carol Sanders, Jen Skerritt, Doug Speirs, Morley Walker, Mary Agnes Welch, Lindsey Wiebe, Paul Wiecek, Paul Williamson

EDITED BY

Shane Minkin, Andrew Maxwell, Jeff Slusky, Chris Smith, Jill Wilson

PROJECT EDITOR: Julie Carl
ART DIRECTOR / PRODUCTION: Gordon Preece
PHOTO EDITOR: Jon Thordarson
ASSISTANT PHOTO EDITOR: Alexandra Paul

ACKNOWLEDGMENT

Free Press writer Paul Wiecek first approached us in the spring of 2008 with a big and bold idea: Throw a provincewide contest to find The Greatest Manitoban, and produce a book on all the chosen finalists. It didn't take long to talk us into it.

The contest itself might have been controversial — after all, who wants to even try comparing Terry Fox to Margaret Laurence? — but the ends clearly justified the means.

We knew the public debate itself would be fascinating. What is greatness, and how does one region claim a celebrity? Is a moment of international renown the same as a lifetime of enduring worth? Are an athlete's achievements on par with a doctor's or a nuclear scientist's?

Even more irresistible was the thought that we could resurrect some of this province's heroes for our readers. Few today recall J.S. Woodsworth's legacy or can quote Nellie McClung, the bestselling novelist of her day. But these people left a legacy in Manitoba that should never be forgotten.

Deputy editor Julie Carl co-ordinated the contest in paper and online, working with CBC Manitoba to get the great debate rolling. Wiecek wrote his heart out for weeks. And as the list of finalists began to coalesce, we breathed a sigh of relief that our readers are highly intelligent, discerning and passionate, and their choices were well worth chronicling.

With the finalists' names in hand, Carl started recruiting *Free Press* writers to write their stories. And the newsroom was full of 'did you knows?' for weeks. Every one of us who claimed a character in this book came away with a new-found respect for their extraordinary lives and achievements and a new understanding of our province and its history.

The Greatest Manitobans represents hours of spirited and thoughtful debate in this province. I'd like to thank all the people who participated, from the readers to the writers.

Most of all, thanks to Paul Wiecek, photo editor Jon Thordarson, assistant photo editor Alexandra Paul, art director Gordon Preece, and deputy editor Julie Carl for putting it all together so beautifully.

I hope you enjoy this book as much as we enjoyed producing it.

MARGO GOODHAND
Editor
Winnipeg Free Press

INTRODUCTION

They're the greatest

BY PAUL WIECEK

THEY come to us from every profession, every walk of life and every epoch of Manitoba's proud history.

There are doctors, such as Alan Ronald and John Bowman, scientists, whose research is credited with saving the lives of hundreds of thousands of people around the world. And there are community activists such as Harry Lehotsky and Anne Ross, whose grassroots work in Winnipeg's inner city has saved many lives, too.

There are writers, such as Carol Shields and Marshall McLuhan, their work recognized around the world for its prescience and clarity of vision. And there are pioneers, such as Tom Lamb and Chief Peguis, their names and works known more locally but their impact felt profoundly just the same.

There are historical figures, such as Nellie McClung and J.S. Woodsworth, who made contributions in the political realm of such a profound nature that they continue to positively affect the daily lives of every single Canadian almost a century later. And there are contemporary figures, such as Lloyd Axworthy and Leo Mol, whose full measure cannot yet be taken because their contributions to our society continue to unfold today.

They are a disparate group, this remarkable group of 30 men and women who come to you in the pages of this book. But they are united by one common feature: They are all Great Manitobans.

IN the summer of 2008, the *Winnipeg Free Press* invited readers to participate in what ultimately proved to be a four-month search for the Greatest Manitoban.

The response was overwhelming. Thousands took part in a nominating process that identified more than 370 Manitobans worthy of consideration. Tens of thousands voted. And hundreds of thousands followed the drama along in the pages of the *Free Press*, on the paper's website and on CBC radio and television as a province attempted to identify the one individual who was its greatest citizen ever.

The question readers were asked was twofold: What is greatness? And what is a Manitoban?

The answers that ultimately emerged provided interesting insights into what the people of the province value in others and, most importantly, in themselves.

There was a sweeping rejection by voters, for instance, of the modern-day notion that fame equals greatness. While many Manitoba actors, musicians and athletes were nominated, voters almost universally turned up their noses. In the end, just two from that group received enough votes to make this final cut — and what a twosome they are: iconic '70s rock group, The Guess Who; and Canada's greatest Olympian, speed skater Cindy Klassen.

In place of celebrities, readers voted en masse for Manitobans who'd made a substantial contribution to the social, cultural and political fabric of the province, the nation and the world — politicians such as Ed Schreyer and Stanley Knowles, horticulturalist Frank Skinner, war hero Tommy Prince, scientist Louis Slotin and British spymaster — and James Bond inspiration — Sir William Stephenson.

The voters were decidedly less fussy about the actual Manitoba roots of our Greatest Manitobans. Marathon of Hope runner Terry Fox, for instance, left Manitoba as a toddler and yet still claimed 12th spot, two spots above Tommy Douglas, who's much better-known as a premier of Saskatchewan and the father of medicare than he is for having been schooled in Manitoba.

The readers were also equal-opportunity voters. Despite being under-represented among the nominees, voters selected three women in the top 10 — Klassen, McClung and Ross. In a nod to the rich contribution of First Nations to the province, four of the Top 30 are aboriginals — Prince, Peguis, Phil Fontaine and Elijah Harper — while a fifth, Louis Riel, is Métis. And, fittingly for a province that is such a vibrant multicultural tapestry, a huge get-out-the-vote effort by Winnipeg's Sikh community helped choose a visible minority in cardiovascular researcher, Dr. Naranjan Dhalla, as the second-greatest Manitoban of all time.

The honour of Greatest Manitoban, however, was reserved — fittingly enough — for a man who was once much maligned for the very same achievement for which he is now celebrated as our greatest citizen ever. Former Manitoba premier Duff Roblin was mocked when he suggested the province build a massive floodway to divert the Red River around Winnipeg and avert a repeat of the disastrous flooding that devastated the Manitoba capital in 1950.

But 50 years later, Duff's Ditch is celebrated as the saviour of Winnipeg and its originator as a man ahead of his time. Midway through the voting for the Greatest Manitoban, as Roblin engaged in a seesaw battle for top spot with the likes of Louis Riel and Chief Peguis, came the announcement that the floodway had been named by the prestigious International Association of Macro Engineering Societies as one of the 16 greatest engineering marvels of all-time, right alongside such feats as Holland's dikes and China's Three Gorges Dam.

Roblin never looked back in the voting after that and the once-embattled premier seems a perfectly fitting first choice for a self-deprecating province that has always been loath to celebrate the disproportionate number of accomplishments our citizens have made in the world at large.

THIS project, from its inception to its conclusion in this book, was first, last and always about the people of Manitoba. Perhaps more than any other endeavour the *Free Press* has undertaken in the nearly 140 years it has brought the daily news to Manitobans, this project gave voice to the people of the province. Through our Internet portal, ordinary Manitobans nominated their extraordinary fellow citizens, debated their merits and then selected the ones they felt were greatest of all. This is as it should have been — the great people of this great province deciding who were our greatest citizens ever.

It was not, to be sure, an easy choice. The extraordinary history of accomplishment by the citizens of this province — in everything from the arts to the sciences to politics to athletics — is vastly disproportionate to our relatively small numbers and flies in the face of our geographically remote location and hostile climate.

Or, perhaps, we are precisely this way because of those things. Perhaps, it is exactly because we do exist, against all odds, in the middle of the windswept Canadian prairie, locked in ice for six months of the year, that our citizenry has always been so unusually driven to make a mark in the world.

We punch above our weight class, we Manitobans. Always have. Still do.

And this remarkable collection of our most extraordinary citizens — assembled by our most ordinary ones — proves it.

CONTENTS

THE GREATEST MANITOBANS

THEY MADE A BETTER PROVINCE AND A BETTER WORLD

BY BUZZ CURRIE

The genesis of greatness

BY BUZZ CURRIE

WHEN the 19th century dawned, there was a curious silence in the heart of what was to become Manitoba. Between the woodlands of the north and the hills far to the south, there was scarcely a human being. The great and fertile Red River Valley was vacant for most of its length, as were the lower reaches of the Assiniboine.

It hadn't always been that way, of course. When the great glacier began receding 10,000 years ago, there were people stepping northward on the cold, damp ground. As the year 1800 approached, many of their descendants still inhabited Manitoba-to-be. In the north woods, where the moose roamed, the Cree people lived, undisturbed except for occasional contact with Hudson's Bay Co. traders at the bay. Even farther north, in caribou country, lived the Dene people. To the south, the Dakota people occupied the Pembina Hills.

But something terrible had happened in the heart of what would become, in the century ahead, Manitoba.

Father Campeau at aboriginal camp near Swan Lake in 1890.

19TH-CENTURY SETTLERS

SCOTS: Selkirk Settlers arrived in 1812, established the Kildonans.

MENNONITES: Refugees from Russia, they arrived in 1874 and settled up the Red from Winnipeg.

FRENCH-CANADIANS: Arrived in 1875 from Quebec and Vermont, settling in and near towns along the Red.

ICELANDERS: Arrived in 1875 and created New Iceland north of the 'postage-stamp' province of Manitoba.

UKRAINIANS: Arrived in 1890, settling north and west, seeking areas with plenty of wood.

POLES: Arrived in 1890. Like the Ukrainians, were denied choice of homesteads and consequently had poor access to rail.

WINNIPEG FREE PRESS ARCHIVES

Furs, including beaver, wolf, fox and muskrat pelts, hang in the warehouse of the Old Stone Fort, at the Lower Fort Garry national historic site.

French fur traders had reached the plains in the 1730s. Unlike the Hudson Bay English, who preferred to wait at their York Factory seaport for the Cree to bring in the furs, the French built far-flung outposts. For the first time, Europeans and aboriginals were in close quarters. Inevitably, that meant smallpox.

Smallpox, we now know, arose once humans began herding livestock. Europeans, with hundreds of years of farming in their heritage, had developed a resistance to it. To them, it was a frightening killer.

But to aboriginals, it was devastation.

Sometime late in the 18th century, smallpox struck the valleys of the Red and Assiniboine rivers. These lands were inhabited by the Assiniboine tribe, relatives of the Dakota people to the south who had broken away. Smallpox destroyed them.

About the same time in Europe, France and England ended the Seven Years' War, one of the succession of clashes between the two countries that dominated the century. France ceded its North American holdings to England and the French pulled out of their western posts. The forts crumbled and the bison roamed undisturbed.

But not for long.

First came the Anicinabe, also called the Ojibwa or Chippewa or Saulteaux, paddling westward from their land north of what is now Sault Ste. Marie. There were about 65 men in the party that paddled into Lake Winnipeg in about 1790, so we can estimate a band of perhaps 200 men, women and children. At their head was a young man in his 20s, named Peguis.

Peguis and his people paddled down the east and south shore of the big lake, past Victoria and Grand beaches, and on to the mouth of the Red River. There they found the last of the Assiniboine people, still alive but in the death agonies of smallpox. Peguis's band moved a little way up the river from the Netley marsh and made their home at Sugar Point.

Nor was the Montreal fur trade long to lie dormant. The Scots who re-organized the trade, forming the North West Co., established their main depot at the west end of Lake Superior. There, furs were brought by canoe from the northwest and loaded into bigger Great Lakes canoes for the trip to Montreal and on to Europe by ship. Almost immediately, the half-French, half-Ojibwa coureurs de bois who lived along the network of waterways began to congregate at Red River. They would power the fur convoys, they would farm and they would run buffalo — pemmican was the fuel of canoe flotillas. And they would travel far, opening up the northwest.

By 1800, repopulation was underway.

Up until then, it was opportunity — better hunting, more furs — that brought newcomers. But the next waves were not just led by hope; they were driven by despair.

KEN GIGLIOTTI / WINNIPEG FREE PRESS ARCHIVES

A dilapidated York boat rests on the bank of the Red River at the Lower Fort Garry national historic site.

Andrew McDermot

The poorest Prairie settlers built homesteads out of sod. Few had timber or logs at hand to build homes.

PROVINCIAL ARCHIVES OF MANITOBA

In Scotland and Ireland, landlords were driving small farmers from their fields to make room for livestock. In 1811, a small group of them, sponsored by a cutthroat-businessman-turned-philanthropist, the Earl of Selkirk, sailed into Hudson Bay and wintered at York Factory. Over the winter, they built York boats — wide, shallow-draft workhorse freighters — and when the ice cleared, pointed them to Red River, 1,000 kilometres south. There were 37 portages on the way and a climb of 281 metres from sea level to The Forks. Sometimes the boats had to be emptied and carried overland, other times the displaced crofters laboured along the treacherous riverbanks, long-lining the heavy boats. The journey took 78 days.

Among the newcomers was young Andrew McDermot. Surely to most of the settlers, the Hayes-Nelson route must have been a hellish passage that closed forever their connection with Europe. But young McDermot saw it as a road to riches. In those days, the Montreal route was closed to everything but the Nor'Westers fur trade, nor was there a viable connection to the U.S. Whatever could not be produced in Red River — tea, sugar, gunpowder, pig iron — had to come up the 37 portages from York Factory. In time, McDermot and his son-in-law, Alexander Bannatyne, ran nearly as many York boats as the Hudson's Bay Co.

When the Bay bought out the North West Co. after years of fierce and sometimes bloody rivalry, the route

Immigrants in Winnipeg's 'foreign quarter,' modern-day
Point Douglas, circa 1909.

PROVINCIAL ARCHIVES OF MANITOBA

Galician immigrants outside Clement's tailor shop
in Winnipeg circa 1912.

PROVINCIAL ARCHIVES OF MANITOBA

THOMAS HOY COLLECTION / PROVINCIAL ARCHIVES OF MANITOBA

The moose team that won the Brandon Fair race in 1905.

through the Great Lakes reopened and there was a trickle, growing to a flood, of settlers from Upper Canada. They brought with them entrepreneurial skills and a vision of the northwest aligning itself with the Canadas.

And, it must be admitted, they brought a militant anti-Catholic prejudice that would threaten to set the plains ablaze.

One of them was Jimmy Ashdown, trained as a tinsmith in Upper Canada and seeking his fortune in the West. He walked into Red River in the summer of 1869, with a grasshopper plague turning the valley into a dust bowl. He scraped together enough money to open a shop and, now a businessman who saw profit in having Red River annexed by Canada, was a political opponent of the Métis firebrand, Louis Riel. By the end of the year, the Métis had seized control and Ashdown was Riel's prisoner in Fort Garry.

When an army from Canada marched in the next year and occupied the fort, young Ashdown turned a profit by making space heaters — sheet-metal stoves — for the troops. It was a huge boost to his hardware business. By 1880, Ashdown's store near the Portage Road had made him the richest man in the territory, supplanting Bannatyne.

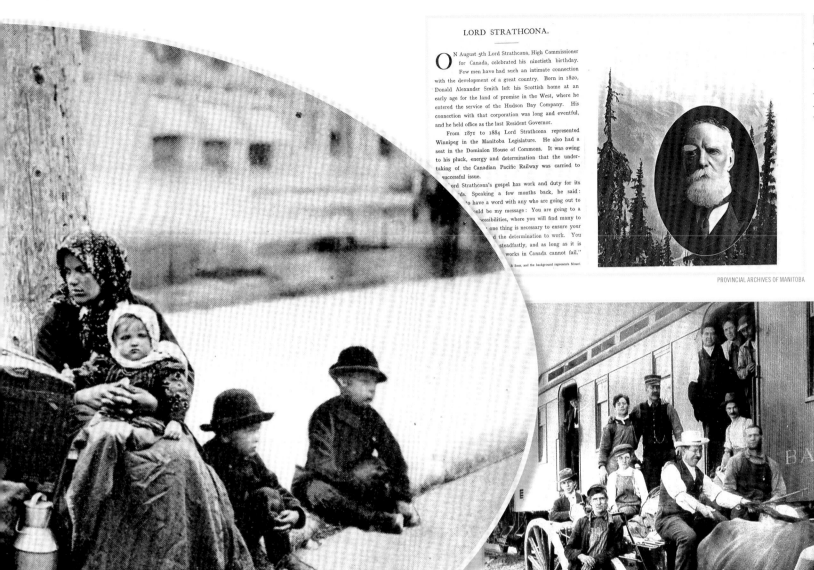

PROVINCIAL ARCHIVES OF MANITOBA

LORD STRATHCONA.

ON August 5th Lord Strathcona, High Commissioner for Canada, celebrated his ninetieth birthday. Few men have had such an intimate connection with the development of a great country. Born in 1820, Donald Alexander Smith left his Scottish home at an early age for the land of promise in the West, where he entered the service of the Hudson Bay Company. His connection with that corporation was long and eventful, and he held office as the last Resident Governor.

From 1871 to 1884 Lord Strathcona represented Winnipeg in the Manitoba Legislature. He also had a seat in the Dominion House of Commons. It was owing to his pluck, energy and determination that the undertaking of the Canadian Pacific Railway was carried to successful issue.

Lord Strathcona's gospel has work and duty for its ...ds. Speaking a few months back, he said: ...o have a word with any who are going out to ...ould be my message: You are going to a ...ossibilities, where you will find many to ... one thing is necessary to ensure your ...d the determination to work. You ... steadfastly, and as long as it is ... works in Canada cannot fail."

...& Sons, and the background represents Mount

PROVINCIAL ARCHIVES OF MANITOBA

Donald A. Smith was a poor Highland Scots boy who rose to wealth and influence in the Canadian fur trade. As a rail baron, he helped open the West for settlement. To thank this empire-builder, Queen Victoria made him Baron Strathcona.

Settlers moved goods from railway cars straight to the Prairie in parts of the West. This photo was taken in Manitoba in the 1880s.

A peasant woman and her children, likely newly arrived in Winnipeg, sit on the curb on Higgins Avenue outside the CPR station circa 1907.

PROVINCIAL ARCHIVES OF MANITOBA

PROVINCIAL ARCHIVES OF MANITOBA

Immigrants in 1909 in Winnipeg's 'foreign quarter,' now Point Douglas.

PROVINCIAL ARCHIVES OF MANITOBA

PROVINCIAL ARCHIVES OF MANITOBA

Polish woman and her children at Winnipeg's All Peoples Mission in 1910.

PROVINCIAL ARCHIVES OF MANITOBA

Families on a Winnipeg street circa 1909.

Hudson Bay Co. senior official Donald A. Smith called in a $5,000 loan to Icelandic settlers in this 1877 letter. HBC made the loan to the settlers in 1875.

Two more immigrant waves rolled into Manitoba — it was now a province of Canada — in the decade following the uprising. The Mennonites, German-speaking pacifists who had moved to Russia and were now being persecuted, struck a deal with Canada. In return for their farming skills — which proved to be formidable — they would be free from conscription and would be allowed to run their own schools. They settled up the valley, in southern Manitoba, beginning in 1875. The next year, as the textile business declined in southern Quebec and its U.S. neighbour, Vermont, French-speaking settlers sought a better life along the Red. Their descendants live in towns like Letellier and St. Jean-Baptiste, between Winnipeg and the U.S. border.

Icelanders, driven from their land by economic depression and a deadly volcanic eruption, arrived in 1875, too. They settled just north of "postage-stamp" Manitoba, establishing a self-governing New Iceland in what was then still Canada's Northwest Territories. Smallpox struck the infant colony along with near-starvation — accustomed to the ocean, the Icelanders failed at first as lake fishermen.

But there could be no retreat, and New Iceland survived to become a prosperous part of an expanding — in area and population — Manitoba.

Then came the railroad.

To pay for that massive infrastructure project and make it profitable, the West had to be filled with farmers to produce freight. The call went out across Europe and the last two waves of 19th-century immigration, from Poland and Ukraine, came in response.

Manitoba had been a beacon of hope for all its newcomers, but it was also a hard and unforgiving land. The eastern Europeans who arrived in 1890 may have faced the hardest time of any.

Earlier homesteaders had been allowed to claim land as they saw fit. But the Poles and Ukrainians were assigned their homesteads by federal bureaucrats, apparently chosen for their xenophobia. Thus, the newcomers tended to get farms far from rail access. E.M. Hubicz, an early historian of the Polish immigrants, tells of a family that arrived in Sifton to find their land was 16 kilometres into the bush. The farmer had to hack his way through the forest with his yoke of oxen before he could even begin to clear some land.

Another family — a couple and two children — arrived at the Selkirk immigration hall on the east bank of the Red. They were destined for Winnipeg Beach and it cost them all their cash — 10 cents — to cross the river by ferry. There they took to the railroad track and walked to Winnipeg Beach, carrying their bundles and their children. They spoke no English, they could not find a relative who had come on ahead and they knew no one. They sat down on their bundles and wept.

But they stayed, for there was no turning back. And they prospered, because the alternative was to die.

Manitoba was populated with survivors, people with backbones of iron. The unforgiving land was the anvil and the harsh elements the hammer that forged them into steel. The 20th century was dawning.

From such beginnings, greatness would inevitably follow.

Smallpox struck the infant colony along with near-starvation — accustomed to the ocean, the Icelanders failed at first as lake fishermen.

LANDNÁM 1874

PROVINCIAL ARCHIVES OF MAANITOBA

Stylized engraving depicts the arrival of Icelandic settlers at Willow Point, dated 1874.

CHIEF PEGUIS

2

BY ALEXANDRA PAUL

Peguis the peacemaker

HISTORY hails Chief Peguis as the native leader who introduced literacy to his people. The same could be said of farming skills and Christianity — and surviving by adapting to the influx of white settlers.

But his most important achievement was bringing peace to the Red River Valley. Peguis' search for peace was something that shaped his destiny.

Perhaps it helped that the Ojibwa leader was a newcomer himself, arriving on the Red River by canoe in the early 1800s.

Like the white settlers, he was a transplant, too, born among the Ojibwa people on Lake Huron, the site of the current-day Sault Ste. Marie. He was born to a Saulteaux woman in about 1774. But she abandoned him at birth, likely out of shame. Peguis suspected his father was a French fur trader who'd abandoned his mother.

An elderly woman found the baby on a wood-chip pile and adopted him. Peguis means Little Chip, some say.

A stylized portrait of Chief Peguis by artist William Tkach.

GREATNESS

Manitoba would look very different in the 21st century if Peguis hadn't been an aboriginal leader in the 19th century. Soldiers, settlers, traders and aboriginal people alike looked to him for leadership.

His accomplishments include:

The first settlers' treaty with Lord Selkirk in 1817.

The first successful aboriginal and European farming settlements located practically side by side.

Saving the lives of his own people and the settlers by maintaining his neutrality to the warring factions of settlers and fur traders.

Saving Louis Riel's family, decades before the Métis leader was born. Peguis sheltered Marie Ann Gaboury Lagimodière and her children in his own camp after he persuaded her husband, Jean Baptiste Lagimodière, to make a 2,900-kilometre trek to Montreal to warn Lord Selkirk of a murder plot against him. The Lagimodières were the grandparents of Riel, the Métis leader.

Kindness. Letters he dictated and accounts of meetings with Hudson's Bay traders, settlers and ministers all say the same thing: Peguis was a kind, honest man and a great leader.

The Peguis First Nation, a Cree and Ojibwa community, 220 kilometres northwest of Winnipeg, also bears his name.

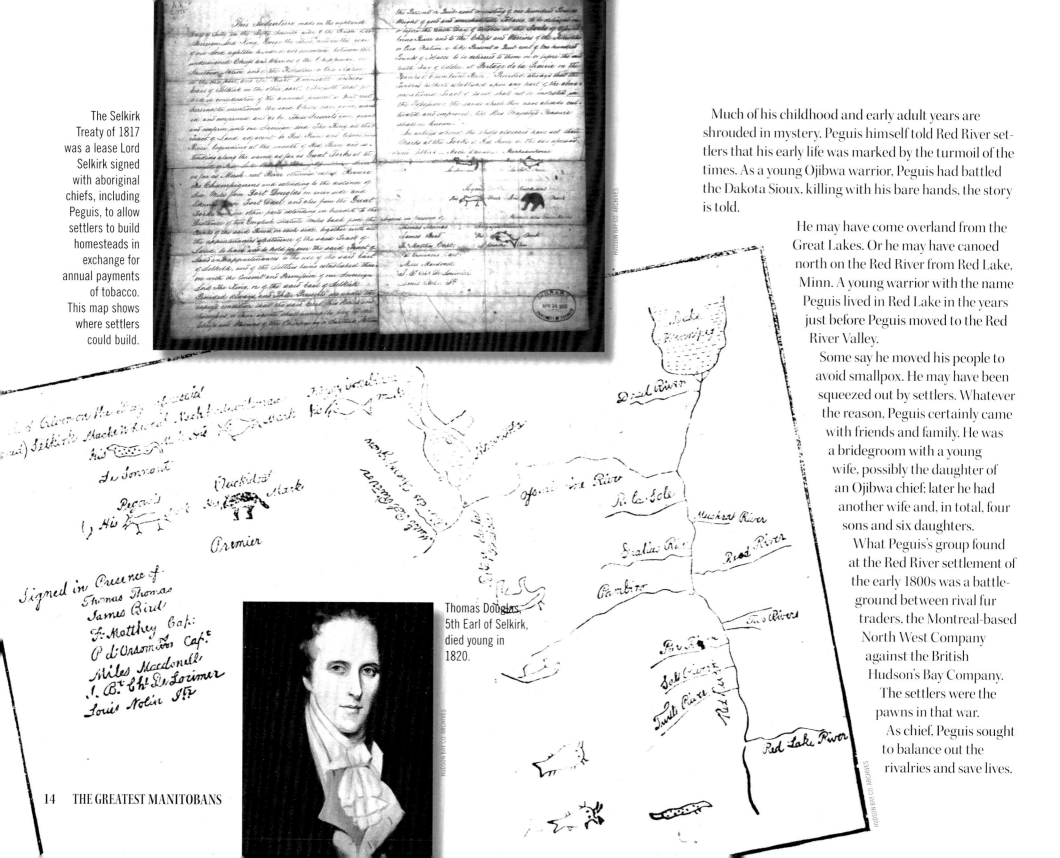

The Selkirk Treaty of 1817 was a lease Lord Selkirk signed with aboriginal chiefs, including Peguis, to allow settlers to build homesteads in exchange for annual payments of tobacco. This map shows where settlers could build.

Thomas Douglas, 5th Earl of Selkirk, died young in 1820.

HUDSON BAY CO. ARCHIVES

Much of his childhood and early adult years are shrouded in mystery. Peguis himself told Red River settlers that his early life was marked by the turmoil of the times. As a young Ojibwa warrior, Peguis had battled the Dakota Sioux, killing with his bare hands, the story is told.

He may have come overland from the Great Lakes. Or he may have canoed north on the Red River from Red Lake, Minn. A young warrior with the name Peguis lived in Red Lake in the years just before Peguis moved to the Red River Valley.

Some say he moved his people to avoid smallpox. He may have been squeezed out by settlers. Whatever the reason, Peguis certainly came with friends and family. He was a bridegroom with a young wife, possibly the daughter of an Ojibwa chief; later he had another wife and, in total, four sons and six daughters.

What Peguis's group found at the Red River settlement of the early 1800s was a battle-ground between rival fur traders, the Montreal-based North West Company against the British Hudson's Bay Company. The settlers were the pawns in that war.

As chief, Peguis sought to balance out the rivalries and save lives.

HUDSON'S BAY COMPANY ARCHIVES / PROVINCIAL ARCHIVES OF MANITOBA

A painting by Charles William Jefferys depicts the Seven Oaks Massacre in 1816.

The Ojibwa lifestyle depended on a peaceful life. Peguis used his considerable oratory powers to find common ground among the competing cultures on the river: Assiniboine, Cree, Ojibwa, Scottish, Métis and French.

Peguis's people continued with their traditional ways, living by the seasons. They hunted and fished, harvested wild rice and tapped maple trees, picked berries and planted Indian corn.

In 1817, along with four other Ojibwa and Cree chiefs,

Peguis brokered the Selkirk Treaty, an indentured-style land lease on the Red River that allowed the Red River natives room to settle permanently. It was the first British settlement of its kind in Manitoba.

"Had it not been for the zealous attachment of Peguis and his kinsman, the colonists would have suffered great want," said one early settler's account in John Henry Pritchett's book *The Red River Valley*.

Peguis wanted stability, but the rivalries did not disap-

pear overnight, despite his best efforts.

In June 1816, before what came to be known as the Seven Oaks Massacre, Peguis caught wind of the plans for an attack on the Red River settlers at Fort Douglas (modern-day Point Douglas) by the Métis loyal to the North West Company at that company's stronghold at The Forks.

Fishing on the Red River, left, at St. Peters circa 1880.

An Indian log house, below, still stood north of Peguis, in 1965.

PROVINCIAL ARCHIVES OF MANITOBA

Men log by horse and wagon, right, near Selkirk circa 1880.

PROVINCIAL ARCHIVES OF MANITOBA

Peguis warned the settlers at Fort Douglas. He met with Red River Colony governor Robert Semple and offered to defend the fort — but the governor dismissed the chief.

"Do not interfere," Semple said.

Peguis held his tongue but quietly moved his camp to the riverbank across from Fort Douglas, miles from its usual spot near Lake Winnipeg.

He and his people looked on helplessly as the Métis attacked. Cuthbert Grant led 60 armed men against the settlers across from Peguis's encampment. Semple followed British army manual procedures, a tragic mistake, and led a force of 20 men out of the safety of the fort to battle the Métis on the exposed bank.

The two sides faced off, traded taunts and then gunfire. Peguis and his camp watched, devastated, as the outnumbered settlers were slaughtered. Later, they went to collect the dead.

They gathered up the bodies of the Selkirk settlers as if they were their own people.

Peguis himself lifted Semple's body and carried it, cradled in his arms, into Fort Douglas.

"The old chief carried him home to the fort, washed his body and wept for him as if he'd been his only son," says one entry of a diary kept by Rev. William Cockran,

PROVINCIAL ARCHIVES OF MANITOBA

TREATY TIME, ST. PETERS, MANITOBA, 1880

Traditional teepees stand near European-style frame homes in St. Peters in 1880.

ROBERT BELL / PROVINCIAL ARCHIVES OF MANITOBA

an Anglican missionary close to Peguis.

From his earliest years on the Red, Peguis worked at being kind, but at one point, that kindness, expressed in support for the settlers, threatened his people. By the 1830s growing numbers of settlers were crowding out game and wild plants were disappearing in the face of cultivated farm fields. Peguis watched his people nearly starve while the new farmers all around them thrived.

And Peguis made a decision that changed his people's lives.

Until then, Peguis had held out against entreaties to live like the settlers. After famine hit his camp in 1831, Peguis agreed to live, with the rest of his people, in log cabins in a parish town as the settlers did.

He moved into the first house built in the first aboriginal town in the Red River Valley at St. Peter near Selkirk, and his community followed. He also took on a Christian name: William King.

The Ojibwa and Cree excelled with the plow and spinning wheel and other tools of that sort of civilization, and their town prospered. Within 20 years, the town had the only harness-maker and the only tinsmith on the Red River.

Peguis allowed the first mission school to teach the native children to read and write, and the first church, where adults gathered in the evening to translate English hymns into their own Ojibwa and Cree languages.

The farming, the literacy, the Christianity and what they did for Peguis's people are how he is remembered. But the chief put his legacy in simpler terms.

"I can say, with a clear conscience, I have been faithful to both the whites and the Indians," he dictated to a son writing his will in 1858.

"This paper I hope will be handed down through my generations so that all may know what life I have lived."

Six years later, Peguis died peacefully in his sleep.

MANITOBA-NESS

PEGUIS predates Manitoba, but he helped mould what the province was to become. In the 1830s, he was among the first aboriginal leaders to give up traditional life on the land for life in a town. He supported the first Protestant missionaries and both the town's first Anglican church and first school.

He was an ardent royalist, a plain-spoken aboriginal-rights advocate and a politician with a nose for opportunity and the skill to turn it to his advantage.

5 THINGS YOU DIDN'T KNOW

1. He was a brilliant mimic with a wicked sense of humour and some of his more outrageous posturing, mostly targeted at fur traders, makes for hilarious reading.

2. He was called the cut-nose chief. The tip of his nose was bitten off when he stepped into the wrong brawl one night.

3. He was in his early 20s when he arrived at The Forks and within a short time, set up a winter camp at Netley Creek. He likely moved human bones to make room for that first camp. The name of the camp is a translation of the French Dead River. Smallpox wiped out entire villages in the 1780s and as late as 1815, bleached bones of the dead were still scattered on the ground in the Red River Valley.

4. He didn't believe in women's rights. And he was not a handsome man. But he had at least two wives; most accounts put the number at four.

5. His hunting prowess was legendary. He traded pelts exclusively with the Hudson's Bay Company for 38 years.

'Good Old Peguis. He was the best friend the settlers ever had'

— Selkirk settler Thomas Truthwaite, 1909

The Father of Manitoba

BY MARY AGNES WELCH

I N 1885, he was reviled as an insane traitor, a half-breed who deserved to hang.

The *Ottawa Free Press* said he "opened the gates of rapine and murder and for that offense deserved the severest penalty possible." The *Globe and Mail* called him a traitor-agitator and called news of his capture "glorious."

More than 100 years later, Louis Riel's got a bridge, a February holiday, a school division and a hotel named after him.

The shorthand description of him nowadays is "the Father of Manitoba," the romantic hero who led us into Confederation, no longer the madman murderer.

"It just shows that's how much it's changed," said Joseph Riel, Louis Riel's great-grand nephew. "As a child, it wasn't like we sat around the table and talked much about the story because it was all negative in the books. Having the name Riel, my grandfather and even my father would take it a little from the English kids. For my dad, who was born in Riel House, there were very few silver linings. In my case, there are institutions named after him and monuments and holidays. There are so many things he did to be proud of."

Louis Riel in 1876.

LOUIS RIEL

1844-1885

3

GREATNESS

Louis Riel was the Métis rebel who helped lead Manitoba into Confederation and championed the rights of aboriginals, francophones and ultimately all minorities.

Riel was a clear choice as spokesman for the Red River Resistance of 1869, in which Métis farmers defended their land by repelling federal government surveyors.

Under Riel's leadership, the Métis turned back a Canadian government party, seized Fort Garry, created a bill of rights and formed a provisional government.

Prime Minister Sir John A. Macdonald agreed to almost all the Métis' demands and passed the Manitoba Act, bringing the province into Confederation on May 12, 1870. Fifteen years later, after the failed North West Rebellion, Riel was hanged for treason.

It took decades for Canada to recognize Riel's greatness. Now, he is considered the Father of Manitoba. In 1992, Tory cabinet minister Joe Clark championed a resolution in Parliament recognizing Riel as the founder of Manitoba.

'It is all too easy, should disturbances erupt, to crush them in the name of law and order. We must never forget that, in the long run, a democracy is judged by the way the majority treats the minority. Louis Riel's battle is not yet won'

— Prime Minister Pierre Trudeau at the unveiling of Riel's monument in Regina, Oct. 2, 1969.

Riel's provisional government executed Thomas Scott, which led to Riel's downfall.

Riel, centre, is surrounded by his supporters in the Red River Resistance.

Riel is arguably Canada's most confounding historical giant, and there may be no other whose popular image has undergone such a radical rehabilitation. There are huge gaps in the historical record of him, especially his many sojourns in the United States, and the religious, racial and economic forces at work during the province's creation are among the most nuanced and difficult to understand. Riel and his times defy history's tendency to simplify pivotal events into black or white, good guys versus bad guys.

And he was on the vanguard of all the issues with which we still grapple today — aboriginal land and cultural rights, the West's struggle with Ontario's WASP-ish establishment, French-language protection, anti-Americanism, even the stigma of mental illness.

Riel was born in 1844, the oldest child of Louis Riel Sr. and Julie Lagimodière, whose mother was a Gaboury, all monikers familiar to modern-day Manitobans that gave Riel an excellent pedigree.

At a young age, Riel was sent to Montreal to study for the priesthood, but went to work instead as a law clerk. In 1868, just a year before the rebellion broke out, Riel returned to the Red River Settlement, a community of long, skinny lots that stretched along the banks of the Red and Assiniboine rivers.

Riel returned to a Red River Settlement much changed by an influx of Protestant anglophones from Ontario. And the settlement was gripped by fears and rumours the Canadian government was about to take wholesale control of the area from the Hudson's Bay

Trial of Louis Riel in Regina in 1885.

*'I know that through the grace of God
I am the founder of Manitoba'*

— Louis Riel in his defence speech in Regina, July 31, 1885

Company without properly consulting or accommodating the Métis majority, who believed their lands, leased long-term from the HBC, were their birthright.

The Red River Resistance erupted in the fall of 1869 when Métis farmers stopped surveyors sent from Ottawa to begin marking out new townships on what was not yet Canadian territory.

By Canadian standards, things happened remarkably quickly after that. Riel's Métis militants turned back a Canadian government party at the United States border, seized Fort Garry, created a bill of rights, formed a provisional government and imprisoned pro-Canadian Anglos — all before Christmas.

Riel, because he was educated and a fine orator, became the rebellion's spokesman and moral centre, articulating better than anyone the Métis struggle for basic land and language rights. He was also somewhat reclusive and sombre and deeply religious, his support among the powerful priests in the Red River Settlement lending him legitimacy.

But in March 1870, Riel committed what historian George Stanley called his one contemptible act in a rebellion that had been almost bloodless: the firing-squad execution of Thomas Scott for counter-insurgency. Scott's death fanned the flames of racial and religious passion, according to Stanley's 1937 book, *The Birth of Western Canada*, one of the first attempts at a more balanced take on Riel.

Those flames would engulf Riel 15 years later when Riel's nemesis, Prime Minister Sir John A. Macdonald, gave in to Ontario voters baying for blood and allowed Riel to hang.

But first Macdonald agreed to pretty much every Métis demand and passed the Manitoba Act that brought the province into Confederation — and kept it out of the hands of the Americans, who'd been eyeing it — on May 12, 1870.

But, with the arrival of Gen. Wolseley's troops in Manitoba, there began a cat-and-mouse game between Riel and Ottawa that lasted for years. For much of the next 14 murky years, Riel lived an itinerant life in exile in the United States as the question of his amnesty or arrest underscored much of the power struggle between Quebec and Ontario back home. Riel was elected three times to Parliament, sneaking into Ottawa to formally sign the register, risking arrest. It was also through that time that Riel's religious fanaticism and his belief in his self-appointed status as the divinely chosen leader of the Métis emerged, along with mental instability that plagued him and his reputation forever.

"When they say he was crazy, what he had was a nervous breakdown," said Joseph Riel. "If you led your people at the age of 25, and went into exile and had a price put on your head and left your family and had to make decisions with huge implications for your people... He was human, that was the whole point."

In 1884, while living in Montana, Riel was lured back to Canada by Gabriel Dumont, one of the leaders of the Métis in Saskatchewan.

PROVINCIAL ARCHIVES OF MANITOBA

Demonstrators hang Riel in effigy on Main Street, Winnipeg in July 1885.

The Regina courthouse during Riel's trial in 1885.

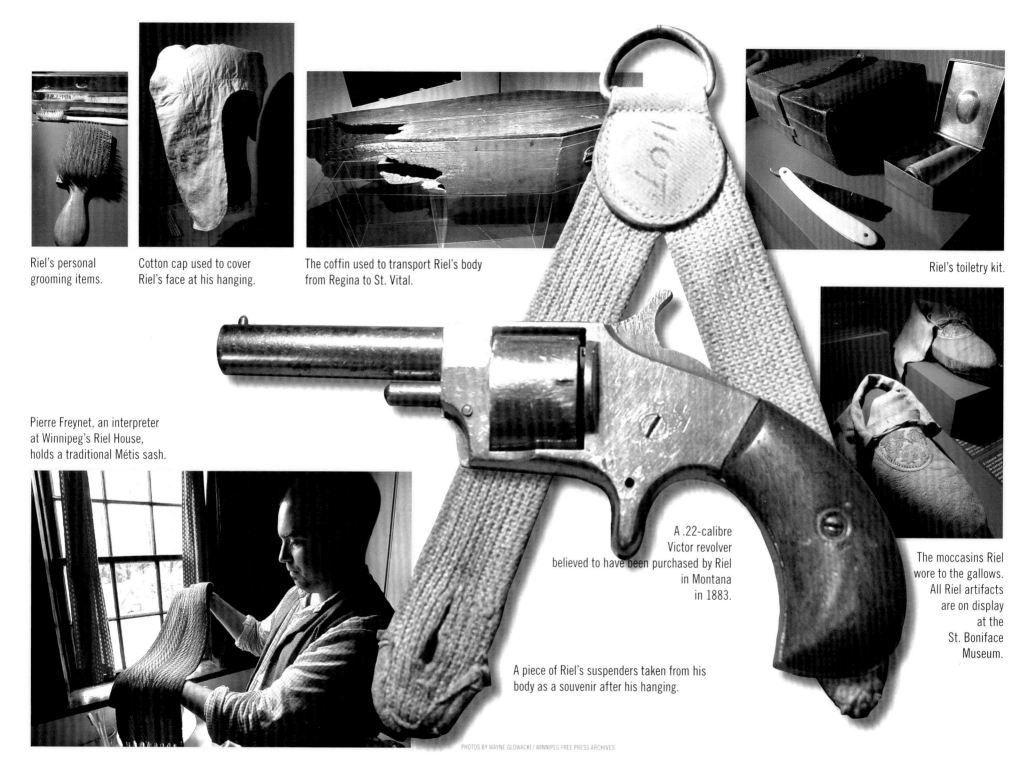

Riel's personal grooming items.

Cotton cap used to cover Riel's face at his hanging.

The coffin used to transport Riel's body from Regina to St. Vital.

Riel's toiletry kit.

Pierre Freynet, an interpreter at Winnipeg's Riel House, holds a traditional Métis sash.

A .22-calibre Victor revolver believed to have been purchased by Riel in Montana in 1883.

The moccasins Riel wore to the gallows. All Riel artifacts are on display at the St. Boniface Museum.

A piece of Riel's suspenders taken from his body as a souvenir after his hanging.

PHOTOS BY WAYNE GLOWACKI / WINNIPEG FREE PRESS ARCHIVES

The Northwest Rebellion — this one more violent and ultimately unsuccessful — began early in 1885 and ended with the Métis defeat at the Battle of Batoche, which Canadian novelist Rudy Wiebe once called one of the pivotal events in Canadian history, akin to America's Gettysburg.

From there, Riel was arrested and tried for treason in Regina in a five-day court case that made daily headlines in the *New York Times*. A jury of English and Scottish Protestants found him guilty, despite Riel's elegant defences of his innocence, his sanity and the rights of the Métis people.

On Nov. 16, 1885, Riel was hanged. He's the only Canadian ever tried for high treason, according to Manitoba's premier historian J.M. Bumsted.

Outside of Quebec and the Métis diaspora, it took a solid 50 years for Canadians to begin the slow process of reconsidering Riel, and real progress wasn't made until the 1970s, when Manitoba celebrated its centenary with a controversial statue of a tortured Riel that in itself forced debate about the rebel's legacy.

Not long after, Saskatchewan laid claim to Riel with a sizable celebration to mark the anniversary of his death. In 1992, Tory cabinet minister Joe Clark championed a resolution in Parliament recognizing Riel as the founder of Manitoba, and by then school curricula had begun offering a more nuanced version of Métis history. In fact, 11 different Manitoba schools nominated Riel as the namesake of the province's new February holiday.

Meanwhile, Riel's famous headshot with the flowing hair and the long moustache adorns hip T-shirts with the words "Keepin' it Riel," and a highly acclaimed comic-book version of Riel's life by Chester Brown has helped restore his folk-hero cachet.

"Sometimes it takes a century for the real truth to unfold," said Manitoba Métis Federation president David Chartrand. "It's taken us over a century to get to where we are, but I think we're richer for it."

RUTH BONNEVILLE / WINNIPEG FREE PRESS ARCHIVES

MANITOBA-NESS

L OUIS Riel was the Métis rebel who helped lead Manitoba into Confederation and championed the rights of Aboriginal Peoples, francophones and ultimately all minorities.

He lived for years in exile in the United States, but still managed to get elected to Parliament three times in absentia.

An enigmatic and mentally unstable man, he also led a more violent and ultimately failed military rebellion in Saskatchewan that resulted in his arrest for treason. He was hanged in 1885 in Regina and has since become a folk hero.

5 THINGS YOU DIDN'T KNOW

1. **He had a rocky love life.** He was first engaged to a Montreal woman to whom he wrote passionate poems, but her parent's put the kibosh on the union, perhaps because Riel was Métis. Next, following the Red River Rebellion and during Riel's most mentally unstable period, he courted the sister of an oblate friend. Too poor to propose, Riel saw the courtship fizzle when the woman failed to follow him back out west. When he was almost 40, Riel finally married Marguerite Monet Bellehumeur, a pretty and quiet Métis woman.

2. **He was an avid pool player.** Along with Gabriel Dumont, Riel enjoyed a good game of billiards and frequently played in pool halls in Winnipeg.

3. **He gave up his seat for George-Étienne Cartier.** The giant of Quebec politics, father of Confederation and prime minister Sir John A. Macdonald's francophone lieutenant lost his seat in Montreal in 1872. Meanwhile, Riel was preparing to run in Manitoba's Provencher riding. Hoping Cartier would champion an amnesty for the Métis rebels, Riel stepped aside, and Cartier was acclaimed as Provencher's MP. Cartier never visited Manitoba. He died the following year.

4. **He was a Republican.** While in Montana in the early 1880s, Riel sought American citizenship and sided with the rabble-rousing Republicans in local politics, especially as he championed the rights of Montana Métis. That's according to historian J.M. Bumsted. Years later, during his trial, Riel appealed for help from Washington and President Grover Cleveland.

5. **When Winnipeg was battling the flood of 1950,** the dike on Tache Avenue sprang a leak, despite a frantic sandbagging effort. The dike was within moments of collapsing, which would have flooded all of old St. Boniface, when the priest at St. Boniface Cathedral agreed to allow flood-fighters to bulldoze a half-metre of mud off the top of the historic cemetery where Riel's body lies. Through the night, the headstones were moved to one side, to be replaced when the mud was returned.

'He wasn't a politician or a rock star, he was just interested in making where he lived a better place. And he did. Look around'

— Hugh Skinner, son of renowned Manitoba horticulturalist Frank Skinner

He changed the Prairie landscape

BY GERALD FLOOD

WHEN Frank Skinner built his dream house at Dropmore in 1907, he could see from its second-storey windows the grain elevator at Saltcoats — 70 kilometres to the west in Saskatchewan. A century ago, the Prairies were all but devoid of trees, and that was certainly true at Dropmore, 400 kilometres northwest of Winnipeg, where the climate was cold and the growing season short. It was not for nothing — or perhaps it was for nothing — that the Prairies were called bald. It was widely believed that trees could not be grown on the vast grasslands.

The house still stands 101 years later, although for how much longer is anybody's guess and likely will be decided by a north or south wind of change.

But, oh, what change it already has witnessed! Today, if you were to risk crossing its threshold and brave the climb up the rotted stairs to the collapsing second floor, you would find there no longer exists a view west — it is blocked everywhere by trees, towering giants that Skinner either imported to the site or hybrids created through the horticultural skills for which he was renowned the world over.

Frank Skinner, in February 1956.

WINNIPEG TRIBUNE / UNIVERSITY OF MANITOBA ARCHIVES

Skinner at work in the field in the late 1950s.

CLIFF SHAW / FAMILY SUBMITTED PHOTO

GREATNESS

Skinnner was the most accomplished horticulturalist in Western Canada, having individually introduced 248 species of plants to the region, 144 of which were new, improved varieties.

In 1926, his Lily Dropmore Concolor won the British Horticultural Society Award of Merit.

He topped that in 1933, winning the Cory Cup, the society's highest award, for developing the Lilium Maxwill, a lily he created by dusting a Chinese lily with Korean lily pollen to create a beautiful, hardy, sturdy-stemmed plant. It was the first time anyone outside the U.K. won the award.

In 1932, the Manitoba Agriculture College awarded him an honorary diploma and he won the Stevenson gold medal for achievement in horticulture.

In 1943, he was made a Member of the British Empire.

In 1947, he was awarded an honorary doctorate of law by the University of Manitoba.

In 1967, he was inducted into the Royal Order of the Buffalo Hunt by Premier Duff Roblin.

His portrait hangs in the Canadian Agriculture Hall of Fame in Toronto.

*'He was a
giant among
horticulturalists
and a giant
among his peers.
I lift a hand
in gratitude to him.
Manitoba owes him
a great debt'*

— Wilbert Ronald, former horticulturalist
at the Morden Research Centre who now operates
Jeffries Nurseries near Portage la Prairie

Skinner as a young man,
circa 1912, about the time he
started to become a serious
horticulturalist.

FAMILY SUBMITTED PHOTO

FAMILY SUBMITTED PHOTO

The original Skinner family home, circa 1940.

To even attempt to see the grain elevator at Saltcoats, one would have to climb 20 metres to the top of one of the countless trees on the property, which today is an arboretum, a garden of trees — and a Manitoba Historic Site.

Even from the treetops, the view west would be blocked by bush and forest everywhere, all crowding the horizon and blocking out Saltcoats.

The bald prairie is bald no more.

That, in part, is thanks to Skinner and his curious desire to grow plants and trees hardy enough for Manitoba's harsh climate while also pleasing to the eye.

It would be wrong, of course, to give more credit to Skinner for the changed landscape than he deserves.

The fact is it was settlement that made it possible to grow the trees and shrubs and flowers that Skinner gave to Manitoba and to posterity.

In the millennia before Skinner arrived in Manitoba from Scotland in 1895, the Prairies region was a vast grassland that lived, died and was reborn according to the coincidence of dry spells and lightning strikes

that set fires raging across thousands and thousands of hectares.

The wildfires renewed the grasses, but they killed any tree that dared to grow far from ready water in rivers, streams and lakes. That was where what trees there were made their stands, all but surrendering the vast plains to grasses.

With settlement, however, the free range was chopped into sections, grasses that burned like napalm were turned under, tilled fields became barriers across which wildfires could not leap and slowly the balance tipped from grasses to cultivated crops — and trees.

Skinner, fortuitously for everyone, arrived in Manitoba on the cusp of that transformation 113 years ago at the age of 13.

His father had been a successful fish merchant in Scotland until the tides turned against him after an El Niño event caused stupendous fish catches and the collapse of prices.

Broke, depressed and usually drunk, his dad sent Frank, his mother and some of his siblings to stay with

an aunt in Aberdeen. Part of the aunt's estate had been made into a convalescent home, its gardens a source of succour for shattered soldiers. The gardens were the place where Frank found his first true love — plants.

Although no more than a boy, and a sickly one at that, he soon became fast friends with the gardener, who nurtured the love that one day would make Skinner's reputation and earn him a place among The Greatest Manitobans.

His father, meanwhile, sobered up, literally and figuratively, and over a five-year span raised the money needed to emigrate to Manitoba, where family members had already established themselves. In his auto-biography, Skinner recalls he and his brother thought they were coming to the land of adventure they read about in James Fenimore Cooper novels.

It wasn't anything like his imagining. And it was as different from the gardens of Scotland as could be imagined — a blank, bleak landscape of poor soils and little water.

"One of the northern outposts of farming settlement,"

he diplomatically called it in later life.

He went to school on opening day, discovered the teacher had no more education than the Grade 7 Skinner obtained in Scotland and never went back.

Instead, he planted a flower garden, which by 1900 was well-known in the district, and went into the cattle business with his brother.

A bout of pneumonia cost him the lower lobe of his right lung, and forced him to take it easier, to garden.

And so he did, throwing not so much his back into the work, as his brain.

Don't forget Skinner had only a Grade 7 education. But also don't forget it was an education of the times — literate times in which by Grade 7 he would have had a solid grounding in reading, writing and arithmetic, with no time wasted on MuchMusic, the Internet or an iPod.

Still, that he self-taught himself to be a horticulturalist from a remote homestead in an obscure part of a vast and little-settled nation remains in the minds of his many contemporary admirers the signal measure of his greatness.

He began collecting books and corresponding with horticulturalists the world over. He wasn't shy, forging lasting relationships with many of the greatest experts of the day, reaching out to plant breeders and experts for specimens of plants that grew in similar climates — Manchuria, Siberia and the Scandinavian countries — crossbreeding and grafting in the pursuit of trees, shrubs and flowers that could thrive and blossom despite the long, bitter winters and short, 90-day, frost-free window between thaw and freeze-up.

He was fortunate, too, in that he was untutored — he simply followed his interests wherever they led. In time, he was creating and introducing not just trees (Dropmore elm, silver maples, Swedish aspens) and shrubs (maidens blush and Pocahontas lilacs) and fruit trees (pear, cherry, plum and apple) but also many varieties of Manitoba hardy flowers — clematis, lilies, irises,

roses and catnip.

The Dropmore elm, by the way, became the standard shelterbelt tree in Central Canada.

Before he was done, he "individually accomplished more than any other horticulturalist in Western Canada by introducing 248 species of plants to the region, 144 of which were new, improved varieties," according to a Manitoba government booklet published in 1981 and entitled simply *Dr. Frank Leith Skinner*.

Evidence of his work is everywhere in Manitoba, but it is not always evident that this tree or that lily or those lilacs are his. He worked at a time when there were no breeders' rights or patents, and in time, the sources of what was growing in gardens or along the streets of cities and towns were lost.

Of the 248 species he introduced, perhaps 30 are still common in catalogues.

He married Helen Cumming of Teulon in 1947, the year he was awarded a doctorate of law by the University of Manitoba, and the year he turned 65.

They had five children. One of them, Hugh, a university-trained horticulturalist, lives at the original homestead, operates a nursery there and tends the arboretum.

He remembers there were always people around. They beat a path to the nursery from all over the province, the continent and the world.

"He was very generous with his time and knowledge," Hugh said.

"He was easy to get along with. He had high expectations for himself and for others. But he seldom got angry and rarely raised his voice. I think it was too much a waste of energy for him."

Frank Skinner died at 85 in 1967, the year in which then-premier Duff Roblin inducted him into the Royal Order of the Buffalo Hunt and the year in which his book *Horticultural Horizons*, part autobiography and part textbook, was published.

Skinner, above, circa 1932.

PROVINCIAL ARCHIVES OF MANITOBA

MANITOBA-NESS

FRANK Skinner was born in Scotland and didn't arrive in Manitoba until he was 13. By some lights, the fact that he wasn't born here diminishes his Manitoba-ness.

But those lights are dim.

Consider:

He lived and worked here for 70 years, raised a family here and died here.

He could have left. He was a horticulturalist renowned the world over. He would have been welcome anywhere, particularly anywhere with a climate as disagreeable as Manitoba's. But unlike many Manitobans who are born here, he stayed.

Had he not been born in Scotland, had he not found his love and passion for plants in an Eden by Manitoba standards, then he would not have known what could be, he would not have given his life to creating it here, and we would not be enjoying the fruits and flowers of his labours today.

Skinner was not simply a man who lived in Manitoba, he was a man who helped shape the way Manitoba lives.

5 THINGS YOU DIDN'T KNOW

1. **FRANK IN THE FREEP:** Skinner wrote Nature Notes columns for the Winnipeg Free Press.

2. **AS THE CROW FLIES:** While the Skinner nursery is considered to be in the Dropmore district between Russell and Roblin in northwestern Manitoba, it has been physically cut off from the hamlet that gave the district its name for more than 30 years. The building of the Shellmouth Dam and subsequent flooding that created Lake of the Prairies, also flooded the Dropmore road on which the nursery still operates. The distance to Dropmore remains eight kilometres as the crow flies, but the drive to the hamlet from the nursery has increased to 42 kilometres.

3. **PLAGUE OF EPIDEMICS:** Frank Skinner was a bachelor until 65. His son Hugh says his father had a sweetheart in his younger days, but she died in one of the many epidemics that plagued Manitoba in the first half of the last century.

4. **FRUIT FOR NUTS:** Frank Skinner grew the first pear tree in Prairie Canada. It still grows at the Skinner Arboretum 31 kilometres north of Russell. Visitors, however, are well-advised to resist the temptation to test its tartness.

5. **COLD WARRIOR:** Frank Skinner had contacts in communist Russia and China who smuggled plants to him.

A row of Scotch pines Skinner planted in the 1920s in what is now the Skinner Arboretum.

HUGH SKINNER PHOTO

The last great frontiersman

BY BILL REDEKOP

I N 1902, trappers, mainly aboriginal, harvested more than 850,000 muskrat pelts in Manitoba. By 1926, the muskrat had virtually disappeared. A mere 40,000 were trapped that year. In 1930, a provincial government survey estimated just 26,000 muskrats remained in all of Manitoba.

The demise was not well-understood. It wasn't over-trapping — muskrats breed like rabbits and cancelled seasons did not improve their numbers. The loss of the muskrat population, combined with the Great Depression, which battered fur and fish markets, left many northern aboriginal people destitute.

Into this catastrophe stepped Tom Lamb, whose risk and sacrifice placed him on the road to becoming one of the Greatest Manitobans. Lamb later launched Lambair Ltd., the first northern airline. He became perhaps Canada's greatest aviation pioneer, opening up Northern Canada and flying thousands of northern rescue missions, supply drops and industry and mineral exploration flights, such as the ones that led to the discovery of the Thompson nickel belt.

KEN GIGLIOTTI / WINNIPEG FREE PRESS ARCHIVES

Tom Lamb was the model for the famous Leo Mol statue of a man in a fur-trimmed parka cranking an airplane propeller.

Tom Lamb circa 1973.

TOM LAMB

5

GREATNESS

In 1926, Tom Lamb, 28, bought out his father's trading post at Moose Lake, 70 kilometres southeast of The Pas. From the post he launched a sawmill, commercial fishing operation, muskrat ranch, winter tractor freighting business, and the first cattle ranch north of the 53rd parallel.

Tom Lamb started Lambair Ltd., the first northern air service, in 1935. Lambair had up to 20 airplanes and 40 pilots.

In 1969, Lamb, whose formal education ended after Grade 3, was awarded an honorary doctorate of law from the University of Manitoba.

In 2007, the Nunavut government honoured the remaining Lamb family, who all learned how to speak Cree and Inuit languages, with a ceremony in Rankin Inlet.

In 2008, the Manitoba Aviation Council awarded the Lamb family its Pioneer of Flight Award.

The famous Leo Mol statue of a man in fur-trimmed parka — gripping an airplane propeller as if to crank it to start — is of Tom Lamb. The statues are in the Richardson Building lobby, The Pas Airport, the Leo Mol Garden in Assiniboine Park, and the Western Aviation Museum.

He earned many nicknames in his lifetime: Mr. North, by Manitoba newspapers; Mr. Frontier-Buster; by the *Star Weekly* magazine in 1952; and *The Last Great Frontiersman*, the title of a book about Lamb by Pulitzer Prize-winning American journalist Leland Stowe.

But in the early 1930s, when no one knew him outside of The Pas area where he ran a trading post, Lamb was simply called crazy. Lamb had gone more than $300,000 in personal debt (in 2008 dollars) on a hare-brained scheme — or so many people thought — to bring back the muskrat.

The muskrat is the staple of the fur industry. Other pelts may fetch higher prices, but they aren't harvested in the quantity of muskrat. Muskrat is prized for its waterproof fur that resembles seal and once was frequently misrepresented as seal, mink or sable.

It was during a 10-hour dogsled run from his Moose Lake trading post to The Pas — a 45-minute drive today now that there's a road — that the idea hit Lamb. Water levels had been falling in marshes around The Pas. Lamb believed the lower water levels must be killing the muskrats.

Muskrats live in shoreline burrows below the water and search under the ice for food plants in winter. When water levels fell, the ice may drop so low that the critters couldn't access food supplies.

Lamb's theory made sense. It was his proposed solution that raised eyebrows.

He wanted to lease 54,000 acres of marshy Crown land near The Pas and build a dike and ditch system to raise water levels.

Lamb must have seemed like a crazed backwoodsman to the bluebloods running the Manitoba legislature at the time. He prowled the legislature hallways, needing government to lease him the marsh. He sat for whole days on the benches outside the offices of assistant and deputy ministers, only to be turned down three times.

Supporters told Lamb not to give up, even if it meant cornering Premier John Bracken, leader of the Progressive Party. It was in Natural Resources Minister Donald G. MacKenzie, a Scottish farmer who knew something about drainage, that Lamb found a kindred spirit. The two became lifelong friends.

MacKenzie could see right off that Lamb's plan offered the province a chance to restore incomes to northern aboriginal people with minimal sacrifice. He got Bracken's approval immediately. Lamb's lease cost $1,084 a year for 10 years. But then Lamb had to deal with the bureaucracy again. Government officials treated Lamb as if he were leasing property at Portage and Main. They insisted he have the entire 54,000 acres professionally surveyed and post signs around the marsh, the signs spaced ridiculously close together. It all added to Lamb's costs.

Lamb hired a crew of 30 local Cree men. They

WINNIPEG TRIBUNE / UNIVERSITY OF MANITOBA ARCHIVES

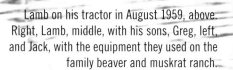

Lamb on his tractor in August 1959, above. Right, Lamb, middle, with his sons, Greg, left, and Jack, with the equipment they used on the family beaver and muskrat ranch.

FAMILY SUBMITTED PHOTO

received a dollar a day. Equipped with just shovels, they hauled rock in from Moose Lake by barge. Teams of horses hauled mud. They diverted water from the Saskatchewan River into the marsh. They built 16 dams and four dikes and deepened and cleared existing channels.

Lamb borrowed from banks as much as they would allow, and as much as local merchants could spare. "I owed so much money around town, I was afraid to go down the street in daytime," he wrote in a memoir for his children.

Local families also had to agree to a moratorium on muskrat trapping for three years. Lamb promised to do whatever he could to keep them afloat until then. By the second year, people wanted to started trapping but Lamb convinced them to wait.

Lamb and his crew raised water levels in the marsh by a full metre. By the third year, muskrat lodges in the marsh increased to 8,600 from 40. Cree trappers began harvesting muskrat in numbers they hadn't seen in a generation. In the spring of 1934, Cree trappers hauled in 34,000 muskrat pelts to Lamb's trading post. Local trappers saw their incomes go to an average of $1,200 from $50 a year.

The American Mercury, a magazine launched by journalist and social critic H.L. Mencken, called Lamb's project "possibly the most successful relief effort in all of North America." Local newspapers hailed Lamb as The Muskrat King. Lamb promptly paid back every last bank and merchant.

The muskrat "ranches" didn't stop there. The province, on Lamb's advice, built dikes and ditches on 130,000 acres along the Summerberry River, also in the northwestern Manitoba. In five years, the number of muskrats there went to 400,000 from 325. (A female muskrat

WINNIPEG TRIBUNE / UNIVERSITY OF MANITOBA ARCHIVES

Lamb in Flin Flon in 1927, above. Left, with his daughter, Sheila, in 1945, roasting meat on a stick over an open fire, ponask, the Lamb family called it, borrowing a Cree word.

FAMILY SUBMITTED PHOTO

can give birth to up to 30 young a year.) About 400 trappers took 122,000 muskrats out of Summerberry by the fifth year. Similar dike and ditch work began at Netley Creek near Selkirk, Delta Marsh on Lake Manitoba and Fisher Bay on Lake Winnipeg, resulting in a boost in income for aboriginal people. Lamb did well financially, too. But he didn't get rich as he would have if the government had approved his proposal for the Summerberry project. But he parlayed the money he made into launching Canada's first northern airline in 1935.

The idea for an airline came to him while freighting fish with a Caterpillar tractor from Moose and William lakes to a railway siding for pickup. His equipment kept breaking down. On one breakdown in January, a bush plane happened to fly past and landed to lend a hand. It hauled out Lamb and his fish. Lambair was born.

To transport fish by plane was considered an extravagance. But Lamb realized he could transport fish by plane at a profit, provided he had the volume. His air service made it possible for more aboriginal communities to market fish commercially.

By the end of 1952, Lamb's flights over northern Canada equalled in total distance 50 trips around the world.

All six of his sons — Greg, Donald, Dennis, Jack, Doug and Connie — eventually joined the airline as pilots. The airline operated until 1982 when it was taken over by Calm Air, founded by Carl Arnold Lawrence Moberg (whose initials spell out CALM.)

'No one may ever know exactly how many mercy flights were made by Tom and his sons, nor how many lives were saved or how much suffering was relieved.' (At one point, Tom flew rescue missions on 16 straight Christmas days.)'

— Robert "Bud" Simpson, former MP for Churchill, in a dedication address following Tom's death

FAMILY SUBMITTED PHOTOS

Lambair workers, above, dig out a plane in northern Manitoba. Left, Lamb, circa 1938, with a new plane he bought from Stinson Aircraft Corp. near Detroit, Mich.

Lamb also restored beaver populations around The Pas. The beaver had been trapped out of northwestern Manitoba since the end of the First World War.

In 1937, Lamb began restocking beaver and forbidding trappers to harvest them. Within 10 years, the beaver population grew to 700 on his 54,000-acre leased marsh.

In 1946, Lamb even stocked Tierra del Fuego on the southern tip of South America with 50 beavers. The Argentine government of the day hired him as part of a cockamamie economic development plan to start a fur industry.

However, the beavers have no natural predator in the area and have decimated forests in bulldozer-like fashion. Today, there are more than 100,000 beavers wreaking environmental havoc on the island of Tierra del Fuego.

Tom also once flew a planeload of live pigs and chickens to a customer in Nelson House. He once flew lynx from South Indian Lake to The Pas. "These lynx were the most vicious and meanest cargo I ever flew," he said.

MANITOBA-NESS

TOM Lamb was born in Grand Rapids in Manitoba's Interlake in 1898. Tom was one of 11 children born to T.H.P. (Thomas Henry Peacock) Lamb, originally from Yorkshire, England, and Caroline, née Marks, from Portsmouth, England.

In 1900, T.H.P. Lamb, a teacher, moved the family to Moose Lake, southeast of The Pas, to open an independent trading post. They were the only white family in Mosakahikan Cree Nation. The Cree people welcomed them with open arms as Lamb represented competition for their furs with the Hudson's Bay Company.

Tom married Jennie Armstrong on May 5, 1925. Jennie's father was an Armstrong—half-Irish, half-Scottish but "at our wedding he was half scotch and half rye," Tom quipped in his family memoir. Tom and Jennie had nine children, three girls and six boys. In order of birth: Sheila, Carol and Phyllis (Skippy), Greg, Donald and Dennis, Jack, Doug, Conrad.

The Moose Lake post traded with aboriginal people for furs like muskrat, beaver, red fox, coyote, mink and otter. It remained in the Lamb family until 1997 — almost a century. Tom Lamb's daughter and son-in-law, Carol and Jock McAcree ran it after him. It is now part of the Northern Store chain.

Tom quit school on the remote reserve after Grade 3. "Elijah Constant, an Indian from The Pas with a Grade 2 education, took over the school teaching job. There was no sense in me continuing school as I held one grade higher than Elijah," Tom explained.

Tom Lamb died of heart attack on Dec. 27, 1969, while he and Jennie were on vacation in Honolulu.

For more on Lamb, go to the family's website, www. lambair.com

5 THINGS YOU DIDN'T KNOW

1. Perhaps least-known about Tom Lamb is his childhood growing up the only white family on a remote Cree reserve east of The Pas. Before he died, he reminisced about his childhood in a 100-page memoir he left to his children.

2. Growing up, Tom loved sleeping in the Cree's birchbark tents. The tent floors were covered in balsam boughs, which lay flat and made the best beds, not like spruce bows, whose needles stick up and prick you. Tom learned the Cree language and had a traditional aboriginal grandfather, Nemoosim, from whom he learned things like how to snare rabbits and groundhogs. He also learned how to build deadfalls (a camouflaged pit) to catch animals as large as bears. He learned to stuff his mitts with fluff from cattails to keep his hands warm.

3. Lamb knew so many stories about the North. One was about medicine man Me-ke-wam, who had killed two white men by holding them underwater by their long hair.

Lamb in August 1957.

WINNIPEG TRIBUNE / UNIVERSITY OF MANITOBA ARCHIVES

The Cree at Moose Lake knew other whites wouldn't trade flintlock and knives with them if nothing was done about it. They made plans to kill Me-ke-wam but no one had the nerve to carry it out. So they did it together, emerging at once from teepees and firing him full of arrows and flintlock. Even the women attacked him with fish spears and pemmican stones until he finally succumbed.

4. "(The Cree people) never had any boxes or stools to sit on... Everyone sat cross-legged on the balsam floor. Birch-bark rogens (pouches made of sewn up birch bark) held dried-pounded fishmeal, berries and water baskets. Hollowed-out wooden plates and basins were in every teepee," Tom recalled.

5. Snow-blindness was a problem in springtime, and so Tom's dad sold "snow glasses." "Snow glasses were little wire mesh things with a green glass. They fit almost inside your eye socket. They were better than the green mosquito netting or cheesecloth, anything that would help snowblindness in April."

JAMES A. RICHARDSON

6

The father of commercial aviation in Canada

BY GEOFF KIRBYSON

HE wasn't a pilot or a daredevil or an inventor.

But James A. Richardson's contributions to aviation were as important to Canada as the Wright brothers' were to the U.S. Richardson masterminded the use of airplanes during peacetime, which led to the development of Canada's North and ultimately to the creation of a national passenger airline.

In the 1920s, few considered aviation outside of combat anything but a frivolous pursuit, said Shirley Render, executive director of the Western Canada Aviation Museum.

"Richardson saw planes as a way to open up and develop the North. There were no roads or railways (in the North). The railway was coast-to-coast, but it was only in the southern part of the country," she said.

"Until planes went into the bush, it would often take mineral explorers anywhere from two to six months just to get to a site. With a plane, they were there in three or four hours. They no longer had to paddle a canoe in the summer or travel by dogsled in the winter."

James A. Richardson, circa 1940.

GREATNESS

James A. Richardson was the father of commercial aviation in Canada. He was the fourth president of James Richardson & Sons Ltd., a role he held from 1918 to 1939.

He had a vision to use airplanes during peacetime to further Canadian commerce. The popular view at the time was that planes were tools of war.

He founded Western Canadian Airways in 1926, a company that pioneered the exploration of Canada's North. It also started passenger service between Winnipeg and Edmonton. Eventually, through various mergers, it became Canadian Airlines International, the second-largest passenger carrier in Canada.

He was president of the Winnipeg Grain Exchange and a director on many boards, including the Canadian Pacific Railway, the Canadian Imperial Bank of Commerce, International Nickel, the National Trust Company Limited and the Great-West Life Assurance Company.

He was a member of Canada's Aviation Hall of Fame.

Skis for planes and heaters for their engines helped the airline adapt to the realities of servicing the North.

DEPARTMENT OF NATIONAL DEFENCE

Richardson was prepared to overcome the "geographic immenseness" of the country, she said, to show there was value to the airplane, a concept grasped in other countries but virtually ignored in Canada.

"He wasn't a pilot, but he was able to gather people together who he could work with to overcome these immense obstacles. A lesser person would have shrugged their shoulders and said, 'We've got the railways, who cares about the North?' He cared," Render said.

Richardson launched his first airline, Western Canada Airways, in December 1926. Its fleet of 52 planes — the second-largest aviation company in the British Empire, trailing only London-based Imperial Airways — could land almost anywhere. In winter, the planes landed on skis on the frozen Red River at the foot of Brandon Avenue. In summer, they landed on floats.

Western Canada Airways provided regular access to remote northern areas, making Canada a world leader in bush flying. But Richardson was convinced transporting people from A to B was needed and his company was best-positioned to do it. Soon, the company launched passenger service between Winnipeg and Edmonton, an initiative that was rewarded with a government contract for a trial airmail service.

In 1930, the Canadian National Railway and Canadian Pacific each ponied up $250,000 to participate in Richardson's transcontinental airline venture. Canadian Airways Ltd. formed with Richardson as its president.

He'd planned to parlay the airline's experience and size into a government-backed national airline, but he was double-crossed by C.D. Howe, then minister of transport, who initially told Richardson he wanted Canadian Airways to be the national operator. Instead, Howe created Trans-Canada Airlines, the precursor to Air Canada.

Canadian Airways was sold to Canadian Pacific Airlines in 1941. Decades later, after a number of mergers, it became part of Canadian Airlines International, Canada's second-largest airline.

Barry Rempel, president and CEO of the Winnipeg Airports Authority, said despite being acknowledged as the father of commercial aviation in Canada, Richardson has never received the recognition his accomplishments deserved.

"There were lots of daredevils prior to him, people who were in it for the exploitation of aviation. Richardson was the first to see a commercial application. He truly believed Canada's North could be opened up through aviation in a way that would benefit Canada," he said.

For all these reasons, Winnipeg's airport was christened the James Armstrong Richardson International Airport on Dec. 10, 2006, exactly 80 years to the day after he incorporated Western Canadian Airways.

Richardson never had a chance to implement other plans that could have changed the course of Canadian history. He died of a heart attack at 54 in his Wellington Crescent mansion on June 26, 1939.

His death shocked the Winnipeg and Canadian business community. On the day of his funeral, trading activity at both the Winnipeg Grain Exchange and the Montreal Stock Exchange came to a standstill. Many businesses closed for the day, and across the country, flags were lowered to half-staff.

The Winnipeg Grain Exchange passed a resolution of condolence. It read: "In his death, Winnipeg has lost her leading citizen; Western Canada has lost a staunch and faithful friend; the many commercial and other boards on which Mr. Richardson sat as a member, have lost a wise counsellor. Canada has lost one of her most illustrious sons and the Winnipeg Grain Exchange, with whose growth and development the name Richardson was synonymous, has lost a real leader."

The stories of Richardson's kindness were told and retold. He was famous for his lack of pretence and the time he always had for the little guy.

A university professor, having just finished his thesis

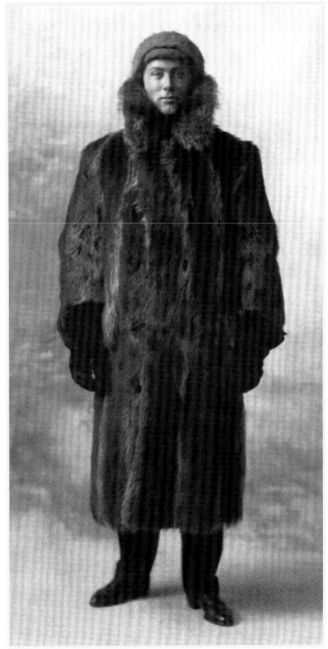

ARCHIVES JAMES RICHARDSON & SONS, LIMITED

Richardson in a fur coat, a symbol of his fondness for the North, in the 1930s.

'In his death, Winnipeg has lost her leading citizen; Western Canada has lost a staunch and faithful friend; the many commercial and other boards on which Mr. Richardson sat as a member, have lost a wise counsellor. Canada has lost one of her most illustrious sons and the Winnipeg Grain Exchange, with whose growth and development the name Richardson was synonymous, has lost a real leader'

— a resolution of condolence passed by the Winnipeg Grain Exchange in 1939

after months of work, didn't have the $1,000 it would cost to publish it. A fellow member of the faculty suggested he ask Richardson for help.

"I don't know the man," the professor said.

"Well, go see him anyway," his colleague replied.

The professor called upon Richardson and was greeted with a cheery, "Come in." After hearing the story, Richardson paid him $1,000 from his personal account.

Another story is of a young trader in the Winnipeg Grain Exchange who was having trouble making ends meet. He borrowed money from Richardson, but when he went to pay it back a few weeks later, Richardson had cancelled the debt upon learning the man's wife was ill.

Richardson's death may have cut short other plans he had, but it set the stage for James Richardson & Sons Ltd., the family company of which he was president, to break even more new ground when his wife and closest confidante, Muriel, succeeded him. She was the first woman to be inducted into the Canadian Business Hall of Fame after her 27-year reign, before she turned the company over to her sons, George and James.

Richardson was truly a visionary. So much of what the Winnipeg Airports Authority, the non-profit that runs Richardson International, is trying to do today, Rempel said, is rooted in that vision. That includes building critical mass in aviation, developing polar routes and building manufacturing and support facilities in Winnipeg.

"I thought we were doing great and wonderful things, but I've come to realize it's not truly original thinking," Rempel said. "Richardson was already thinking that way."

But for all his success, adventure, riches and fame, Richardson may have yearned for a simpler life, at least from time to time. He once told a taxi driver who drove him home, "Boy, I would trade jobs with you any day."

Lucky for Manitoba, the cabbie declined his offer.

Richardson and Winston Churchill leave the Winnipeg Grain Exchange in 1929.

ARCHIVES JAMES RICHARDSON & SONS, LIMITED

MANITOBA-NESS

Richardson, then chancellor of Queen's University, with Prime Minister Mackenzie King and President Franklin D. Roosevelt in 1938.

NATIONAL FILM BOARD OF CANADA

J AMES A. Richardson wasn't born in Manitoba, but he spent most of his life in the province. Perhaps the most important step he took was moving the head office of James Richardson & Sons Ltd. from Kingston, Ont., his hometown, to Winnipeg, in 1923, four years after becoming the firm's president.

His wife, Muriel, who ran the company for 27 years after his death in 1939, and their descendants, created the biggest family-owned business in Manitoba and one of the biggest in Canada, all based from its head office at Portage and Main.

As president of Canadian Airways Ltd., he launched its first passenger route from Winnipeg to Edmonton.

In December 2006, Winnipeg's airport was renamed the James Armstrong Richardson International Airport in his honour.

He died of a heart attack in his Wellington Crescent mansion on June 26, 1939, at age 54.

5 THINGS YOU DIDN'T KNOW

1. Richardson was not well-known to politicians and business people in Eastern Canada. Once he picked up a high-profile mover and shaker at the airport, and the man, thinking Richardson was the driver, offered him a tip at the end of the trip.

2. He was not one for small talk. His chief contribution at board meetings was often a recommendation that others "quit talking and do something."

3. He was rumoured to have made $10 million on International Nickel Company stock.

4. He enjoyed squash, golf, tennis, curling and had an active interest in swimming and fishing.

5. He also enjoyed the simple life and loved nothing more than putting on old clothes and puttering around his St. Vital farm, inspecting buildings, fences and repairing broken gates.

ARCHIVES JAMES RICHARDSON & SONS, LIMITED

Richardson, fourth from left, with managers of Canadian Airways in Montreal in 1933.

The original suffragette

BY MARGO GOODHAND

IT'S a shame the commemorative stamp Canada Post issued in 1973 to honour Nellie McClung, 100 years after her birth, depicts a rather grim elderly matron, the stereotypical suffragette.

That's not the woman Manitobans knew and loved, who brought a packed house at Winnipeg's Walker Theatre to its feet at the height of her public career in 1914.

It was the defining moment in the suffrage debate in Manitoba and in Canada, and McClung — an attractive, charismatic, witty 41-year-old — was centre stage.

One day earlier, she had joined a delegation of Manitobans pressing for women's right to vote. As the representative of the newly formed Political Equality League, McClung must have secretly been delighted at Premier Sir Rodmond Roblin's patronizing response.

Because the next night in a Mock Women's Parliament at the Walker — depicting a world where men couldn't vote and she was premier — McClung threw Roblin's words back at him. To the great amusement of the crowd, she captured the Conservative premier to a T, thumbs tucked in her lapels, twiddling her pinkies, teetering on her heels.

Nellie McClung, left, at her writing desk. Right, Canada Post issued a stamp in 1973 commemorating McClung 100 years after her birth.

Canada 8

postes postage
Nellie McClung 1873-1951

B.C. ARCHIVES

GREATNESS

Bestselling novelist, with 16 books to her credit. Her first novel, Sowing Seeds in Danny (1908) sold more than 100,000 copies, and earned more than $25,000. Eight others were also bestsellers.

Leading advocate for prohibition and women's rights, credited with the campaign that gave Manitoba women in 1916 the right to vote and hold public office — the first in Canada.

1914: After her husband was transferred to Edmonton, McClung joined the Edmonton Equal Franchise League. Alberta would follow Manitoba's lead on women's suffrage within two months.

1916: Embarked on a six-week, 40-city tour of the U.S. as a speaker for women's suffrage. American women would get the vote in 1920.

1921-26: Elected Liberal party member of the legislature in Alberta.

1926-29: Was one of the Famous Five of Alberta who petitioned the Supreme Court of Canada to get women declared "persons" under the BNA Act of 1867, which would grant them the same legal rights and privileges as men and the right to run for the Senate. They lost in 1928. A year later, they appealed to the Privy Council in London, England.

Continued on Page 47

Her "loud masterful commanding voice" rode roughshod over the delegation of men pushing a wheelbarrow full of petitions on stage, asking the all-female legislators for the vote.

"Man is made for something higher and better than voting," she said piously as the audience roared with laughter. "It may be that I am old-fashioned. I may be wrong. After all, men may be human. Perhaps the time will come when men may vote with women ..."

That was "Our Nell" — smart, feisty and fun — at her best.

McClung at five years old. At seven, she moved with her family to homestead in the Souris Valley in Manitoba.

It's hard to find an equal to Helen (Nellie) Letitia Mooney McClung, even a century later.

Try to find someone who wrote 16 books, raised five children, became a provincial politician, a syndicated newspaper columnist, a phenomenally popular public speaker and an eloquent advocate for prohibition, women's rights, health care, education and social reform.

Try to find someone who changed the lives of generations through her passion for the underdog — in a nation where "No woman, idiot, lunatic or criminal" was allowed to vote, according to the Dominion Franchise Act.

Growing up on a farm in south-central Manitoba in the 1880s, Nellie knew what she couldn't do. She couldn't run with the boys; she couldn't play ball in the schoolyard (for fear her legs might show); she couldn't be "too forward;" she had to stop "showing off."

Women couldn't be lawyers, judges, politicians. They were not considered "persons" under the British North America Act.

One of the few career paths open to women in the 1890s — other than life as a homemaker — was to become a writer or a teacher.

Nellie became all three.

And despite the odds, she grew up to be one of the most remarkable Canadians in history.

"I loved her sassiness, her determination and her spunk," says MLA Myrna Driedger, who hopes to one day see a monument to McClung at Manitoba's legislature.

"She's the one who started banging on the glass ceiling. I thought it was time we acknowledged her significant contributions to the lives of women in this province."

Young teacher Nellie Mooney's career as a political activist began in 1891 in Manitou, where she was introduced to the Women's Christian Temperance Union by her soon-to-be mother-in-law Annie McClung.

Alcoholism was a huge issue at the turn of the century, cutting a wide, sad swath through families and communities. The WCTU was also a place where women could talk about other issues, politics and current affairs. As McClung began to raise a family with her husband Wes, the WCTU offered a welcome window on the world.

McClung gave her first public speech at a national conference of the WCTU in Manitou in 1907. She never looked back.

"For the first time, I knew I had the power of speech," she wrote. "I saw faces brighten, eyes glisten, and felt the atmosphere crackle with a new power. I knew what could be done with words ..."

A year later, the young mother of three published her first novel, *Sowing Seeds in Danny*. It became a bestseller, propelling her into book tours and speaking engagements across the nation.

But it was when the family moved to Winnipeg in 1911 that Nellie McClung became the most famous women's activist in North America.

She had four children and was pregnant with her fifth, but she immediately joined her slick city mentors, the pioneering female journalists of the *Manitoba Free Press*, at the Canadian Women's Press Club.

In 1912, she also joined the Council of Women, which sought social reforms such as better conditions for factory workers. And that year, she had her first run-in with the Conservative premier when she and Mrs. Claude Nash met Roblin to press for a female factory inspector in Winnipeg.

They took him on a tour of two inner-city sweatshops that so shocked Roblin, he bolted, sputtering he "never knew such hellholes existed."

Still, he scolded them later, saying the inspector's job was "no job for a woman," and that he didn't "want a hyena in petticoats talking politics at me. I want a nice gentle creature to bring me my slippers."

The confrontation pushed McClung into a new

Nellie's Childhood Home

...a Road, one mile from Chatsworth, Ontario, in the County of Grey (nine mile south of Owen Sound) where she was born on Oct. 20, 1873.

...ch of the original Mooney log home, near Chatsworth, Ontario. Made from an original photograph.

Miss Nellie McClung, grand-daughter of the famous author, officiating at the unveiling, in 1957, of the Cairn located on the site of the old farm home, erected by the Women's Institute of Grey County, in loving memory of Nellie McClung. The plaque reads: "Nellie (Mooney) McClung — Lecturer, Legislator, Teacher, Writer. Ardent advocate of women's rights in Canada."

'S FATHER

...MOONEY, who came from... in 1830 at the age of 18.

MOONEY CREST

HER SISTERS

HANNAH (Mrs. H. M. Sweet)

ELIZABETH (Mrs. Tom Rae)

HER BROTHERS

HER MOTHER

WILLIAM

JACK

GEORGE

...LETITIA (McCurdy) MOONEY — from Dundee, Scotland. Married in 1858.

9

---

organization, the Political Equality League, which would go on to stage the mock parliament that turned the tide of public opinion on women's suffrage.

She campaigned for the Liberal party in 1914 and again in 1915, speaking to packed houses from Minto to Melita. She was burned in effigy in Brandon and went from being "Our Nell" the popular novelist to "Calamity Nell" in the Conservatives' eyes.

By all accounts, McClung was a terrific speaker. She made people laugh, she was quick on her feet, she always had a witty response for hecklers. No audience stayed hostile.

And though the Liberals lost in 1914, they won the year later, and kept their promise to give women the vote in 1916.

Jan. 27, 1916, the Bill for the Enfranchisement of Women passed in Manitoba — the end of a "bonny fight, a knock-down drag-out fight, uniting the women of Manitoba in a great cause," McClung wrote.

The gallery was packed with women dressed in purple and yellow, the suffragette colours, watching as the men down below passed the historic bill. A lone, high, proud voice began to sing *O Canada*, and legislators and suffragettes, men and women, all joined in.

A telegram went out from the house to McClung, now living in Alberta. It read: "From the women voters of Manitoba to Mrs. McClung, for the great service she has rendered her cause in Manitoba."

They won on Oct. 18, 1929. The headlines read: "Privy Council declares that women are persons." The five women are honoured in a beautiful statue on Parliament Hill in Ottawa: Emily Murphy, Nellie McClung, Henrietta Edwards, Louise McKinney and Irene Parlby.

1936: First woman to serve on the board of governors of the Canadian Broadcasting Corporation.

1938: The only female Canadian delegate to the League of Nations in Geneva, Switzerland.

Wrote a syndicated newspaper column for years, Leaves from Lantern Lane, from her retirement home in Victoria, B.C.

She fought for old age pensions, mothers' allowances, education and social reform, better working conditions for labourers, prohibition, birth control, more liberal divorce laws — the underdog, always. When she and Wes retired to B.C. in the 1930s, she took up the cause of unjustly interned Japanese-Canadians.

MANITOBA ARCHIVES

McClung's first home with her husband Wesley, built in Manitou in the 1880s.

'Never retract, never explain, never apologize — get the thing done and let them howl'

— McClung's famous slogan on the campaign trail, not found in her literature, but credited to her in the preface of her 1915 book, In Times Like These

'I do not want to pull through life like a thread that has no knot. I want to leave something behind me when I go; some small legacy of truth, some word that will shine in a dark place'

— this quote from McClung is on the plaque at the little Wolseley park that bears her name

'If I were only a few years younger, I'd move tomorrow to Winnipeg with its blizzards'

— an ailing McClung near the end of her life to a visitor in Victoria who remarked on her beautiful garden

MANITOBA-NESS

BORN Helen Letitia "Nellie" Mooney, Oct. 20, 1873, in Grey County, Ont. Died Sept. 1, 1951 in Victoria, B.C. But she grew up in Manitoba and reached the pinnacle of her public career here in 1914 and 1915.

The Mooney family was part of the great wave of homesteaders who arrived in Manitoba in the 1880s. McClung spent her first night in Manitoba at the age of six in "Tent City" at The Forks in 1880, with hundreds of other hopeful settlers, and then moved to a rental house in St. James while the men in her family built a log home southeast of the Brandon Hills.

The buffalo had disappeared just one year prior. Between 1880 and 1883, towns such as Treherne, Manitou and Carberry sprang up.

Growing up on a remote homestead near current-day Wawanesa, 128 kilometres southwest of Portage la Prairie, McClung couldn't even read until she was 10 years old, because there was no school. But she became a teacher by the time she was 16, passing her exams in Winnipeg in 1889.

She taught school for five years in south-central Manitoba — at Hazel, Manitou, Treherne and Northfield schools — and it was here she became part of another great wave, at the turn of the century, as women began to seek equal rights with men.

In 1896, she married Wes McClung, who owned a drugstore and was mayor of Manitou for a term.

She wrote three books while in Manitoba, including *Sowing Seeds in Danny.*

In 1911, her husband took a job with a life insurance company and moved the family to Winnipeg, then the third-largest city in Canada. The family bought a lakeshore cottage at Matlock Beach and a home in the bustling new suburb of Wolseley at 97 Chestnut St., with a writing room for McClung.

In 1914, the Political Equality League and a host of other delegates asked the Manitoba legislature for voting rights for women — and were dismissed by the premier, Sir Rodmond Roblin. The next night, the league presented a mock parliament with McClung playing Roblin. Despite criticism that she was "neglecting" her five children, McClung toured Manitoba that year, campaigning for the Liberals. They were narrowly defeated in the July election. In October, McClung and her allies marched on the legislature to demand temperance legislation. Roblin ordered his Tories to leave the house.

In 1915, McClung returned to Manitoba to campaign for the Liberal party, again playing to packed houses. This time, they won.

"It is acknowledged throughout Manitoba that the most powerful speeches of the recent political campaign were made by a woman, Mrs. Nellie McClung," claimed the post-election editorial in the *Grain Growers Guide.*

5 THINGS YOU DIDN'T KNOW

1. There's a Nellie McClung Collegiate in Manitou and a little Nellie McClung Park on Winnipeg's Wolseley Avenue. The house she lived in from 1904 to 1911 in Manitou was relocated to the Archibald Historical Museum at La Riviere, Man., and restored as a museum. There's a bust of her at Winnipeg's Assiniboine Park Citizens Hall of Fame. McClung's Winnipeg house at 97 Chestnut St., from which she gained international renown, is a private home, slowly and beautifully being restored by its owners. "If this house was in any other city — any other city in Canada — it would be a landmark," says owner Kurt Markstrom. And if Myrna Driedger gets her way, a statue of McClung will one day grace the legislature's west side.

2. A number of Nellie McClung's relatives still live in Winnipeg. One of Nellie's great-great-great nieces, Emilie Anderson-Gregoire, didn't find out she was related to the famous suffragette until she was halfway through a Grade 6 social studies project. "My mom told me," says the now-19-year-old with the warm brown eyes. "I thought it was the coolest thing ever. I was so proud to be related to her."

3. Nellie was inspired herself in part by the sharp and sassy female journalists at the Free Press. She wrote three pages in her memoir on a single encounter in 1890 with agricultural reporter E. Cora Hind, at the Manitou train station, entitled "I Saw E. Cora Hind." The 17-year-old country schoolteacher never got the courage to speak to Hind that day, but noted Hind's "little hat, fresh and lovely colour on her face and fine dark blue eyes beaming with health and friendliness. I had never seen prettier shoes." She wrote away for a book on shorthand immediately after, hoping it would pave the way to a career in newspapers.

4. A meagre Wikipedia entry notes McClung was an advocate of eugenics — sterilization of mentally handicapped girls. She's not around to defend herself, but it was a tenet of its time. It's sad that a life's work could be diminished to 20 lines — two of them devoted to a purported cause that doesn't even make her memoirs.

5. In an ironic twist, the woman who spent her life fighting for prohibition ended up watching at least two of her youngsters battle alcoholism.

A portrait of the young McClung at the start of her writing career.

NATIONAL ARCHIVES OF CANADA

JAMES SHAVER WOODSWORTH

8

BY DOUG SPEIRS

Man on a mission

A portrait of Woodsworth hangs in the stairwell of J.S. Woodsworth House in Winnipeg.

MIKE APORIUS / WINNIPEG FREE PRESS ARCHIVES

James Shaver Woodsworth presides over an early strategy meeting of the Co-operative Commonwealth Federation. From left are Tommy Douglas, Andus MacInnis, A.A. Heaps and Woodsworth.

IT was 1985 — *Back to the Future* was a box-office smash, *We Are the World* rocked the airwaves and *Calvin and Hobbes* arrived in 35 newspapers — when Winnipeg academic and author Allen Mills made his way to the National Archives in Ottawa.

For Mills, a University of Winnipeg politics professor, it was a research trip, a chance to immerse himself in the personal papers of a Manitoba and Canadian icon — James Shaver Woodsworth.

As he rummaged through Woodsworth's dusty documents and books, Mills made a curious discovery — a hatbox, about a foot-square, covered in a faded paisley pattern.

"I wondered to myself, 'What the heck is this?'" a bemused Mills recalls in an interview. "I opened the box and there it was — a life-size crown of thorns! It was the kind of thing you see in depictions of Christ in any Catholic church.

"In 1906, J.S. Woodsworth went to Palestine on holidays, and he apparently bought a crown of thorns as a souvenir. In many ways, it's a perfect metaphor of his life. He was a kind of latter-day Christ, a suffering servant of change. He gave himself to the world."

GREATNESS

As a founder and first leader of the Co-operative Commonwealth Federation — the forerunner of the New Democratic Party — Woodsworth helped establish a multi-party political system in Canada. For the first time, the left became a third-party force at the national level.

While superintendent of Winnipeg's All Peoples' Mission in the North End, he began writing two books — Strangers Within Our Gates (1909) and My Neighbour (1911) — required reading for students of social reform in Canada.

Considered one of the founding fathers of socialism in Canada, his tireless efforts to create a fairer society — he helped lay the groundwork for unemployment insurance and medicare — earned him the nickname "the conscience of Canada."

We are indebted to Woodsworth for the corner-stone of Canada's social security system — the old-age pension. In 1926, Woodsworth offered to support the fragile government of Mackenzie King in return for a pledge to pass pension legislation. King agreed.

He is the most well-known advocate of the so-called social gospel — a creedless movement of social reform calling for the establishment of the Kingdom of God "here and now." He represented the riding of Winnipeg Centre from 1921 until his death in 1942.

Latter-day Christ? As metaphors go, that's hard to top. But for Mills and others touched by Woodsworth's sweeping legacy it's not far off the mark.

Woodsworth certainly didn't walk on water, but he definitely walked the walk. As a cleric, social activist, longshoreman, author, missionary, member of Parliament and driving force behind Canadian social-

PHOTO COURTESY OF CENTRE FOR CHRISTIAN STUDIES

Woodsworth married Lucy Lilian Staples in 1904.

ism, Woodsworth dedicated himself to making life a little more tolerable for the huddled masses.

Consider the evidence: Without Woodsworth, Canadians might not enjoy the benefits of many things we now hold sacred — old-age pensions, unemployment insurance, medicare and a multi-party political system. Not a bad list by any measure.

"I would say he is the most significant politician at the national level to come out of Manitoba," declares Mills, author of *Fool for Christ: The Political Thought of J.S. Woodsworth.*

"He helped form a national party (the Co-operative Commonwealth Federation, which later morphed into the New Democratic Party) that reshaped the national political debate in this country.

It doesn't take much prodding to get NDP MP Pat Martin to wax poetic about Woodsworth, who represented the same riding as Martin, Winnipeg Centre, from 1921 to his death in 1942.

"For most of the 20th century, my riding has been represented by two of the greatest champions of social justice our country has ever known — J.S. Woodsworth and Stanley Knowles," gushes Martin, whose grandfather was Woodsworth's friend.

"Politicians like J.S. Woodsworth don't grow on trees. Our party is lucky to have had quite a few — Tommy Douglas, Knowles, Bill Blaikie — all men of the cloth and all rooted in the finest tradition of selfless public service. But it was J.S. Woodsworth who blazed the trail."

Like many great Manitobans, Woodsworth wasn't actually born in this province. The oldest of six children, he was born in Etobicoke, Ont., on July 29, 1874. The family moved to Brandon in 1885 when Woodsworth's father became head of Methodist missions for Western Canada.

Woodsworth went into the family business, becoming a Methodist minister. But, as Mills notes, no sooner had he entered the ministry than he wanted out.

NATIONAL ARCHIVES OF CANADA

Woodsworth addresses a crowd in 1935.

'He deserves to be remembered because he was a political leader in the very best tradition of selfless public service. A champion of social justice who entered politics for one reason only — to elevate the living and social conditions of the people he represented. A great Manitoban'

— NDP MP Pat Martin, whose Winnipeg Centre riding was represented by Woodsworth from 1921-1942

Canadians of To-morrow

By J. S. Woodsworth

Some ten years ago at a Children's Festival in Toronto, I witnessed a pageant illustrating the historical development of the Canadian people. First came a band of little Red Men dressed in blankets and feathers and beads. Then across the stage danced a gaily dressed group of Habitants. Next followed a mixed company representing the John Bulls and Sandy Macs and Paddys from Cork. Then came the "hit" of the evening—an outlandishly dressed row of little Doukhobors. The Doukhobors had just arrived in Canada.

Such a conception fairly presented the national elements that composed our population ten years ago. But to-day all is changed. An ordinary stage would not be large enough to hold the fifty groups of immigrants that are now crowding to our shores.

What a picturesque array! The parti-colored flags, the quaint costumes, the strange folk-dancers, the medley of songs, the ensemble is utterly bewildering yet full of charm. Probably it is this picturesque aspect of our immigration that first arrests our attention. To meet the immigrant trains is almost as interesting as to travel through Europe. Bits of Europe and Asia transferred to Canada, and intermingled in endless combinations. Put in a background of pioneer conditions and a natural beauty not yet revealed to the world.—What a field for an artist!

Then comes the dis-illusionment. The quaint costume smells to heaven. The attractive dance ends in a brutal fight. Our

Polish Peasant Woman and Polish Children in Kindergarten of All Peoples Mission.

ARCHIVES OF CANADA

One of Woodsworth's social justice handbills.

Disillusioned by the church's emphasis on the hereafter, he became a leading advocate of the "social gospel" — a movement calling for the establishment of the Kingdom of God "here and now."

He moved from the pulpit to the streets in 1907 as superintendent of All Peoples' Mission on Stella Avenue in Winnipeg's North End, where he spent six years witnessing the horrific conditions endured by new immigrants and the poor.

"He made the mission a centre for social justice," says Mills, "It agitated for social causes. The mission period is very important to him. It taught him the importance of action, not just sermonizing."

As Pat Martin tells it, Canada might have lost another legend of the left if it weren't for Woodsworth's six years at the Winnipeg mission.

"One of those families he helped was that of the young Tommy Douglas, who would have lost his leg at age nine or 10 had the mission not found a doctor willing to operate on him pro-bono," Martin explains.

Woodsworth's radical writing made him the darling of social reformers across the country, and he left Winnipeg in 1913 to become secretary of the Canadian Welfare League.

But Woodsworth was adamantly pacifist, a belief to which he would cling all his life. He was fired from a government research job in 1917 for his opposition to the First World War. He returned to the ministry in B.C., but resigned in 1918 because of the church's support of the war.

After working as a longshoreman to support his family — he married Lucy Lilian Staples in 1904 and had six children; his daughter Grace Woodsworth MacInnis served as an MLA and MP from Vancouver and received the Order of Canada in 1974 — he changed careers again, touring as a speaker for workers' rights, which landed him back in Winnipeg in 1919 just as the Winnipeg General Strike began.

"He's often thought of as the great leader of the strike, but he wasn't," Mills says. "It's a myth. He was really a bit player."

Woodsworth did deliver stirring speeches to strikers, but he emphasized peace and orderliness. "He's a socialist, but he's not a Marxist or a revolutionary," Mills notes.

Then, when the editor of the strikers' newspaper was jailed, Woodsworth famously stepped into the role and quickly found himself locked up on charges of seditious libel for "promoting treasonous ideas."

Laughs Martin: "The language he was accused of using to incite the strikers turned out to be quotes from the Bible, the book of Isaiah, in fact."

Woodsworth spent five days cooling his heels in jail, but the case was never prosecuted. A turning point for Woodsworth? Mills says no, it wasn't. But getting locked up gave him serious street credentials among Winnipeg's working people.

That paid off in 1921, when Woodsworth was elected the Independent Labour Party member of Parliament for Winnipeg North, with the slogan "Human Needs before Property Rights."

The first bill he pushed concerned unemployment insurance. It didn't go far, but Woodsworth was nothing if not dogged. Every year, Woodsworth, a master of parliamentary procedure, brought a motion calling for the creation in Canada of a "co-operative commonwealth."

"He wanted the state to ease poverty and suffering," Mills says, "instead of a dog-eat-dog world, a place where people looked at each other as brothers and sisters."

In 1926, Woodsworth swapped his vote and that of a colleague to win a pledge from the fragile government of Mackenzie King for an old-age pension plan.

"Stanley Knowles would go on to achieve huge improvements to old-age security over the years, but it was Woodsworth who pried this huge concession out of the hands of the party of big business and the whole country should thank him for it," the NDP's Martin says.

Woodsworth's shining moment came in 1933 when he changed Canada's political landscape forever: Working with socialist and labour groups, he founded and became the first leader of the CCF, the forerunner of the NDP. The two-party system was broken; the left had a voice in Ottawa.

Always a slight man of uncertain health, Woodsworth was handcuffed by his pacifism. While other members of his party saw the need to use force to stop Hitler, he alone rose to record his opposition to going to war in 1939.

His days as a party leader were done. In 1940, he won his last election, and in the spring of 1942, weakened by a stroke, J.S. Woodsworth died.

By all accounts, he was not a fun guy. He was a single-minded man on a mission. Few know he was an early advocate for birth control, the vote for women and equality among the sexes in marriage. He also vehemently opposed smoking and gambling.

"As far as I can see, he never cracked a joke in his life," Mills concedes when asked if the man had a lighter side. "He was a very serious individual, probably too serious for his own good.

"He was sort of a one-dimensional man — his politics was his life. I really think he drove himself to an early grave."

Woodsworth probably wouldn't care that he has largely faded from memory today. He'd likely just be content the social reforms he fought for made Canada a kinder, gentler place.

In hindsight, maybe that crown of thorns wasn't such a strange souvenir after all.

Woodsworth, back row second from right, with his class at Wesley College, circa 1896.

Woodsworth as a young man.

NATIONAL ARCHIVES OF CANADA

MANITOBA-NESS

J.S. Woodsworth House on Maryland Street in Winnipeg.

Lucy Woodsworth on the veranda of the family home in 1945.

WHO could ever forget J.S. Woodsworth? Well, as it turns out, a lot of you.

And that's a shame. We owe a tremendous amount to J.S. Woodsworth, who is widely regarded as one of the pre-eminent politicians in Canadian history.

In 2004, a CBC contest rated Woodsworth as the 100th Greatest Canadian of all time. He deserves a much higher ranking in our list of Greatest Manitobans.

Born in Etobicoke, Ont., in 1874, Woodsworth entered public life as a Methodist minister around 1900 in rural Manitoba. His pioneering views on social reform were largely forged during his time as head of Winnipeg's All Peoples' Mission, where he spent six years helping the city's impoverished immigrant community.

During the First World War, he became a prominent opponent of conscription and was jailed during the Winnipeg General Strike on charges of seditious libel. The case was never pursued, but it made Woodsworth's name among the working classes, who sent him to Ottawa in 1921 as the MP for Winnipeg Centre.

Woodsworth served that riding until his death in 1942. Along the way, he reshaped Canada's political landscape by founding the Co-operative Commonwealth Federation in 1933. That party, the forerunner of the NDP, broke the two-party system and gave the left a voice at the national level.

Another shining moment came in 1926 when he and a fellow labourite, A.A. Heaps, held the balance of power in the Commons and forced the King government to pass old-age pension legislation, the cornerstone of our country's social security system.

But, above all, he was a Manitoban. He preached here, he taught here, his visionary ideas were formed

PHOTO COURTESY OF CENTRE FOR CHRISTIAN STUDIES

'There are few men in this Parliament for whom I have greater respect than the leader of the Co-operative Commonwealth Federation. I admire him in my heart, because time and again he has had the courage to say what lays on his conscience, regardless of what the world might think of him. A man of that calibre is an ornament to any Parliament'

— Prime Minister Mackenzie King, on Woodsworth's opposition to Canada's entry into the Second World War in 1939

here. Backed by the people of Winnipeg Centre, he moved from the pulpit to politics and helped a young nation understand the meaning of "social justice."

At one time, he was called a saint, a prophet, and "the conscience of Canada." Politicians of all stripes revered this frail man from Manitoba.

Is he forgotten today? "In a way, yes, he is," laments U of W politics professor Allen Mills, an expert on Woodsworth's life, "Social pioneers often leave a legacy that lives on and people don't know who is responsible."

We may not remember J.S. Woodsworth, but we have a lot for which to thank him.

5 THINGS YOU DIDN'T KNOW

1. Canada's father of medicare, Tommy Douglas, might not have been around if it weren't for Woodsworth's time spent running All Peoples' Mission on Stella Avenue in Winnipeg. The story goes that Douglas would have lost a leg at about age 10 but a mission doctor saved his life and limb.

2. A leading opponent of conscription and a lifelong pacifist, Woodsworth was the only MP to rise and record his opposition to Canada entering the Second World War. Even his Co-operative Commonwealth Colleagues voted for war. Not even Tommy Douglas, who had just returned from Europe, could persuade him force was needed to stop Hitler.

3. As editor of the strikers' newspaper during the 1919 Winnipeg General Strike, he was arrested and jailed for five days on charges of "seditious libel." As it turns out, the shocking comments in question were taken from the Bible. To be precise,

the book of Isaiah. Myth has it Woodsworth was a key leader of the strike. In fact, his role was minimal.

4. Few people are aware that Woodsworth was ahead of his time on a number of moral issues. For example, he swam upstream as an early advocate for birth control, the vote for women, men and women being equal in marriage, as well as his opposition to smoking and gambling.

5. This year we are marking the 75th anniversary of the founding convention of the CCF, forerunner of the NDP. The closing sentence of the Regina Manifesto states: "The CCF will not rest content until every person in this land and in all other lands is able to enjoy equality and freedom, a sense of human dignity and an opportunity to live a rich and meaningful life as a citizen of a free and peaceful world. This is the Co-operative Commonwealth Federation, which the CCF invites the people of Canada to build with imagination and pride."

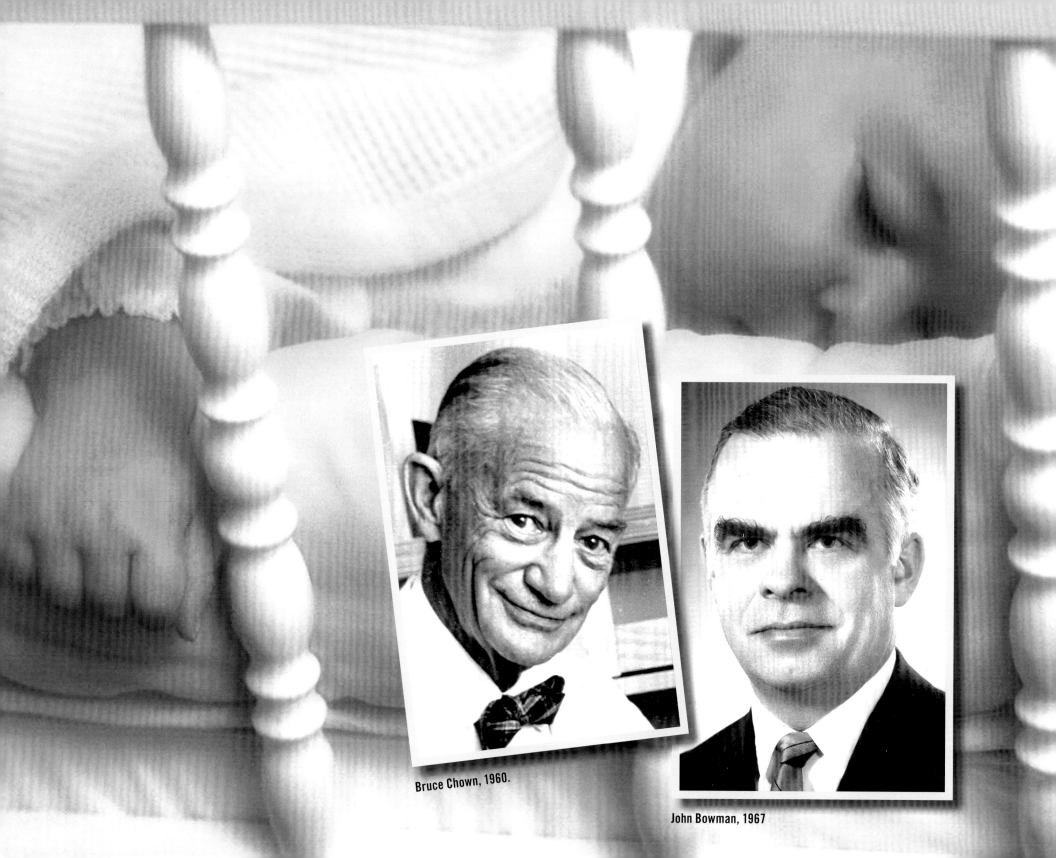

Bruce Chown, 1960.

John Bowman, 1967

BY MEGHAN HURLEY

Pediatric pioneers

DR. JOHN BOWMAN

DR. BRUCE CHOWN

9

DR. John Bowman faced a dilemma. A devoted father of five, the renowned pediatric researcher knew the day of his daughter's wedding was to be a happy one for his close-knit family.

But another of Bowman's children, a baby yet to be born to one of his patients, might enter the world the day of the wedding — and instantly, this child would face problems that could prove fatal without Bowman's help.

Bowman and his research partner, Dr. Bruce Chown, saved thousands of babies who would have died of rhesus disease. They gained worldwide recognition in 1968 when they developed WinRho, a vaccine that prevented the disease.

Before that, mothers with Rh-negative blood who carried an Rh-positive fetus developed antibodies that made her body react against the fetus. In later pregnancies, if she carried another Rh-positive fetus, that immune reaction generally caused a miscarriage or was fatal to the baby shortly after birth.

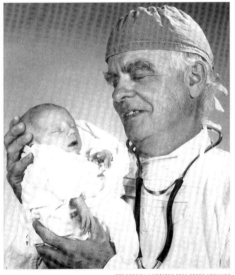

JEFF DEBOOY / WINNIPEG FREE PRESS ARCHIVES

John Bowman with a very tiny patient in June 1980.

GREATNESS

Dr. Bruce Chown
Made an Officer of the Order of Canada: 1968
Founded the Winnipeg Rh Institute: 1968
Developed WinRho: 1968
Awarded the Karl Landsteiner Memorial Award: 1971

Dr. John Bowman
Became clinical director of the Rh Lab: 1961
Completed the first successful intrauterine transfusion in North America: 1964
Developed WinRho: 1968
Made an Officer of the Order of Canada: 1983

Chown and Bowman
Dr. Bruce Chown and Dr. John Bowman, both born in Winnipeg, pioneered treatment for babies born with rhesus disease and eventually a vaccine that prevented the fatal illness.
The doctors gained worldwide recognition when they developed WinRho in 1968.
Before WinRho was discovered, Rh-negative mothers who carried an Rh-positive baby developed antibodies that treated the fetus like an intruder in the mother's body.

Continued on Page 61

WINNIPEG FREE PRESS ARCHIVES

Bowman sits with pictures of babies his work saved.

Before the vaccine, doctors used blood transfusions to save many of these babies.

Bowman knew the baby due on his daughter's wedding day would need such a blood transfusion. He discussed with his colleague, Dr. Molly Seshia, what he should do if the baby arrived on time.

"If she delivered the same day as his daughter's wedding, he didn't know whether he should go to his daughter's wedding or whether he should go to the delivery," Seshia said. "It made such an impact on me that I still remember the name of the patient. The good thing is she didn't have the baby on the day of his daughter's wedding because I honestly think it would have caused him a major dilemma."

It's telling that Bowman struggled between his own family and one of the many, many families his life's work helped create.

Chown and Bowman were not early researchers on Rh factor disease.

Austrian-American physician Karl Landsteiner discovered the cause of the disease in 1940, and after that, the Manitoba doctors were among many worldwide who developed treatments for these babies and researched a vaccine to avoid the disease.

They performed thousands of blood transfusions that saved the lives of newborns.

Maxine Bambridge is one of the mothers whose child was saved by Chown and Bowman.

If not for their early work, Bambridge would never have brought home from hospital Jim — now 43 and with children of his own, grandchildren Bambridge would not have had.

"When I see how healthy my son is and what he's accomplished, it's quite a treasure," Bambridge says.

"It would have been a sad homecoming without bringing Jim home. When I packed the clothes up, it was one of the hardest things because I didn't know if I was going home with Jim or not."

She remembers watching Jim lying in the hospital nursery, limp and listless as a rag doll. Her heart was breaking as she packed up the new baby clothes to take home from the hospital, unsure Jim would live to wear them.

But Jim was a lucky baby. Chown and Bowman's use of blood transfusions to treat babies with rhesus disease saved him.

That work led to their eventual breakthrough of the vaccine that prevented the disease, which put Winnipeg on the neonatal map. Pregnant women from as far away as Brazil, Mexico and the United States came to Winnipeg for treatment.

Chown took a long route to his work in the labs of Winnipeg's Children's Hospital. After graduation from

McGill University in 1914, he enlisted as a Canadian Armed Forces artillery officer in the First World War.

After the war, he earned his medical degree at the University of Manitoba then spent three years at Columbia, Cornell and Johns Hopkins universities where he completed his specialty training in pediatrics.

In 1922, he married Gladys Webb. The couple had four children. The Chown family returned to Winnipeg in 1925, where he began his 52-year medical career at the Children's Hospital. There were few trained pediatricians in Canada at the time, and Chown may have been Manitoba's only one.

A brilliant man, Chown's colleagues jokingly called him the professor of "rareology" because he was so adept at diagnosing and treating rare illnesses.

In 1944, Chown accepted a grant from the National Research Council to create the Rh Lab in the basement of the Children's Hospital. The same year, Chown offered free Rh testing for pregnant women in exchange for examining the Rh-positive babies after birth. It was a bold step forward in public health policy to offer such widespread testing, and Manitoba was the only jurisdiction to do so.

By the mid-1940s, doctors had adopted blood transfusions for Rh-positive babies of Rh-negative mothers as an effective treatment that saved thousands of babies.

Chown's work made *Winnipeg Free Press* headlines in 1953 when he set a record, having used blood transfusions to save four children in the same family.

"For the first time, in the opinion of Dr. Bruce Chown, professor of pediatrics at the University of Manitoba," an unnamed reporter wrote, "four members of one family have been saved from destruction or imbecility caused by a deadly agent in their mother's bloodstream."

Florence Seepish had already given birth to two healthy children, but a third died shortly after birth. Without Chown's pioneering treatment, Seepish's other Rh-positive babies would have died.

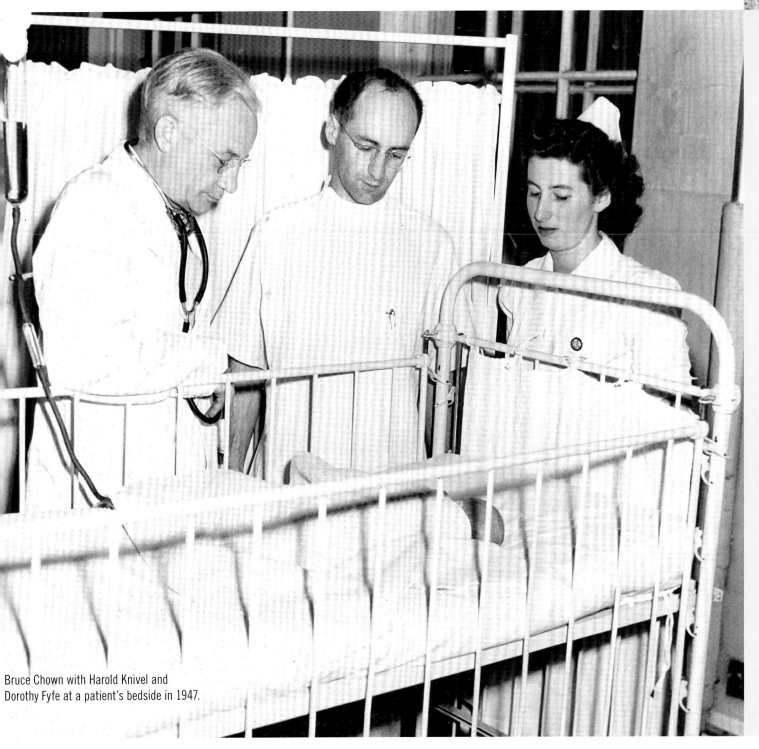

Bruce Chown with Harold Knivel and Dorothy Fyfe at a patient's bedside in 1947.

The mother would be able to carry a healthy first child to term, but following pregnancies could be affected. Generally, the reaction causes a miscarriage or is fatal to the baby shortly after birth.

Chown and Bowman's work put Winnipeg on the neonatal map. Rh-negative women pregnant with Rh-positive babies travelled from around the world for treatment.

Both Chown and Bowman graduated from the University of Manitoba and completed advanced training in the United States. They both returned to their hometown to practise medicine and do research.

WINNIPEG TRIBUNE / UNIVERSITY OF MANITOBA ARCHIVES

Bowman receives Winnipeg Children's Hospital's first annual Teddy Award from Arnold Naimark.

'When I see how healthy my son is and what he's accomplished, it's quite a treasure. It would have been a sad homecoming without bringing Jim home. When I packed the clothes up, it was one of the hardest things because I didn't know if I was going home with Jim or not'

— Maxine Bambridge, whose son, Jim, was saved by blood transfusions

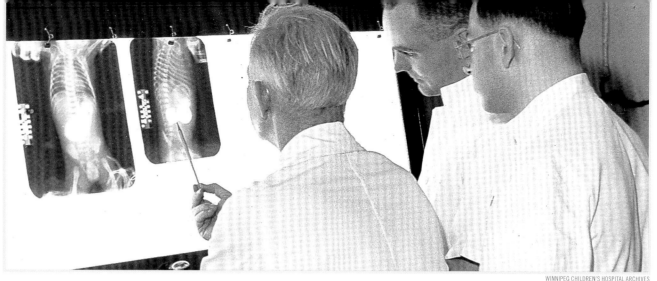

WINNIPEG CHILDREN'S HOSPITAL ARCHIVES

Chown teaches residents in 1947.

By 1963, Chown's work had saved six Seepish children — Ken, Linda, Frank, Theresa, Marie and Tom.

"I wouldn't be here today so it's pretty amazing," said Theresa Gallop, one of the Seepish daughters. "I didn't really think about it until I was older. Now, we're all very healthy."

Chown's dedication showed in his sometimes absent-minded approach to practical matters in life. A young intern — actually the twin brother of Dr. John Bowman, later Chown's research partner — recalls heading out to Winkler with Chown in the dead of winter to deliver a baby. At 40 below, Bill Bowman knew they wouldn't last long once he realized Chown had driven his sad little British car until the tank was empty. But as was so often the case for Chown, luck was on his side.

"It was pitch-black and bitterly cold. We stopped in front of a gas station which was pitch-black and nobody was there. But it was a two-storey so the tenant lived above," Bill Bowman said.

"They came out, filled our gas tank, and we went on our way. It saved our lives. The good Lord was looking after Bruce."

A lucky man perhaps, but Chown's life was not without sadness. His wife Gladys died after a stroke in 1948, and he married Allison Grant in 1949.

The couple had a son.

Chown might well have been content to know he'd pioneered a treatment that saved so many babies with Rh disease. But a true researcher at heart, he believed there had to be a better way. There had to be a vaccine or some other way to stop the disease from developing before the damage was done.

So in his 60s, when he might have chosen retirement, he turned all his attention to research. He began working full-time in the Rh Lab he'd established 10 years before.

It was after almost 15 years of hard work in that lab before Chown — with his young research partner, Bowman — unveiled the vaccine that *Time* magazine hailed as one of the Top 10 medical discoveries of the 1960s. The magazine reported 50,000 babies in the U.S. alone had been saved in the 10 years after the vaccine's development.

THERE is something to be said for sibling rivalry. When Dr. John Bowman — Jack to his friends — realized his identical twin brother, Bill, was working with the great Dr. Bruce Chown, Jack decided that was the work for him, too. It was ever thus.

As boys, the twins saw their doctor father too often get up at 3 a.m. to deliver babies. Both decided engineering would provide a good life.

"(We) swore we would never be doctors because it was too hard," Bill said.

"I got a summer job working on mustard gas in a lab, and I found it fascinating. So I thought I would go into medicine after all."

That's when Jack thought he'd better go into medicine, too.

Jack Bowman graduated from the University of Manitoba's medical school in 1949, the same year he married Constance. Eventually, their family included five children, two boys and three girls.

Bowman started a family practice in Oakville with Constance working by his side as nurse, bookkeeper and accountant.

After two years as a rural doctor, Bowman did postgraduate training at hospitals in Manitoba and the United States. He certified in pediatrics in 1956 and studied and lectured at Queen's University in Ontario for a year.

But sibling rivalry pulled him back to the West. Bowman returned to Winnipeg in 1957 to join his brother in the Manitoba Medical Clinic's pediatric department.

There, he took his first step toward his breakthrough work on Rh disease. He started working with the great Dr. Bruce Chown in the Rh Lab. Bowman administered blood transfusions to treat babies with Rh disease. Under his care, the survival rate of those babies soared to 90 per cent from 75.

About that time, Bill Bowman was lured to England by a fellowship, leaving his research work with Chown in the Manitoba lab. That's when Jack Bowman stepped in.

"He became more and more interested in Rh disease and the management of it and more specifically neonatology, diseases of the newborn," Bowman's son, Tom, said. "He gradually switched over to doing that full-time and stopped doing general pediatrics."

Bowman pushed the cause forward in Canada, introducing a method of performing blood transfusions intrauterine — before the baby was born — which increased babies' survival rate even more.

But this was not enough for Bowman. He was keen to do research work with Chown.

All research is built on the work of researchers who came before, and Chown knew that. He always made time to mentor young people who would continue his work after him. Bowman was one of the researchers Chown mentored.

Bowman's twin credits their lifelong competition — with his brother always riding his bicycle a few feet in front, always trying to top him in school — giving Bowman the determination a researcher needs to keep at a task until the problem is solved. Certainly, those who worked with Bowman say they were inspired by his drive.

"Jack had to be first. We were very good students, and he was always first in the class and I was always second," his twin brother joked.

"To compete with Jack would have been just fatal. I was OK with him being first as long as I was second."

Chown and Bowman wondered if they could make a vaccine from the plasma of Rh-negative women who had given birth to Rh-positive babies. That was the breakthrough they'd sought.

But it's a sad fact that the key to ending the heartbreak of the infant deaths came from the tragedy of mothers who'd lost children.

It wasn't until Bowman's own children were old enough to understand Rh disease that they realized the magnitude of their father's work. Tom Bowman is a doctor at Winnipeg's Grace Hospital where he routinely prescribes WinRho to save babies.

"What always strikes me is that when we find out a woman is Rh-negative, at the stroke of a pen, I write the order, and with a simple injection we prevent a huge tragedy down the line."

MANITOBA-NESS

DR. Bruce Chown and Dr. John Bowman were both born and raised in Winnipeg.

They both graduated from the University of Manitoba — albeit decades apart — and completed advanced training in the United States. Each returned to their hometown where they practiced medicine and eventually did research together.

They gained worldwide recognition when they developed WinRho in 1968, putting Winnipeg on the neonatal map. Their vaccine saved thousands of babies and brought Rh negative mothers carrying Rh positive babies from around the world to Winnipeg for treatment.

Chown and Bowman each had five children which they raised in Manitoba.

Chown died July 3, 1986 at 92 in Victoria, B.C.

Bowman died May 22, 2005 at the Grace Hospital in Winnipeg. He was 79.

5 THINGS YOU DIDN'T KNOW

DR. JOHN BOWMAN

1. For a doctor with such a passion for medicine, Bowman tended to neglect his own health. In his 50s, he was denied life insurance because of his high blood pressure. That woke him up and he started walking.

2. There had never been a set of twins in medical school in Manitoba before the Bowmans. But in the Bowman brothers' class, there were two sets.

3. Bowman was known as Jumping Jack because he was always in a hurry.

4. He refused to profit from creating WinRho, which would have made him a millionaire. Instead, all profits went to the Rh Institute and its research.

5. He had a bulletin board full of baby photos and letters from mothers. He personally wrote back to every single woman.

DR. BRUCE CHOWN

1. Outside of medicine, he spent much of his time in the country at his cottage in Lac du Bonnet where he loved to garden.

2. Chown was awarded a medal of bravery when he served as a Canadian Armed Forces artillery officer in the First World War.

3. Chown travelled north to study the red blood cells of Inuit and aboriginal people.

4. He wasn't very good with financial matters. He had a drawer in his office stuffed with uncashed cheques.

5. He won the Gairdner Foundation's $25,000 award of merit in 1968 for his knowledge of blood groups and treatment and prevention of Rh disease in newborns.

CONFIDENTIAL

Bond.
(Intrepid)
Bond.

BY BARTLEY KIVES

MORE than a million Canadians fought in the Second World War and almost 100,000 were killed or wounded. Many saved the lives of buddies or entire platoons and were deemed heroes.

But only one combatant can be credited with saving the lives of millions of people around the world.

Sir William Stephenson, as the head of British intelligence on North American soil, oversaw a vast communications network that helped crack the Enigma code, a feat historians believe hastened the end of the Second World War by about two years.

But Stephenson was also directly and indirectly responsible for hundreds of other less well-known intelligence achievements. That impressive list includes supplying early evidence of military buildup in Germany before the war, ensuring — before the Japanese attack on Pearl Harbor — that the United States supported the British war effort and co-ordinating the information-gathering and code-breaking capabilities of Canada, the U.S. and the U.K. throughout the duration of the war.

1897-1989

SIR WILLIAM STEPHENSON

GREATNESS

A confidante of both Winston Churchill and Franklin Delano Roosevelt, Sir William Stephenson is Canada's most celebrated spymaster and the inspiration for several characters in Ian Fleming's spy novels.

Among Stephenson's accomplishments:

Earned both the Military Cross and Distinguished Flying Cross as a First World War pilot.

Despite a lack of education, became a wireless technology inventor and amassed millions as an industrialist, controlling steel, film and aviation companies, among others.

Supplied British MP Winston Churchill with intelligence about the Nazi arms buildup before the Second World War.

Undercover as a passport-control agent in New York City during the Second World War — and under Prime Minister Churchill's orders — set up and ran British Security Co-ordination, an office that eventually functioned as the American headquarters for all British intelligence services.

Before Pearl Harbor, used his office to sway U.S. public opinion in favour of joining the war and diverted U.S. ships and other supplies to the U.K.

Continued on Page 67

Stephenson's proponents believe the man played as pivotal a role in the defeat of Adolf Hitler and Nazi Germany as did British Prime Minister Winston Churchill and U.S. President Franklin Delano Roosevelt.

Detractors, however, have attempted to diminish his achievements over the decades, claiming lazy or unscrupulous biographers have exaggerated the legend of the spymaster most famously lionized as *The Man Called Intrepid.*

And in recent years, as pop culture takes precedence over historical knowledge, Stephenson has gained renown as the inspiration for three of the most famous characters created by his friend, the novelist Ian Fleming.

As a spymaster, Stephenson served as the template for M. As a lover of gadgets, he resembled Q and as a charming and gallant socialite who loved cocktail parties and massive martinis, he shares many characteristics with James Bond, the literary epitome of British cool.

The latter is ironic, given Stephenson was actually an uneducated Icelandic Canadian born to an impoverished Winnipeg family who grew up in the shadow of a red-light district that made Winnipeg infamous after the turn of the 20th century.

William Samuel Stephenson was actually born William Samuel Clouston Stanger, the son of an Orkney Islander father and an Icelandic mother.

After his father William died, his mother Sarah could not afford to raise him. So he was handed over to Vigfus and Kristin Stephenson, an Icelandic couple who lived on Syndicate Street in what's now the east side of North Point Douglas.

The young Stephenson left school after Grade 6 and worked as a delivery boy and telegraph operator before signing up with the Winnipeg Light Infantry and shipping overseas to join the British effort in the First World War.

NORMA FELLER PHOTO / COURTESY BILL MACDONALD, THE TRUE INTREPID

Vigfus and Kristin Stephenson, circa 1912, adopted William Samuel Clouston Stanger and renamed him William Stephenson.

He competed as a boxer and eventually became an airman, shooting down anywhere from 12 to 26 enemy planes — the records are inconsistent — before crashing and being taken prisoner by German forces.

As biographer Bill Macdonald notes, it's difficult to tell what actually happened to Stephenson behind enemy lines. According to legend, but quite possibly in fact, the young Winnipegger stole a can opener from one of his German captors and saw the metal artifact as an opportunity to launch a career as a businessman.

After escaping his prisoner-of-war camp and returning to Winnipeg a decorated flyer, he patented the stolen can-opener design and launched a hardware supply company with his friend Charles Russell.

Stephenson convinced members of Winnipeg's Icelandic Canadian community to invest thousands of dollars in his fledgling company, which flopped like a stale vinarterta cake within three years.

And that's when the story of Stephenson begins to become stranger than any spy novel. Despondent over his failed business, the uneducated delivery boy-turned-soldier returned to England — and was soon feted as a genius inventor in the field of wireless radio operations.

Winnipeg author Macdonald calls the young Winnipegger's sudden success in the U.K. the greatest mystery about a man whose life story was already remarkable to the point of being improbable. Macdonald's Stephenson biography, *The True Intrepid,* documents dozens of errors and inconsistencies about Stephenson in the earlier books *The Man Called Intrepid* and *The Quiet Canadian.*

"It's unexplainable. I have him bankrupt on Victor Street, and months later, he's being hailed as a great inventor by the (London) *Daily Mail,*" says Macdonald. "For a while, I thought I was researching two entirely different people."

Macdonald suspects some of the money Stephenson raised from Winnipeg's Icelandic community may have fuelled his sudden success. But the entrepreneur clearly had his own motivation.

Within months of inventing a wireless photo application, Stephenson began a business career that eventually saw him amass millions of dollars, creating and acquiring stakes in companies that manufactured steel, made films, built airplanes and even helped erect Vancouver's Lions Gate Bridge.

Eventually, Stephenson's business dealings around Europe would give him a first-hand look at the industrial renaissance taking place in Germany, a country that was devastated by the First World War and bound by treaty not to rearm.

By the mid-1930s, Stephenson was supplying Churchill, then an MP, with intelligence about the arms buildup in Nazi Germany. Stephenson soon began working undercover as a British intelligence agent: He ceased all contact with his family back in Winnipeg, actively obfuscated aspects of his past and did not even acknowledge the death of his mother.

In 1940, with the Nazis threatening to invade the U.K., Churchill — by then Britain's prime minister — sent Stephenson to New York City.

Churchill asked the Winnipeg industrialist to set up and run British Security Co-ordination, an organization that would eventually serve as the U.S. headquarters for the entire U.K. intelligence effort during the Second World War. Stephenson was not such an illogical choice; his outsider status meant he had no ties to British elites, some of whom Churchill suspected of harbouring sympathies for, or being in outright collusion with, the Nazis.

The only known photo taken during the war of Sir William Stephenson, far left, turning his head away from the camera.

After Pearl Harbor, ran a communications and spy network that intercepted and decoded enemy messages. The collective Allied intelligence-gathering effort is believed to have hastened the end of the war by two years.

Set up spy training centre Camp X in Ontario, where thousands of U.S., British and Canadian operatives trained during the war.

Convinced Roosevelt to create the U.S. Office of Strategic Services, which eventually became the CIA.

Knighted by the U.K., awarded the U.S. Presidential Medal of Merit and received the Order of Canada.

Aspects of his personality were incorporated into several Ian Fleming characters, particularly M (Stephenson was a spymaster) but also James Bond and Q (Stephenson loved both martinis and gadgets).

> *"I want to assure you that as long as Americans value courage and freedom, there will be a special place in our hearts, our minds and our history books for the 'Man Called Intrepid'"*

— Then-U.S. president Ronald Reagan in a 1983 letter to William Stephenson, as documented in Bill Macdonald's biography

NATIONAL SECURITY AGENCY PHOTO / COURTESY BILL MACDONALD, THE TRUE INTREPID

The German cipher machine, Enigma. Stephenson headed a vast network during the Second World War which helped break the Enigma code, a feat historians believe hastened the end of the war by two years.

"Churchill needed an outsider and chose this 'bumpkin' from Winnipeg to head up his secret service," says Macdonald, noting that few people in England or the U.S. knew what Stephenson was doing.

Under cover as a passport-control officer, Stephenson began recruiting Americans and Canadians to aid with propaganda and information-gathering efforts. Initially, his main job was to sway public opinion in the U.S. toward joining the allied war effort, diverting U.S. resources to Britain and keeping tabs on Nazi agents and sympathizers across the Americas.

But after Japan attacked Pearl Harbor, Stephenson's mission changed dramatically. His own organization evolved into a massive and far-flung information-gathering and code-breaking network that employed a small army of typists and translators.

Instead of keeping track of the Nazis in the U.S., he was responsible for more obscure spy operations in Latin America. And as a Roosevelt confidante, he convinced the U.S. president to place his friend Bill Donovan in charge of American intelligence. Donovan established the Office of Strategic Services, an information-gathering agency that eventually became the CIA.

Stephenson also founded Camp X, a southern Ontario spy-training institution that taught covert operations to thousands of Canadian, American and British trainees. By the end of the war, he was the single most powerful intelligence operative in the Western Hemisphere.

But Stephenson's penchant for secrecy wound up enshrouding his achievements. Few people — certainly not his family back in Winnipeg, or even most of his friends — knew what he was actually doing in New York City during the war. His work remained obscure until the publication of the biographies that would forever make him famous as *The Man Called Intrepid*.

Long after the U.K. made him a knight and the U.S. hung a presidential medal around his neck, he was awarded the Order of Canada. And up to the day he died — in Bermuda in 1989, at the age of 92 — he continued to obfuscate aspects of his life before, during and even after the Second World War.

"Why this was kept up after the war remains a mystery," Macdonald says.

Perhaps, Stephenson feared assassination by remnants of the Nazi regime. Just as plausibly, he worked undercover too long to be able to live a public life — or even enjoy the accolades he deserved as the spymaster who helped prevent Hitler's Nazis from conquering the planet.

According to Macdonald, Stephenson only visited Winnipeg once after he retired and did not tell anyone about his visit until he had left.

Forget the martinis, tuxedos and cocktail parties — the mark of a real spy is an aversion to attention.

During the war, Stephenson competed as a feather-weight boxer, was decorated as a pilot and was eventually captured by the Germans.

After returning to Winnipeg, he started up a hardware-supply company that quickly failed, forcing him to leave for the U.K., where he swiftly — and mysteriously — became renowned as an inventor and industrialist.

Stephenson only visited Winnipeg once after he retired and did not tell anyone about his visit until he had left. He retired to Bermuda, where he died in 1989 at the age of 92.

PHOTO COURTESY OF BILL MACDONALD / THE TRUE INTREPID

Stephenson, above, at age 21 in 1918. Left, Stephenson receives the Order of the Buffalo Hunt from Col. Tom Lawson and his wife Miggsie in 1985.

PHOTO COURTESY OF BILL MACDONALD / THE TRUE INTREPID

MANITOBA-NESS

W ILLIAM Stephenson, the Man Called Intrepid, was born in Winnipeg in 1897 as William Samuel Clouston Stanger and given up for adoption at the age of four.

Raised in Point Douglas as William Samuel Stephenson, he worked as a delivery boy and telegraph operator before he sailed overseas to fight in the First World War.

5 THINGS YOU DIDN'T KNOW

1. William Stephenson was actually born William Stanger, but was given up for adoption at the age of four, after his father died and his mother could not afford to raise him.

2. As a pilot in the First World War, Stephenson is believed to have shot down anywhere from 12 to 26 enemy planes.

3. After the war, Stephenson's business failed and he left Winnipeg for the U.K., and he is suspected of running away with thousands of dollars he raised from members of Winnipeg's Icelandic community.

4. Stephenson was so deep undercover during the lead-up to the Second World War, he ceased all communications with his family and did not even acknowledge his adoptive mother's death.

5. Stephenson remained suspicious of his wartime enemies decades after the Second World War ended and continued to obfuscate aspects of his background until his death at 92.

BY CAROL SANDERS

Canada's conscience

'He pleaded the cause of the common man from one end of Canada to the other'

— Pierre Trudeau in 1975 on the 40th anniversary of Douglas's arrival in the House of Commons

Tommy Douglas speaks in November 1965.

YOUNG Tommy's leg, maybe his life, hung in the balance.

But his parents, Tom and Anne Douglas, didn't have the money to pay for treatment of the 10-year-old's serious bone infection. If not for a visiting surgeon who offered to treat the boy in exchange for letting medical students watch, Tommy Douglas would certainly have lost his leg.

The die was cast.

One hundred years after his birth, shaped thus by the profound experiences of a Manitoba childhood, Douglas, long dubbed Canada's Father of Medicare, was named the Greatest Canadian in a nationwide CBC poll.

"I felt that no boy should have to depend either for his leg or his life upon the ability of his parents to raise enough money to bring a first-class surgeon to his bedside," Douglas is quoted as saying in *T.C. Douglas, The Making of a Socialist.* "And I think it was out of this experience, not at the moment consciously, but through the years, I came to believe that health services ought not to have a price tag on them, and that people should be able to get whatever health services they require irrespective of their individual capacity to pay."

GREATNESS

Considered Canada's Father of Medicare. As Saskatchewan premier and later MP, Douglas was the leading advocate for the adoption of medicare as national public policy.

He served Canada on many levels.

In 1935, he was elected to the House of Commons representing the Co-operative Commonwealth Federation (CCF).

In 1942, he returned to Saskatchewan as leader of the provincial CCF.

In 1944, with Douglas as leader, CCF won the first of five consecutive majorities in Saskatchewan.

In 1961, Douglas became the first leader of the New Democratic Party at its creation but was defeated in the federal election. He was later elected to Parliament as MP for Burnaby-Coquitlam.

In 1962, Douglas's greatest political ambition was realized when Saskatchewan's provincial government instituted socialized medical care for all residents.

In 1979, he retired from politics and died in 1986.

The hard times — and good times — in Manitoba planted the seeds of his social-justice agenda.

Douglas, born in Scotland in 1904, grew up in Winnipeg where his family struggled to make ends meet. He dropped in and out of school along with his two younger sisters to work and help support the household.

Douglas served as church minister in Weyburn,

Tommy Douglas is congratulated by trade unionist Claude Jodoin, CCF president David Lewis and British labour leader Hugh Gaitshell as Douglas wins the NDP leadership in 1961.

Sask., during the Dirty 30s before entering politics and becoming the premier of Saskatchewan. He went on to establish labour laws, medicare, public car insurance, paved roads, sewage systems and electricity for rural Saskatchewan households, all while reducing the provincial debt by millions of dollars.

Douglas took his Saskatchewan policy successes to Parliament as a federal MP and the NDP's first national leader. His ideas were instrumental in the development of national programs such as social welfare, universal medicare, old age pensions and mothers' allowances.

As a teen, he was a paperboy for the *Winnipeg Free Press* and witnessed police officers shooting unarmed protesters on Bloody Saturday during the 1919 Winnipeg General Strike. He learned his family's church pastor, J.S. Woodsworth, was imprisoned for practising the social gospel he preached. Woodsworth walked with the demonstrators demanding better wages and working conditions.

Douglas's faith was nurtured at the Point Douglas Presbyterian Church his family attended while they lived on Gladstone Street in Point Douglas.

In 1924, he left Winnipeg for Brandon College — a liberal arts college run by the Baptist Church at the time. He continued his long involvement in scouting there, serving as Cub master and Scout troop leader in Brandon, Carberry, Strathclair and Shoal Lake.

He met his wife, Irma, a music student from Carberry at Brandon College — now Brandon University.

Some of the fight in Douglas was literal. He was Manitoba's lightweight boxing champ for two years after the 1922 title bout that left him with a broken nose. His ability to go the distance was put to the test in the long, drawn-out battles to come — with political opponents, big business and public opinion.

When he was pushing universal health care in Saskatchewan, Douglas faced the wrath of the American Medical Association.

"All of the PR men from the AMA were brought up,"

THE CANADIAN PRESS ARCHIVES

Douglas, new premier of Saskatchewan, visits a Canadian Army hospital in 1945. Two years later, Douglas legislated the first paid hospital stays in North America.

he said in a *Free Press* interview more than 40 years ago. The agents for the powerful professional association distributed brochures, propaganda against medicare, to doctors' waiting rooms throughout the province.

"It said all interviews with doctors would be tape-recorded and the information sent to the Department of Health. It said there would be no confidential discussions... If a woman was pregnant, the government would decide whether or not she should have the child."

Douglas wasn't afraid to take on other big projects and set out to see basic services such as sewer, water and electrical power extended to 55,000 family farms in Saskatchewan.

"I never got so much kick in my life as I did seeing the first privies being burned and the fire being put out with a hose attached to the farmer's water system," Douglas told the *Free Press*'s John Dafoe in an interview in 1960.

Douglas showed that government could help improve people's lives as well as the economy, said *Free Press* columnist Val Werier.

"Saskatchewan was on the brink of bankruptcy when he took over," said Werier, who had often interviewed Douglas.

"The so-called socialist — alleged not to be able to run a hotdog stand — ran the province into the black."

Small of stature, Douglas wasn't an imposing figure who commanded attention but a personable, popular guy who attracted people with a great sense of timing and humour, said Werier. All joking aside, Douglas said his mission wasn't to make them laugh.

"I didn't come into this world to be a standup comedian," he once said. "I recognize the value of laughter, it's a means of building a rapport, but there must be a message. The world demands it."

In the 1970s, he was besieged by autograph hounds as the father-in-law of actor Donald Sutherland following the release of the movies *M*A*S*H* and *Kelly's Heroes*. His daughter Shirley Douglas and Sutherland are the parents of Kiefer Sutherland, the cigarette-smoking actor who plays a secret agent on the right-wing Fox network's TV drama *24*.

His grandfather's real-life role as an outspoken champion for peace and socialist causes attracted real-life RCMP spies who kept tabs on him for three decades. A 1,142-page dossier was released in 2006, 20 years after Douglas's 1986 death. It found little in the way of intrigue, dirt or personal scandal that would make good fodder for a Fox TV series.

It showed that Douglas was the real deal and did in fact practise what he preached.

Today, Canada is defined by its social structures, and Douglas, with his Manitoba upbringing, laid the foundation.

"In so many ways, he has led the way," said Werier.

The Regina Manifesto — the 1933 founding document of Douglas's Co-operative Commonwealth Federation — was more the blueprint for the Canadian society we know today, than the theories of old-line parties:

"Power has become more and more concentrated into the hands of a small irresponsible minority of financiers and industrialists, and to their predatory interests, the majority are habitually sacrificed. When private profit is the main stimulus to economic effort, our society oscillates between periods of feverish prosperity in which the main benefits go to speculators and profiteers, and of catastrophic depression, in which the common man's normal state of insecurity and hardship is accentuated.

"We believe that these evils can be removed only in a planned and socialized economy in which our natural resources and principal means of production and distribution are owned, controlled and operated by the people."

MANITOBA-NESS

SPENT his formative years in Winnipeg. His politics were deeply influenced when, as a *Free Press* newspaper carrier in 1919, he witnessed police officers shooting unarmed protesters during the Winnipeg General Strike.

Attended Brandon University.

5 THINGS YOU DIDN'T KNOW

WINNIPEG FREE PRESS ARCHIVES

1. As a teen, Douglas was a paperboy for the Winnipeg Free Press and witnessed police officers shooting unarmed protesters on Bloody Saturday during the 1919 Winnipeg General Strike.

2. Douglas grew up in Point Douglas. He lived on Gladstone Street and his family attended Point Douglas Presbyterian Church.

3. He was a Boy Scout troop leader as well as a boxer, winning the Manitoba lightweight boxing championship and a broken nose during the bout.

4. He and his sisters dropped in and out of school as they were growing up to work and help support their family.

5. The only person who ever beat Douglas in a college debate was a music student named Irma Dempsey — who became his wife.

He exemplified 'an extraordinarily rare combination of generosity of spirit, good humour, tenacity and courage — not to mention eloquence'

— Former Conservative leader Robert Stanfield

Douglas, right, and Stanley Knowles, longtime CCF then NDP Winnipeg MP, pictured in May 1962.

WINNIPEG TRIBUNE / UNIVERSITY OF MANITOBA ARCHIVES

The conscience of Parliament

BY PAUL SAMYN

BY the time the 1970s rolled around, he was not only a political icon but practically part of Canada's parliamentary furniture.

Sombre but solid, he helped transform the country's political left over four decades in federal politics and was a tireless crusader for social justice with a string of pension victories.

But championing the cause of women's rights?

A young feminist working the NDP caucus never expected that. She figured she'd have a tough time getting the MP from Winnipeg North Centre on board.

"I saw him then as an old-style male politician," Judy Wasylycia-Leis recalls of her initial impression of Stanley Knowles. "But in fact, he turned out to be quite the raving feminist."

Still, Knowles' feminism would go only so far. And when Wasylycia-Leis crossed the line of parliamentary decorum one day, she learned an important lesson about the preacher-turned-politician.

Stanley Knowles in November 1950.

WINNIPEG TRIBUNE / UNIVERSITY OF MANITOBA ARCHIVES

Stanley Knowles sits as an honorary officer of Parliament at the clerk's table on the floor of the House on April 27, 1995.

1908-1997

STANLEY KNOWLES

12

GREATNESS

MP for Winnipeg North Centre from 1942 to 1958 and then from 1962 to 1984.

Praised for leading the fight to improve pensions and improve veterans' rights.

Widely recognized as an expert in parliamentary procedure who used both the rules of the Commons and his words to attack the Liberal government of Louis St. Laurent during the 1956 pipeline debate.

One of the architects of the transformation of the CCF into the New Democratic Party.

Prime Minister Joe Clark made him a member of the Queen's Privy Council.

Prime Minister Pierre Trudeau made him an honorary table officer of the House of Commons in 1984.

Named an officer of the Order of Canada in 1984.

Brandon University Chancellor from 1970-90.

WINNIPEG TRIBUNE / UNIVERSITY OF MANITOBA ARCHIVES

Knowles and a supporter walk along Wellington Crescent in September 1968.

As Knowles sat in his Commons seat one afternoon during question period, Wasylycia-Leis was co-ordinating a demonstration over Liberal cuts to women's programs in the gallery above him.

On Wasylycia-Leis's cue, a group of women stood up, took off their sweaters to reveal a different letter on each of their chests, which collectively spelled out a message to MPs below.

The security guards were on them in an instant. But what really had Wasylycia-Leis worried was the look she got from Knowles as the protesters were ushered out of the gallery.

"Stanley Knowles was not impressed with my efforts to raise the profile of women's rights," says Wasylycia-Leis, who has represented much of Knowles' old riding since 1997. "He shook his finger at me, and I think he scolded me, but it was the look."

It was a look that only someone who was the conscience of Parliament could give. The rules, the traditions, the standing orders of the chamber weren't just words on paper to him. They were the tools Knowles used to his advantage, first as a Co-operative Commonwealth Federation MP, and later as a founding member of the New Democratic Party to prod, push and pressure successive governments into acting on his Christian brand of socialism.

"I think he was more than an MP; he was a person who really cared for his fellow humans," says his son David, who believes his father would despair at the circus side-shows of today's Parliament.

"A lot of our current MPs go into Parliament to be able to control and to make decisions. Dad and his ilk back in the '20s and '30s went into Parliament to achieve change for Canadians that would improve their lives. He and Tommy Douglas and David Lewis would say they achieved things by being a thorn in the side of government. The fact they weren't in charge was secondary. They were a group of people who were elected for the best reasons."

WINNIPEG TRIBUNE / UNIVERSITY OF MANITOBA ARCHIVES

Knowles admires a caricature of his famous expression.

This thorn in the side of government, who would be elected 13 times between 1942 and 1980 with only a defeat in the Diefenbaker sweep of 1958 interrupting his parliamentary run, started life not in Canada but in Los Angeles. While his Methodist family didn't have much, Knowles was blessed with a brain that enabled him to finish high school by the time he was 15.

He lost his mother to tuberculosis when he was 11 and despaired as his father's deteriorating health resulted in his being laid off from his job as a streetcar driver without a pension.

"Of course, Dad looks at this and thinks, 'This just isn't right,' and this is the basis of his belief that he has to fight for a better life," David explained of his father's formative years.

But before that fight could begin, Knowles trekked from Southern California to the family's roots in Nova Scotia and then westward to Carberry where time spent with his cousins would anchor him on the Prairies. He went to Brandon University and then became a United Church minister.

Rev. Earl Gould preached from the same pulpit at

'He changed the way our society regarded the poor and the ill and the aged. He changed minds and he changed the law, and he used the traditions of Parliament to do so. And remember he did this from the ranks of His and then Her Majesty's loyal Opposition. And Canada is a better place for it'

— Knowles' biographer Susan Mann from her eulogy to him

Knowles talks to Canadian Pacific Railway workers in November 1965.

WINNIPEG TRIBUNE / UNIVERSITY OF MANITOBA ARCHIVES

A collection of Knowles memorabilia, including one of his favourite ties.

Kildonan United Church from which Knowles used to thunder in his black robes on Sunday mornings. Copies of those sermons from long ago are now in the care of the University of Winnipeg archives and Gould said reading through them shows the connection between the social gospel and his service in the secular world.

"You can see an evolution of his theology and how his theology impacted on the bent he took in politics," Gould said.

In 1942, Knowles the preacher presided over the funeral of J.S. Woodsworth at Westminster United Church and then became a politician when he took over the CCF's founding leader's seat.

Knowles' arrival in Ottawa as a rookie MP in the middle of the Second World War came as the Mann family was struggling with a $13 hole in their budget. The family was reluctant to get tied down with a full-time boarder. But they figured taking in an MP would be a perfect solution as the boarder would only be there for half a year — plus elections would ensure the politician would eventually move on.

As it turned out, Knowles was the MP the family approached, and before the family toddler, Susan, knew

WINNIPEG TRIBUNE / UNIVERSITY OF MANITOBA ARCHIVES

Knowles election night Nov. 8, 1965 with campaign worker Alan Wade. Knowles won by nearly twice the votes of the closest contender.

it, the dining room was converted into a bedroom for a boarder who stayed more than 40 years.

Over the decades that followed, Knowles became a second father to Susan and her sister, Gretchen. He served up porridge and politics for breakfast.

As a 17-year-old, Susan found herself acting as a sounding board when Prime Minister John Diefenbaker offered Knowles the job of Speaker, an offer he ultimately refused. The Mann family helped him through the stress and the strain of his failed marriage in the 1950s. They marvelled at how he kept his multiple sclerosis in check through sheer willpower.

And they, better than anyone else, understood how important the 1984 honour Prime Minister Pierre Trudeau bestowed upon Knowles was after a stroke in 1981 ended his political career.

In an unprecedented move, Trudeau, made Knowles an honorary officer of Parliament, allowing him to sit at the clerk's table on the floor of the House. It was a role Knowles filled virtually every day for the next dozen years.

"He was the ghost of Parliament past and a reminder of the significance of this place," says Susan Mann who, as a historian, wrote Knowles' biography.

"You'd see him sitting there, and he was a bit of a gargoyle for the Canadian parliamentary system," she said. "He is sitting there very quietly and very still, and he really wasn't able to follow what was going on but most people didn't know that."

Still, the sight of that still and silent figure on duty, watching and listening, continued to make a difference to the House of Commons.

ON June 18, on the 100th anniversary of Knowles' birth, there was an intimate gathering at his Brookside Cemetery gravesite. It was a quiet affair with no hype, no media, no official NDP hoopla — just family, Rev. Gould and that feminist-cum-MP who Knowles chided for her Commons stunt back in the early 1970s.

As much as it was a celebration of all that Knowles accomplished, it was also a time for the family to say things that had never been said, to let loose some of the pain and suffering that came from having a father who devoted so much of his life to that house on Parliament Hill instead of the family's house in Winnipeg.

And then it was off to Kelekis, that Winnipeg institution in his old riding for a birthday party that Stanley Howard Knowles watched from his framed picture hanging on the restaurant's wall of fame.

MANITOBA-NESS

KNOWLES was born in Los Angeles, but he fell in love with the province when he arrived in his late teens.

He is a Brandon University graduate, represented the riding of Winnipeg North Centre for 40 years and is buried in Brookside Cemetery.

5 THINGS YOU DIDN'T KNOW

1. Knowles had such a hate on for the Senate that every year he introduced a bill calling for its abolition.

2. While never in cabinet, Knowles was a minister known to perform marriages on demand. In fact, he once married a couple who showed up at Parliament looking to take their wedding vows.

3. Knowles' body lay in state not once but twice when he died in 1997. His flag-draped coffin was honoured on Parliament Hill and at Winnipeg city hall. His funeral was at Westminster United Church, the same church where he performed the funeral for CCF founder J.S. Woodsworth and where he and Vida Cruikshank married in 1936.

4. During an official tour of postwar Europe in 1945, the pacifist politician was made an honorary colonel in the British Army in order to facilitate his trip home from Berlin.

5. He was the longtime chancellor of Brandon University, and its student union building is named for him and Tommy Douglas.

Knowles makes a point in Parliament
as Ed Broadbent looks on.

THE CANADIAN PRESS ARCHIVES

'Stanley always liked to say that he chose Canada — the better place — after a childhood in the United States. But in some ways Canada chose him, drawing him back by four generations of Nova Scotia roots, roots of loyalty and hard work, of religious conviction, of intellectual endeavours and upright behaviour, roots that spread, by aunts and uncles to the Canadian West, mingled in the prairie farmland and took hold for Stanley in the urban industrial setting of Winnipeg'

— Susan Mann

Knowles sits alone on election night, Nov. 21, 1988.

PHIL HOSSACK / WINNIPEG FREE PRESS

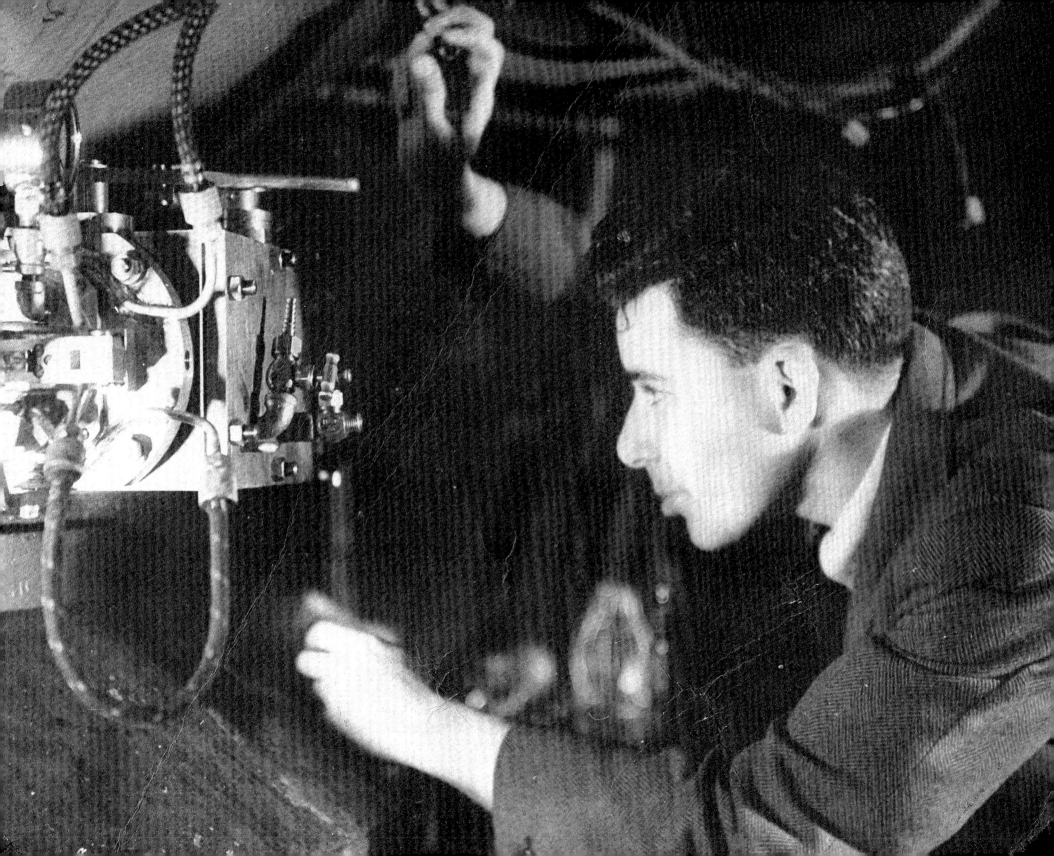

BY ALISON MAYES

Atom smasher

ON July 16, 1945 in the remote New Mexican desert, humankind unleashed its first weapon of mass destruction.

Scientists from the top-secret Manhattan Project watched in awe as their atomic "gadget" detonated at the Trinity test site, igniting the nuclear age.

A brilliant young physicist named Louis Slotin had assembled the very heart of the bomb — its plutonium core — and delivered it to a brigadier-general. He kept the receipt as a memento.

The dark-haired, bespectacled scientist who worked alongside Robert Oppenheimer and other physics legends was raised in Winnipeg's North End. He was one of an extraordinary group of atom-splitting trailblazers who changed the course of the 20th century.

As a research associate at the University of Chicago, Slotin had been present on Dec. 2, 1942 for the world's first controlled, self-sustaining nuclear chain reaction.

"He etched his name in scientific history," says Winnipeg journalist Martin Zeilig, associate producer of a 1999 documentary about Slotin, *Tickling the Dragon's Tail.*

Louis Slotin at work, date and location unknown.

GREATNESS

He worked on a pioneering atom-smashing cyclotron in the late 1930s. It's believed he did important research into the use of radiology to treat cancer and that if he had lived, he would have resumed research into medical applications of radiation.

Slotin was one of the elite minds recruited in 1942 for the Allies' top-secret atomic-bomb program, known as the Manhattan Project. He worked in 1943-44 at the project's site at Oak Ridge, Tenn.

In late 1944, he joined the team of pre-eminent scientists racing the Germans to develop a nuclear bomb at the isolated base in Los Alamos, N.M.

Slotin became a specialist in dangerous "critical assembly" tests of fissionable materials. He was part of the key team that built the world's first atomic bombs, including those dropped on Hiroshima and Nagasaki. His work also helped pave the way for burst reactors used in research.

Slotin is credited with coining the term "dollar," a unit of nuclear reactivity.

In 2002, Slotin became the first Manitoban to have an asteroid named after him — Asteroid 12423 Slotin — by the International Astronomical Union.

Slotin in shorts next to the Trinity,
the world's first atomic bomb.

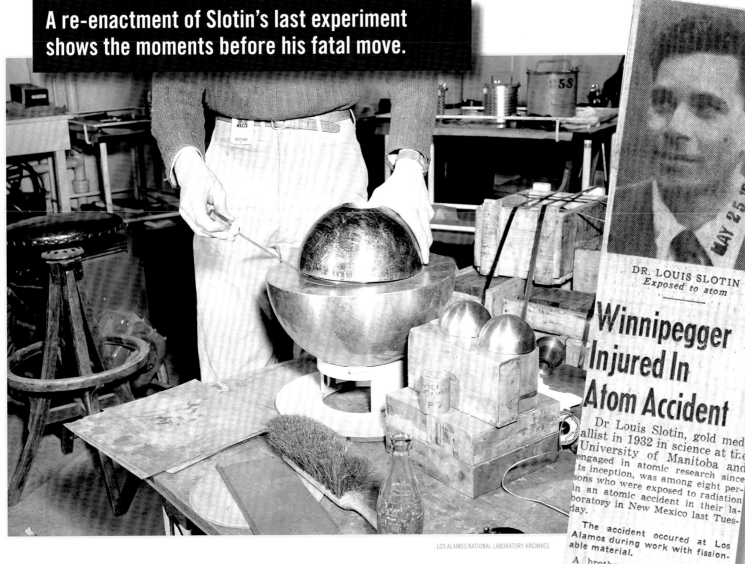

LOS ALAMOS NATIONAL LABORATORY ARCHIVES

WINNIPEG TRIBUNE/UNIVERSITY OF MANITOBA

DR. LOUIS SLOTIN
Exposed to atom

Winnipegger Injured In Atom Accident

Dr Louis Slotin, gold medallist in 1932 in science at the University of Manitoba and engaged in atomic research since its inception, was among eight persons who were exposed to radiation in an atomic accident in their laboratory in New Mexico last Tuesday.

The accident occured at Los Alamos during work with fissionable material.

A brother, Sam Slotin, of 213 Niagara st., told The Tribune Friday: "I talked with my brother by phone this morning and he said he had burns on his hands but otherwise he was feeling fine."

The extent of the exposure is not certain but his parents, Mr. and Mrs. A. I. Slotin of 125 Scotia st. were rushed to Sante Fe by plane Friday. Special priorities were arranged by U. S. authorities here.

Dr. Norris E. Bradbury, project director, said that Slotin's quick work in dispersing the fissionable material when the accident occured probably was instrumental in averting more serious consequences in the accident.

The 35 year-old scientist was born in Winnipeg, he university, graduated from the university here in 19...

Slotin might have gone on after the war to decades of achievement — maybe even a Nobel Prize, suggests his niece, Winnipegger Beth Shore.

But less than a year after hand-assembling the Trinity bomb core, he was dead at the age of 35.

The controversial accident that claimed his life has overshadowed his accomplishments. The tragic slip-up has been recounted — and embellished — in movies,

plays, a novel called *The Accident*, historical books and countless articles. It has mushroomed into a nuclear-age myth that casts Slotin as the martyred saviour of seven lives.

In spring 1946, Slotin had been working at the secret bomb-building compound of Los Alamos,

N.M. for about 18 months. The war was over and he was anxious to get back to the University of Chicago for the fall term. But first, he had agreed to go to Bikini Atoll for navy tests of atomic bombs.

Not much is known about the bachelor physicist's moral perspective on the bomb, though he told his father, "We had to get it before the Germans."

He had not gone overseas the year before to assemble the A-bombs that decimated Hiroshima and Nagasaki because his U.S. citizenship was not finalized.

Still, there is evidence that he was troubled. Two months before his death, Slotin wrote: "I have become involved in the navy tests, much to my disgust... I am one of the few people left here who are experienced bomb putter-togetherers."

On May 21, 1946, Slotin was asked to demonstrate a dangerous experiment known as "tickling the dragon's tail."

Ironically, "this would have been his last time doing the experiment," notes Zeilig, who wrote an exhaustive article on Slotin for *The Beaver* magazine in 1995.

Slotin had done the table-top procedure dozens of times, to test the reactivity of a bomb core. It involved gradually lowering one hemisphere of beryllium-coated plutonium onto another.

He had to bring them close enough to start a fission reaction without allowing them to touch and awaken the dragon's wrath.

With his right hand, Slotin was using a screwdriver to hold the hemispheres wedged apart. His left hand grasped the upper hemisphere. A Geiger counter clicked faster and an instrument graphed the reaction rate in red ink as "criticality" approached.

It seems incredible today that anyone would perform a nuclear test with a screwdriver. But Slotin, who has been described as intense and stubborn, had been taking such extraordinary risks since his days in Chicago.

He had a reputation as "a bit of a cowboy," says his nephew, Winnipegger Israel Ludwig.

The culture at Los Alamos was one of improvisation, habitual urgency and hands-on bravado.

"They cut corners," says Ludwig.

And Slotin may well have been recruited for the Manhattan Project because of his nervy attitude.

"It took a little bit of a daredevil to actually get what he was doing done," says Dwight Vincent, head of the University of Winnipeg physics department.

At 3:20 p.m. on that fateful day, with seven colleagues present in the lab, Slotin's screwdriver apparently

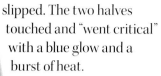

The young physicist's ID badge from the top-secret Manhattan Project.

LOS ALAMOS NATIONAL LABORATORY ARCHIVES

slipped. The two halves touched and "went critical" with a blue glow and a burst of heat.

The "bomb putter-togetherer" had given himself a fatal dose of radiation. Since he was standing nearest to the apparatus, he absorbed most of the impact.

He died nine days later of horrific radiation sickness, blistered and swollen as if he had been standing 1.4 kilometres from a nuclear bomb blast. The other seven men survived, though according to a 1989 story in the *New York Times Magazine*, at least three of their eventual deaths were linked to the radiation exposure.

Slotin's metamorphosis into a folk hero began with the official statements and condolence letter from the U.S. army. Releasing almost no details of the highly classified incident, authorities lauded the scientist for his quick dismantling of the experiment, saying it reflected "the highest type of courage."

Journalists — and perhaps friends and family members — began to embroider the tale. They reported that Slotin "lunged" or "dived" to rip the hemispheres apart, deliberately putting himself in the path of the deadly rays to save the others.

This scenario, reminiscent of a soldier throwing himself on a grenade, is a noble fiction — but a persistent

one.

Winnipeg's only plaque honouring Slotin inaccurately states that he "willingly and heroically laid down his life to save seven fellow scientists" and that he "spontaneously leaped forward, covering the experiment with his body."

First-hand evidence indicates the less romantic reality: Slotin simply reflexively shifted his left hand and dropped the upper hemisphere to the floor.

The story's ultimate irony is that, according to retired Los Alamos physicist Dick Malenfant and other experts, the fission reaction had halted itself in a fraction of a second — before Slotin reacted — due to rapid heating of the plutonium.

Some say it was heroic that Slotin lost his life doing experimental physics in the climate of haste fostered by the arms race. Others see his accidental suicide as a fatal case of hubris.

The University of Winnipeg's Vincent, a Newfoundlander, wishes more Manitobans knew that one of their own was exceptional enough to reach a "critical position" within the inner circle of the Manhattan Project.

"There's no plaque at the University of Manitoba (where Slotin earned bachelor's and master's degrees)," says Vincent. "There's no building called the Slotin Building. And I think it's mainly because he screwed up."

Slotin's death marked the end of a rugged era in which mortals sparred with atomic power as if it were a beast they could slay with a screwdriver. Thereafter, criticality tests were done by remote control.

"It took courage to do what he was doing," says Zeilig, who would like to see a statue of Slotin in Winnipeg. "Certainly, he was a courageous, brilliant, dedicated scientist who gave his life for his work.

"He was a part of us. He was a Winnipegger — a North End Jewish boy."

WINNIPEG TRIBUNE UNIVERSITY OF MANITOBA ARCHIVES

Louis Slotin, second from the left at
Hebrew class, circa 1920.

PROVINCIAL ARCHIVES OF MANITOBA

MANITOBA-NESS

L OUIS Slotin (SLOE-tin) was born in 1910 in
Winnipeg. He was the eldest of three children of
Israel and Sonia Slotin, Orthodox Jews who escaped the
pogroms in Russia. The Yiddish-speaking North End
family prospered in the livestock business.

Growing up on Alfred Avenue, Slotin was a brilliant,
straight-A student at Machray Elementary School and
St. John's Technical High School. Slotin and his brainy
friends sometimes hung out at a grocery store, using up
rolls of butcher paper as they discussed and scribbled
algebraic equations.

Slotin excelled in both chemistry and physics at the
University of Manitoba, winning the gold medal in
science in 1932. He completed his master's degree in
chemistry there, then received a fellowship and earned
a PhD in physical chemistry at the University of London
in 1936.

In 1937, he applied for a job with Canada's National
Research Council. He was turned down, possibly due to

anti-Semitism.

On May 21, 1946 while working on the Manhattan
Project in New Mexico, Slotin accidentally gave himself
a massive dose of radiation. He died nine days later. His
shocked and heartbroken father permitted an autopsy
in the interest of science, though Jewish law forbade
it. The body was flown home to Winnipeg, but not in
a lead coffin — that's one of the myths that surround
Slotin's story.

More than 2,000 people attended Slotin's funeral, held
on the lawn of his parents' house at 125 Scotia St. His
casket was draped with a U.S. flag. The presiding rabbi
paid tribute to him as "one of the most brilliant scholars
ever to come out of this city."

The homegrown physicist who contributed to an
invention of Earth-shattering significance is buried in
Winnipeg's Shaarey Zedek Cemetery.

In 1993, the city created Dr. Louis Slotin Park. The
small green space with a plaque in Slotin's honour is at
the east end of Luxton Avenue on the bank of the Red
River.

5 THINGS YOU DIDN'T KNOW

1. Slotin had a romantic streak and liked to string people along
by mythologizing his past. He claimed to have fought in the
Spanish Civil War — in reality, he went on a walking tour of
Spain — and to have flown fighter jets with the Royal Air Force.

2. The most outrageous risk Slotin took before arriving in Los
Alamos occurred at a Manhattan Project lab in Oak Ridge, Tenn.
He was too impatient to wait a few days for a nuclear-reactor
shutdown and needed something fixed inside a tank of radioactive water. So he simply stripped down, dived underwater and
made the fix. "He'd done the unthinkable," the lab's safety chief
recalled in the documentary Tickling the Dragon's Tail. "He had
unnecessarily risked his own life. Of course, he received a very
large dose of radiation."

3. Exactly nine months before Slotin's fatal accident, his lab
assistant, Harry Daghlian, had a similar lethal slip-up while
working alone — against regulations — testing the same
plutonium core. Both accidents occurred on a Tuesday, on the
21st of the month. Both men died in the same room at the Los
Alamos hospital. After Daghlian's demise, the lab developed
shims that were supposed to keep the plutonium safely apart.
But Slotin didn't use them. The bomb core that killed both men,
dubbed "the Demon core," was used in the "Able" atomic bomb,
detonated July 1, 1946 near Bikini Atoll.

4. In the 1989 movie Fat Man and Little Boy, which tells the
story of the bomb's creation, the American character Michael
Merriman (John Cusack) is based on Slotin. The timing of his
accident is backed up by 10 months for dramatic effect. Rather
than dying after the war, Merriman pleads that the A-bomb not
be dropped on Japan, then dies just minutes before the Trinity
test explosion.

5. Slotin's car was shipped back to Winnipeg after his death.
His family found in the trunk what they believed were numbered
iron moulds for the nose cone and tail fin of an atomic bomb.
For many years while her children were growing up, Slotin's
niece Beth Shore used the moulds as ashtrays in her rec room.
In 1993, Shore visited Los Alamos and donated the items to
the museum of the Los Alamos National Laboratory. She later
received a letter saying the items had been tested and were not
radioactive.

BY MORLEY WALKER

The Manitoban was the messenger

'We march backwards into the future'

...rshall McLuhan
...d the medium
...he message,
...most famous
...nouncement,
...a radio
...vention in 1957.

MARSHALL McLUHAN

14

IN 1974 the Canadian media prophet Marshall McLuhan was at the top of his game.

Sought out by political and business leaders around the globe to explain the meaning of the fast-changing technological landscape, the Toronto-based academic found time to give a playful interview to CBC Radio host Danny Finkleman, a fellow former Winnipegger and alumnus of the University of Manitoba.

"I think it's quite natural to be a person of very wide interests when you live out west," McLuhan offered.

"You're less likely to be a specialist out there."

McLuhan knew of what he spoke. Born in Edmonton in 1911 to Methodist parents, he spent almost 20 years in Winnipeg, from the time he was four until he obtained his master's degree in English at age 23.

To paraphrase Neil Young, all his changes were here.

GREATNESS

Honours and awards of Marshall McLuhan:

A 1953 Ford Foundation grant worth $44,240 to McLuhan and his U of T colleague Ted Carpenter.

The 1962 Governor General's Award for Critical Prose for The Gutenberg Galaxy.

An honorary doctorate of letters from the University of Manitoba in 1967.

A $100,000 grant accompanies his nomination to the Albert Schweitzer Chair in the Humanities at New Hork's Fordham University.

The Companion of the Order of Canada in 1970.

Eight honorary doctorates in total by 1973. The U of M dedicated Marshall McLuhan Hall in University Centre in 2004.

Anointed as a "person of historic significance" in 2007 by the federal Historic Sites and Monuments Board, an honour given 34 other Manitobans to date.

MARSHALL MCLUHAN-ISMS:

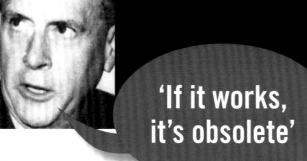

'If it works, it's obsolete'

'The car has become the carapace, the protective and aggressive shell, of urban and suburban man'

'The road is our major architectural form'

McLuhan at about six months on the knee of his mother, Elsis Naomi Hall McLuhan, in Edmonton circa 1911.

McLuhan, above, at three years old, on his trike and, left, at about four, with his dog, Rags, both shots taken at the family's Gertrude Avenue, Winnipeg, home.

McLuhan at seven, right, with his brother Maurice and father Herbert Ernest McLuhan at their Gertrude Avenue home.

COPYRIGHT THE ESTATE OF MARSHALL MCLUHAN

As a boy, he played baseball on the street outside his parents' Fort Rouge home and skated and skied on the Assiniboine River.

As a young man at the University of Manitoba, he joined the debating society and played hockey and rugby.

He nurtured his passion for literature here, fell in love for the first time, and, as an eventual Catholic convert, discovered the authors who influenced his religious and social values for the rest of his life.

"We grew up with him telling us he was a Prairie boy and a 'Winnipigeon,'" his daughter Elizabeth, the fifth of his sixth children, said when she taught at the University of Winnipeg briefly in the early 2000s.

"He always said this is where he was from."

In the years since McLuhan died in 1980, after spending his career as a literary scholar at the University of Toronto, he has been hailed as a seer and a visionary.

Though his gnomic pronouncements resulted in as much confusion as clarification, he was a thinker ahead of his time, an intellectual who laid the groundwork for modern communication theory and a public figure who normalized the academic study of popular culture.

Through such groundbreaking 1960s books as *The Gutenberg Galaxy, Understanding Media* and *The Medium is the Massage*, he did more than anyone to explain the rise of both visual and digital cultures to the often perplexed masses.

Even if they didn't know exactly what he meant, they probably recognized him as the pointy head who coined the phrases "the global village" and "the medium is the message," or maybe as the string bean who did a self-important cameo in American director Woody Allen's 1977 comedy *Annie Hall*.

At the turn of the millennium, when the first international overviews of 20th-century culture were published, McLuhan was routinely the lone Canadian whose ideas made the cut.

The American journalist and novelist Tom Wolfe, a McLuhan acolyte since the mid-'60s, wrote an essay in 2003 in which he compared McLuhan's influence to that of Darwin, Marx and Freud.

Wired magazine, the current bible of the digital age, calls McLuhan its "patron saint."

"We've imagined the world in a way that's been shaped by McLuhan," says Adam Muller, a critical theorist in the U of M's English department.

"His ideas are so powerful and so obviously true that they have erased him as the person responsible for them."

Exactly what were those ideas?

Or, in the words of the late *Laugh-In* comedian Henry Gibson: "Marshall McLuhan, what are you doin'?"

'he specialist is one who ever makes small mistakes hile moving toward the 'and fallacy'

'I may be wrong, but I'm never in doubt'

'People don't actually read newspapers. They step into them every morning like a hot bath'

'All advertising advertises advertising'

'Tomorrow is our permanent address'

'With telephone and TV it is not so much the message as the sender that is sent'

McLuhan holds a display card for his 1964 book, Understanding Media.

THE CANADIAN PRESS ARCHIVES

In a nutshell, he argued that all media — in and of themselves and regardless of the messages they communicate — exert a compelling influence on man and society and change the way people think.

"The better part of my work on media is actually somewhat like a safe-cracker's," he told *Playboy* magazine in a 1969 interview that remains an excellent primer on his prescient world views.

"I don't know what's inside; maybe it's nothing. I just sit down and start to work. I grope, I listen, I test, I accept and discard; I try out different sequences — until the tumblers fall and the doors spring open."

The way McLuhan explained it, prehistoric, or tribal, humans existed in a "harmonious balance of the senses," perceiving the world equally through hearing, smell, touch, sight and taste.

But as civilization progressed, people developed technologies that altered the balance. Even today, in thrall to the computer and Internet age, McLuhan would argue, we are as unaware of the effects of new technology as "a fish is of the water it swims in."

He also believed that the "electric media" — telegraph, radio, films, telephone, television and computers — spelled the end of the reign of the printed word. Human culture would be restored to its oral and aural past in a kind of "global village."

McLuhan's 1933 University of Manitoba yearbook.

NIMAN CHODIRKER
Winnipeg.
Mathematics, Latin, Sociology,
Applied Mathematics.

KATHLEEN MORELAND
Winnipeg.
English History.
Arts Dramatics cast.
Editor The Manitoban Literary
Supplement (1931-32).

HARRY WALSH
Winnipeg
German, Latin, Economics,
Mathematics.

YEAR
NOR
UDENTS

Row—
ecord
asterbrook
oughead
McBride
intoul

rd Row—
Moscovitch
Benidickson
Jones
Finegood
Lavender

cond Row—
Guy
, Park
, McLuhan
, Brock
4. Malcolmson

Bottom Row—
), Gracey
R. Bailey
G. Cousens

There was more, of course. Much, much more. His aphorism "the medium is the message" implied that it was the characteristics of television or computers themselves that affected society, not the content transmitted by them.

He drew a famous distinction between "hot" and "cool" media. The former, like radio and film, he said, filled in most details for audiences.

Television and comic books, on the other hand, were cool media because they required more conscious participation.

He also argued that individuals could be inherently suited to one medium over another. From this took root a truism of 20th century political wisdom — that Richard Nixon lost the 1960 U.S. presidential election to John F. Kennedy because he projected a "hot" personality through the cool medium of TV.

"Kennedy had a compatible coolness and indifference to power, bred of personal wealth," McLuhan explained, "which allowed him to adapt fully to TV."

To this day, every aspiring politician assesses his or TV performance and electability based on criteria set down by McLuhan.

In the '60s and '70s at the U of T, thanks to his visibility in the culture, McLuhan was Canada's first academic pop star. He was as famous as, say, drug guru Timothy Leary south of the border.

And in scholarly circles, he was as controversial as such post-modern European thinkers as structuralist Michel Foucault and deconstructionist Jacques Derrida.

McLuhan's views have not gone unchallenged. Many have said he was a creature of American film and television executives who had a financial stake in a culture in which the printed word no longer ruled.

Others have argued McLuhan failed to properly acknowledge his debt to his U of T colleague Harold Innes, the pioneering communications theorist who died in 1952.

And some, such as U of M English prof David Williams, say McLuhan was essentially a reactionary looking to escape the "tyranny of the book" and return to a Catholic utopia of medieval Europe.

"He set media studies back a generation," says Williams, a novelist and communications theorist. "He could not sustain a systematic or coherent argument."

Still, his ideas continue to cast a giant shadow over the emerging global village of the 21st century.

And here in Winnipeg, we like to believe we provided the fertile soil in which his young mind grew to maturity.

"Winnipeg should take credit for McLuhan's cosmopolitanism," Williams admits. "When he was growing up, aside from Montreal, this was the country's most cosmopolitan city."

McLuhan at about 14.

COPYRIGHT THE ESTATE OF MARSHALL MCLUHAN

MANITOBA-NESS

BORN in Edmonton on July 21, 1911, Herbert Marshall McLuhan was four when his parents, Herbert and Elsie, arrived in Winnipeg after Herbert took a financial bath in the wake of an Edmonton real estate bust. In 1921, after several moves, the family settled at 507 Gertrude Ave., where Marshall lived until he left for England in 1934 with a master's degree in English from the University of Manitoba. Later, in Toronto, where he spent his academic career, he would tell his children he was a Prairie boy and a "Winnipigeon."

5 THINGS YOU DIDN'T KNOW

1. When he was 17, he and two friends in Fort Rouge built a 14-foot sailboat in a neighbour's garage.

2. He landed his first university teaching job, in the English department of the University of Wisconsin, in Madison in 1936.

3. His wife, Corinne, whom he married in 1939, hailed from Fort Worth, Texas.

4. He uttered what is probably his most famous pronouncement, "the medium is the message," as the guest speaker at a radio convention in 1957.

5. In 1967, McLuhan was asked to appear on television with the legendary comedian Groucho Marx, but he turned down the opportunity, citing other commitments.

THE CANADIAN PRESS ARCHIVES

McLuhan outside St. Michael's College, University of Toronto, where he taught from 1946 to 1979.

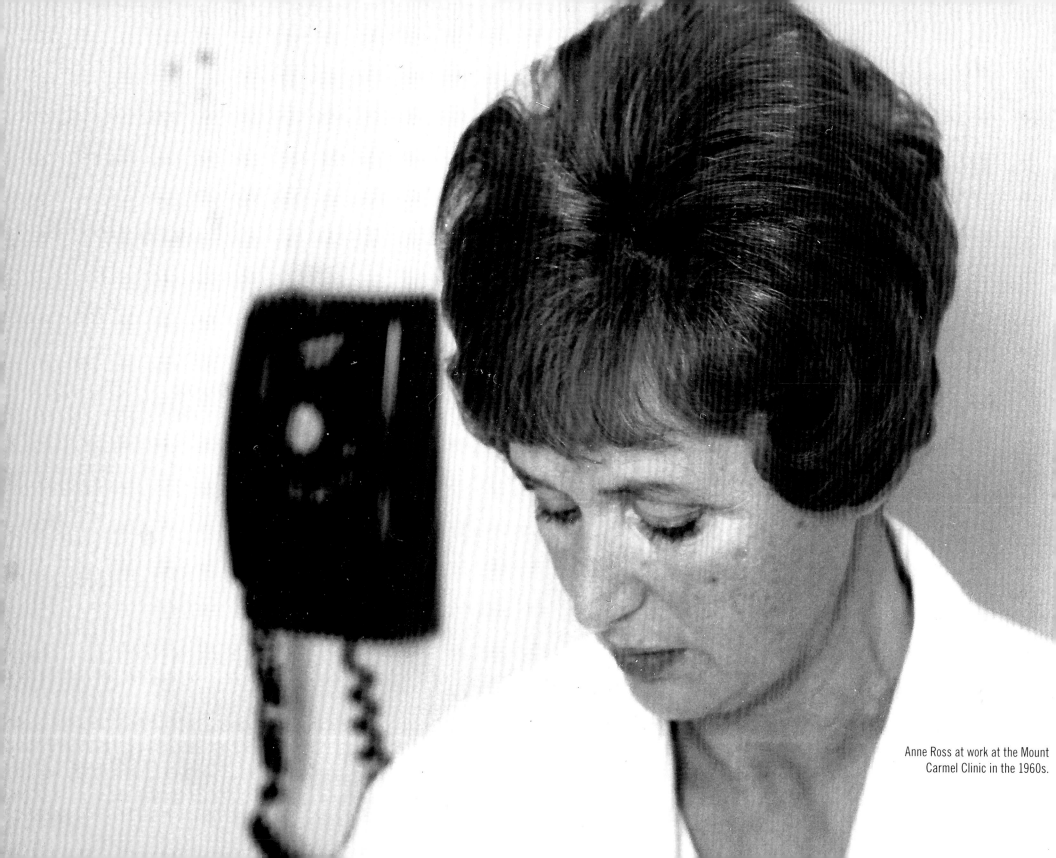

Anne Ross at work at the Mount Carmel Clinic in the 1960s.

ANNE ROSS

15

BY GABRIELLE GIRODAY

Nurse to the needy

S HE never backed down from some of Manitoba's most vicious health-care and social service battles.

Anne Ross knew a sly truth about getting what she wanted: If you can't beat them, simply grin, keep working and wear 'em down.

Thanks to plucky Nurse Ross's efforts from the 1940s to the 1980s, Winnipeg's Mount Carmel Clinic served some of the city's most poverty-battered residents to become Canada's most visionary community clinic.

Whether it was hounding health professionals to volunteer, developing sex education programs, providing women access to abortion or continually haranguing the governments in power to fund her cutting-edge programs, the 5'2" dynamo with the 1,000-watt smile parlayed her considerable charm and indomitable persistence into a vision of health for the clinic's clients.

GREATNESS

Professional Service Award, Radiological Association of Manitoba (1952).

Life Membership in recognition of outstanding contributions, Planned Parenthood of Manitoba (1976).

Community Service Award, City of Winnipeg (1981).

Good Citizenship Award, Tourism Association of Manitoba (1983).

Citation of Merit, Tourism Association of Manitoba (1985).

Citation of Merit, Manitoba Association of Registered Nurses (1985).

Distinguished Service Award, University of Manitoba (1985).

The Order of Canada (1985).

Communications and Leadership Award, Toastmasters International (1987).

The Order of the Buffalo Hunt, Province of Manitoba (1987).

Community Service Award, Burton Cummings Community Centre (1992).

Commemorative Medal: 125th Anniversary of the Confederation of Canada (1992).

Honourary doctorate of laws from Ryerson Polytechnic University (1998).

"In the '50s, she was talking a foreign language to people. Nobody understood or thought it was important what she was doing," said Dee Dee Rizzo, Ross's daughter, a retired teacher and Mount Carmel Clinic board member.

"She was so far ahead of her time in this whole concept of the health of an individual. They talk about it now in all sorts of different terms, but she was the forerunner of the concept of total care, that you cannot look at the health of a person separate and apart from their environment, from economics, from housing, from (their) job, from the emotional and physical."

When Ross became medical services supervisor at Mount Carmel in 1948, the clinic was underused and crammed into an old brick building on Selkirk Avenue. Ross tramped in and out of Point Douglas homes, seeking immigrant families in need. As those needs became apparent, Ross opened the city's first walk-in clinic, then a day hospital, then a dental clinic, then a birth control program, then a pregnancy counselling service, then a day nursery, serving thousands of patients.

Dubbed Anne of the Milk Subsidies for her fight for cheap milk for needy families and free milk for pregnant women, Ross caught the attention of detractors who called her a Communist. She'd also married Bill

Ross at work in the 1970s.

Ross at the Mount Carmel Clinic in December 1967.

FAMILY SUBMITTED PHOTO

Ross, longtime leader of Manitoba's Communist Party of Canada.

But then, given her personal struggles growing up, Ross was used to not blending in to the crowd.

Ross was born Channah Glaz in Samgorodok, Ukraine, and poverty, social alienation and violence against Jews marked her childhood.

"She had an awful, awful upbringing, in the sense she and her siblings and her mother had to cope with very little money," recalls her son, Arthur Ross, a Ryerson University politics professor. "She remembered as a child going out in the field to pick leftover grain... she had a very rough time."

In 1921, Ross's family, her Yiddish-speaking parents and three siblings, emigrated to Winnipeg and settled into an Aberdeen Avenue home. The family changed their name to Glass, an anglicized version of Glaz.

Times were lean, with her father, Aaron Glaz, working as a fisherman and cattle salesman. Her beloved older sister, Gitel Glaz, inspired in her a deep devotion to social justice. Gitel's death at 24 to complications of rheumatic fever hardened her dedication to those ideals.

Ross studied at Winnipeg's legendary I.L. Peretz Folk School, a progressive Jewish institution where she met her husband, then named Cecil Zuken. He later changed his name to Bill Ross to protect his family from repercussions for his Communist beliefs.

Anne was no teacher's pet as she moved through high school and university in the 1920s and '30s, finishing her studies as a registered nurse at the Winnipeg General Hospital in 1934, the only Jewish student in her class of 60.

"Being the only Jew and being outspoken," said Rizzo, "I don't think she was ever rude, but I think if she thought something was wrong, she would have questioned it."

After graduation, she worked in Montreal and Hastings, N.Y. then returned to Winnipeg around 1937

and married Zuken, by then Bill Ross. He'd pursued her tenaciously for 12 years.

While her husband was waging his own political battles — his Communist activism landed him in jail twice — Anne worked as a nurse at the Winnipeg Children's Hospital.

"My mother was not a Communist and never a member of the party... but it was an issue that came up many times in my mother's career and the label was put on her," said Rizzo, who said her mother "shared a lot of common ideals in terms of socialism" with Ross.

Ross took the job running the Mount Carmel clinic in 1948.

"She started walking around the neighbourhood and talking to people and seeing the needs," Rizzo said. "The day hospital got started in the early '50s because my mother was seeing women struggling with children and many of them having difficulty coping... never mind having the medication, even being able to care for the child adequately at home."

Under Ross's guidance, the clinic started a program that sent staff into the community to pick up sick kids and take them to the clinic where they would be taken care of, fed, bathed, their clothes washed and taken home at the end of the day.

As well as designing the programs Ross saw the community needed, she harangued politicians and donors to support the clinic. In 1982, she saw the culmination of her dream when a sprawling $3-million clinic opened at 886 Main St.

Lobbying was one of Ross's greatest gifts.

"She did not simply approach or lobby politicians and public servants, she laid siege," said her son. "Politicians came and went. Anne Ross persisted."

Frank Maynard, the province's deputy minister of health from 1988 to 1994, said Ross wouldn't take no for an answer when he told her to stop calling him at home.

"She phoned again the next week," he said. "She

'I would really rather have her as a relative than an opponent. Her persistence has paid off... I suppose the first reaction to her was "Here comes little Annie Ross." Later, I suppose the reaction was "Look, you can't fight her, so you better join her" '

— Legendary Winnipeg city councillor Joe Zuken, Anne Ross's brother-in-law started calling me on a regular basis. We were having a chat every week after a while. I was able to talk to her about substantive things… we'd get into interesting discussions about children's health, about what the clinic was doing."

After his retirement, Maynard joined Mount Carmel's board because he admired Ross's vision of an integrated system of health care.

By the 1970s, Ross was known for outspoken and frank education about sex. Her views, then considered radical, developed into a radio program that was broadcast across the province.

Then there were the headline-grabbing political attacks about the clinic's role in birth control counselling for women in the '60s and early '70s.

Joe Borowski, then Manitoba's minister of transportation, accused the clinic of "pimping for abortionists" in 1971 after Ross told the *Free Press* she'd sent some women to New York for abortions.

Borowski eventually resigned from provincial cabinet over the remarks, which contradicted the NDP government's stand. But there'd be others to take his place.

Trouble reared up again after authorities launched an investigation into clinic staff dispensing birth control pills. A Winnipeg doctor who opposed the clinic's services had lodged a complaint with the Manitoba College of Physicians and Surgeons.

Ross didn't scare easily. She also held a more nuanced view of the clinic's goals.

"It worried me that people referred to us as 'that abor-

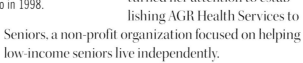

FAMILY SUBMITTED PHOTO

Ross receives an honorary doctorate from Ryerson University in Toronto in 1998.

tion clinic.'

"If Winnipeggers felt that way, my dream was undermined; our intention was to serve the community as a family-oriented health-care facility concerned with the total care of children, troubled teens and their struggling families. Any other definition would be unwarranted and deeply disappointing," she says, in her 1998 book *Clinic with a Heart: The Story of Mount Carmel Clinic.*

"My actions were a natural outgrowth of my philosophy of helping people in need."

In 1978, Ross's book *Pregnant and Alone* was published, a book of short stories and health information for young women.

In 1982, she followed it up with *Teenage Mothers/Teenage Fathers,* which focused on helping young parents and reflected Ross's emphasis on keeping families together by educating parents and helping them meet their children's needs.

She retired from the clinic in 1985 at 74, heralded as "somewhere between Mother Teresa and a political dragon slayer" by the *Winnipeg Free Press,* then turned her attention to establishing AGR Health Services to Seniors, a non-profit organization focused on helping low-income seniors live independently.

Ross died of ovarian cancer in 1998. When she knew she was dying, she told her daughter: "I still have things I have to do."

Rizzo remembers telling her mother, "Mom, no matter how long you live, there will always be things you have to do."

MANITOBA-NESS

SEPT. 25, 1911: Anne Ross, known then as Channah Glaz, is born in Ukraine. Her children think the date may not be accurate due to poor record-keeping.

1922: Ross immigrated to Canada with her mother and siblings, and joined her father Aaron Glaz, who had already moved to Winnipeg.

1920s and 1930s: Ross lives on Aberdeen Avenue and attends St. John's High School, graduating at 16, and studies at the I.L. Peretz Folk School. She takes courses at the University of Manitoba and University of Winnipeg, and in 1934 earns her nursing qualifications at the Winnipeg General Hospital. In 1937, she marries Bill Ross.

1944: Ross has her first daughter, Dee Dee Rizzo. In 1947, she has a son, Arthur Ross.

1948: Ross takes a job at Mount Carmel Clinic as head nurse, but laments the clinic is rundown, relies on volunteer doctors and is "dying slowly" due to lack of patients.

1950s: The Mount Carmel Clinic develops its day hospital and walk-in clinic, and Ross starts sex education programs.

1960s: Mount Carmel launches a birth control program so women can get birth-control pills and stares down heavy political backlash.

1970s: The clinic starts a pregnancy counselling service, where women could get advice and information about their options, including where to obtain abortions. Once again, the clinic becomes a centre of controversy, and the United Way comes under fire for funding it. Mount Carmel starts developing programs to support teen mothers pursuing education and employment.

1982: The new Mount Carmel Clinic opens on Main Street. The new clinic houses the Anne Ross Day Nursery.

Ross and her husband Bill share a quiet moment in Assiniboine Park.

FAMILY SUBMITTED PHOTO

5 THINGS YOU DIDN'T KNOW

1. Anne and Bill were married for 61 years, surviving personal attacks for their work and beliefs. But Anne almost married someone other than her controversial husband. In her 20s, she almost married a doctor she met in Montreal where she was working as a nurse. But Ross captured her heart with letters from Winnipeg and she returned to Winnipeg to marry him. They died within weeks of each other in 1998.

2. Anne Ross considered being a doctor but didn't have the grades or the money to study medicine.

3. She was a lousy teenage waitress but also displayed an early talent for the gift of gab. Working at Lake Louise as what her daughter calls an "absolutely hopeless" 16-year-old server, Anne told her boss if he fired her he'd have to shoulder the guilt of knowing he'd stymied a future doctor. "I think instead of serving customers directly, she was given some jobs in the kitchen, and further along, she graduated to serving customers," said Rizzo.

4. Ross almost quit her job at Mount Carmel after the first year but ended up staying 36 more years. "They were maybe two or three patients, maybe half a dozen patients a week, coming into that place, and she was going crazy out of sheer boredom," said Rizzo.

5. Anne Ross died at her home Aug. 14, 1998. She lived her entire life in the North End, save for her childhood in Ukraine and from 1934 to 1937, when she lived in Montreal and Hastings, N.Y.

STEVEN JUBA

16

By KEVIN ROLLASON

Champion of the common citizen

STEVE Juba grew up poor and Ukrainian. In his childhood, in Winnipeg, those two qualities were enough to block him from any hope of ever sitting in the mayor's chair. But once he took that august seat, they guided him and the causes he championed.

And in many ways, they were the reasons everyday Winnipeggers kept him in that chair.

It was a different world when Juba, already a sitting MLA, was first elected Winnipeg's mayor in 1956. The city's more affluent denizens looked upon Winnipeg's Ukrainian population as second-class citizens. Even though Juba had made a fortune through his Keystone Supply Co., his election shocked many and was widely considered a mistake to be corrected at the next election.

It wasn't. Juba was elected by landslides in the elections to come until he decided to leave office of his own accord in 1977. At the time, he was second only to Montreal's Jean Drapeau as the country's longest-serving mayor.

Steve Juba waves farewell at the last council meeting at Winnipeg's old city hall.

GREATNESS

Steve Juba was colourful and controversial, but Winnipeggers loved him and made him the city's longest-serving mayor.

Juba lost elections in the federal, provincial and civic arenas before finally becoming an MLA in 1953, followed by his election to the mayor's chair in 1956. He overlapped those two posts for three years before stepping down as an MLA. He stayed in the mayor's chair until 1977 when he chose not to run.

Juba's election as MLA shocked the establishment because at the time it was the highest electoral office a person of Ukrainian descent had achieved.

During Juba's years in office he initiated and presided over the 1967 Pan American Games, pushed for a new city hall building, built the Disraeli Freeway, Centennial Library, Winnipeg Convention Centre and co-founded Folklorama.

While an MLA, Juba championed making margarine yellow, allowing Sunday professional sporting events and letting women drink in bars.

Honoured with Order of Canada in 1970.

Presented with honorary doctor of laws from University of Winnipeg in 1974.

City named downtown Stephen Juba Park for him in 1983.

WAYNE GLOWACKI / WINNIPEG FREE PRESS

Juba was a political veteran who launched many a mayoralty campaign.

WINNIPEG FREE PRESS ARCHIVES

Juba signs the deal in 1966 to bring the 1967 Pan Am Games to Winnipeg.

WINNIPEG TRIBUNE / UNIVERSITY OF MANITOBA ARCHIVES

Juba and his wife Elva landed this Marlin on a tropical trip in February 1958.

WINNIPEG FREE PRESS ARCHIVES

Juba makes a point to Premier Ed Schreyer in August 1975.

Juba was a man of contrasts: He spent his entire political career living in a modest home on William Avenue and yet he owned two dozen Cadillacs throughout his life.

"What made Steve Juba so special is that he grew up at a time of tremendous inequality," said Al Golden, former city councillor and family friend.

"He recognized this, he was upset about this and he tried to champion every case where people were not equal. He had to share a pair of shoes with his brother when they were growing up, they were that poor. He never forgot it."

It has been more than 50 years since Juba first sat in the mayor's chair, and more than 30 since he surprised everyone and suddenly pulled his nomination papers out of the ring in 1977.

Juba retired to Petersfield and spent his winters in Florida. He died May 2, 1993.

"I'm surprised people still remember him," said Juba's wife Elva. "He would be surprised, too. Who wouldn't be? I know how much he tried to do and did do, all the things he accomplished. But it would still be a surprise to him.

"But he would be pleased, too."

While many young people today might not know who Steve Juba was, he continues to cast a long shadow at city hall with each mayor who has come after judged using him as the measure.

"He did much more than people realize," said former deputy mayor — and rival — Bernie Wolfe.

"He was able to generate a real identity for Winnipeg. He projected the image of a city on the move. He wasn't bashful about standing up."

Juba was born in Winnipeg on July 1, 1914, to Gregory and Sophie Juba, two Ukrainian immigrants. He had a brother, Daniel, and a sister, Nancy.

Juba was defeated in his first stab at politics, losing to Stanley Knowles in a federal election. He lost again provincially and twice in civic elections. But he was

Juba's April 1971 campaign included a promise to open taverns to women.

WINNIPEG TRIBUNE / UNIVERSITY OF MANITOBA ARCHIVES

lucky the fifth time and was elected in 1953 as an Independent to represent Winnipeg Centre in the provincial legislature. Three years later, he took the mayor's chair, defeating incumbent George Sharpe.

Because there weren't any rules saying you couldn't, he continued as a provincial MLA and was re-elected to that post in 1958. He quit it in 1959.

During the Juba mayoral years, the old gingerbread city hall building was demolished and the current one erected in its place, the Public Safety Building and the Disraeli Freeway were built, the Winnipeg Convention Centre and Centennial Library (now Millennium Library) opened.

Juba also created the idea of twinning Winnipeg with international cities, including Setaguya-Ku, Japan.

The city also hosted the 1967 Pan American Games, but how it got here is a funny story.

Winnipeggers look back at those Games as the sport-ing event that put their city on the global map, a heady time that left it with major sporting facilities including the appropriately named Pan Am Pool, the velodrome (since demolished to make way for stores near Polo Park) and improvements to the Winnipeg Stadium.

But former CJOB broadcaster and *Winnipeg Tribune* city editor Peter Warren says that's not what Juba had in mind a few years earlier when he returned from meeting then-Chicago mayor Richard Daley Sr.

"He was bubbling over when he got off the plane," Warren said.

"Mayor Daley had just announced Chicago had Pan Am and he told Steve you should get Pan Am, too. So when he got off the plane, he was so excited I asked him why. And he said Chicago had Pan Am, and he'd like to see Winnipeg get Pan Am, too.

"He said it would be great to see Pan Am Airlines at Winnipeg Airport. That's how it all started."

With then premier Ed Schreyer, Juba founded Folklorama, a cultural celebration now in its 39th year.

Elva still remembers being there when the idea for Folklorama was germinated.

"I remember him and I walking in Copenhagen in Tivoli Gardens, and he said, 'One of these days, we'll have this in Winnipeg,'" she said.

"When he got back, he called Mary Kelekis and said, 'We have to have something like Tivoli Gardens here.'"

Juba was famous for his media stunts to help him get his own way.

He drove to the Wolseley area and held hands with the women who circled an elm tree preventing civic crews from removing it. When the provincial government refused to let the city fog for mosquitoes, he had all 28 of the city's fogging trucks park in front of the legislative building and dropped all their ignition keys on a table in front of the premier.

He plopped a portable washroom in front of the legislative building when he was unsuccessfully battling the province against the so-called Broadway Biffy, a public washroom built on Broadway across the street from the legislature.

While in provincial politics, Juba led several battles including getting margarine coloured yellow in Manitoba, allowing professional sports events on Sundays, letting women drink in bars and allowing lotteries to raise money for hospitals.

Juba also proposed projects that didn't get off the ground, including a roof for Winnipeg Stadium and perhaps the most famous, constructing a monorail for rapid transit.

Elva said her husband's politics didn't bother his father, but it didn't win him any affection from his mother.

"His mother thought he was the direct descendent of the Devil," she said. "She was a strong Catholic and here he was with the liquor issue and Sunday sports. She was very upset with him."

Elva said Juba ran for a second term as mayor because of his father.

"He wanted to get out after his first term, but he promised his dad he would go two terms, which he did. And then it snowballed. I guess (his dad) knew that if Steve started something, he wouldn't be able to finish it in his first term."

Elva said her husband finally gave up being MLA and mayor at the same time because the grind weighed heavily on him and affected his health.

"It was hard because the house used to sit at night so Steve would go from the mayor's office to the Manitoba legislature. It did take its toll. He had an ulcer and didn't go anywhere without two quarts of milk in the trunk."

Elva said she never pushed her husband to leave politics, even though she knows he could have become a multimillionaire had he turned his full attention to business during those years.

"I let him make up his own mind," she said. "I knew he loved it. I knew he wouldn't be happy at the business without politics."

Elva said it was the failure of getting the monorail that pushed him to leave office.

"He was so disappointed. We had gone to two or three places and got prices. He wouldn't go into something unless he studied it."

Just hours before Juba pulled his name from the election, he expressed pessimism as to how long he would be remembered.

"Nobody will remember what I did 25 years from now. When something blooms in spring, it's fresh and exciting. But when it fades in fall, everybody forgets about it."

But Golden said Juba was wrong.

"He lives on in the tens of thousands of people he helped. He helped people grow. The people he planted seeds of hope in still remember him.

"He gave them confidence, and he gave them hope."

WINNIPEG FREE PRESS ARCHIVES

Juba and other members of Winnipeg's Pine to Palm goodwill tour, left, pose in New Orleans in 1957, top, and on Pembina Highway, bottom, to mark the 40th anniversary of the construction of the New Orleans-to-Winnipeg route.

WINNIPEG FREE PRESS ARCHIVES

ba holds his nose and jumps, above, when he invited Canada's Swimming Hall
Fame to attend a centennial water show at the Pan Am Pool in 1970.

WINNIPEG FREE PRESS ARCHIVES

Juba paid for billboards in 1976 to keep the TCA repair base in Winnipeg.

WINNIPEG FREE PRESS ARCHIVES

Juba makes
a proclamation
in 1973.

WINNIPEG FREE PRESS ARCHIVES

'Steve Juba certainly loved Winnipeg and for more than two decades Winnipeg loved Steve Juba... he was very attentive to people who had a connection with the North End, in particular. He was certainly a man of the people. He was champion of the little guy. He was an individual who had respect and support from all corners of society, all areas of Winnipeg and certainly beyond'

— former premier Gary Filmon

'He would always say that it was important to speak up to be heard, to stand to be seen and to sit down to be appreciated'

— former MLA Darren Praznik

'He didn't take the easy way out. He called the shots as he saw them and not every politician is so frank'

— former Manitoba premier Duff Roblin

WINNIPEG FREE PRESS ARCHIVES

'He identified readily with Joe Citizen, who swears by him as the champion of the little guy. He may drive a Cadillac, but he drives it himself... and the man on the street approves'

— former city councillor Lloyd Stinson

WINNIPEG FREE PRESS ARCHIVES

Juba helps firefighters, hauling hose in 1957 to battle a blaze on Pembina Highway, above, and in 1968, below.

WINNIPEG FREE PRESS ARCHIVES

Juba is kidnapped, above, part of a publicity stunt in 1968 that startled shoppers on Portage Avenue.

WINNIPEG FREE PRESS ARCHIVES

Juba chats with Hollywood star Bob Hope in Winnipeg.

Juba eats a perogy at Dauphin Ukrainian Festival in 1971.

WINNIPEG FREE PRESS ARCHIVES

THE CANADIAN PRESS ARCHIVES

a holds a tiger cub, left, part of a contest in 1959.

Juba at Canadian National Exhibition with Monty Hall and Bobby Hull in 1974.

WINNIPEG FREE PRESS ARCHIVES

MANITOBA-NESS

JUBA was born in Winnipeg July 1, 1914, and died in 1993. He married Elva Campbell, who grew up in Minnedosa and was one of his employees at Keystone Supply Co., in 1952. Keystone was a wholesale company specializing in furniture and appliances for hundreds of dealerships across the country.

'When I was first elected I didn't expect city council to do handsprings for me. I was as welcome as a skunk at a garden party'

— Steve Juba

5 THINGS YOU DIDN'T KNOW

1. As mayor, Juba had a hand in deciding where red lights would be. But he spent a lifetime hating them. Juba would never go through one and would sometimes drive around for blocks to avoid them.

2. During his early political years, Juba was derided by some as being a North End Ukrainian. Juba was proud of being Ukrainian — after leaving politics, he and his wife made Ukrainian decorative eggs and sold them at Folklorama and other places — but he never lived a day of his life in the North End. He lived in the Brooklands area and on William Avenue.

3. Juba wasn't the only mayor in the family. His brother Daniel was elected mayor of Brooklands. Juba Street was named in honour of Daniel.

4. Juba had a secret file on his rivals. He recalled in a Free Press interview in 1989 how he would call a councillor into his office, show them the file, tell them what they were looking at was a copy and the original was in a safe place and tell them what he wanted them to do.

5. Juba had an unofficial circle of advisers — five in all — he used as a sounding board. They included broadcaster and journalist Peter Warren, and journalist and publisher Ted Byfield, but the others are unknown because the group never met and none of them knew who else was in the Juba circle.

Peter Warren   WINNIPEG FREE PRESS ARCHIVES

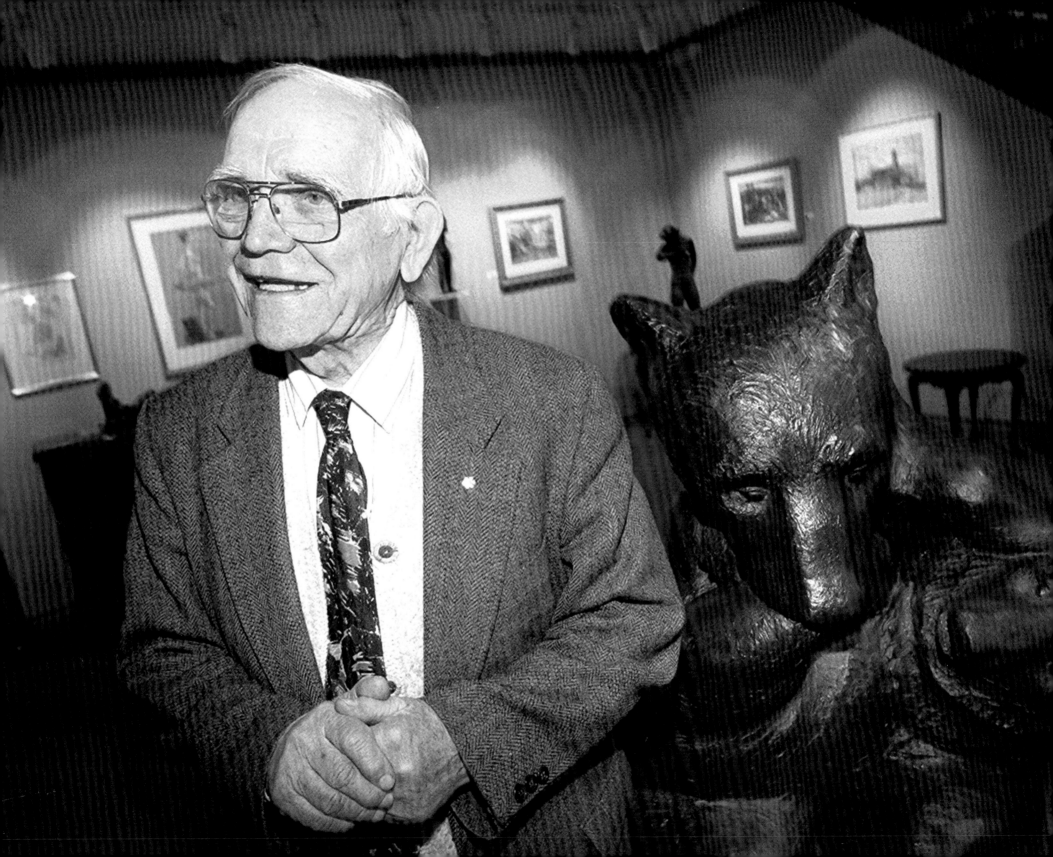

By ALISON MAYES

Master sculptor

WHEN Leo Mol was fleeing Europe in the wake of the Second World War, immigration authorities told him Canada didn't need artists. It needed farm labourers.

So the 33-year-old classically trained Ukrainian sculptor arrived in January 1949 at a frozen grain farm near Prince Albert, Sask.

He and his wife Margareth had $70 to their names. He didn't speak English.

There was nothing to do on the farm except wait for spring. But Mol couldn't stand to be idle. He set out for the nearest big city, Winnipeg. He got off the train and trudged along Main Street.

Eventually, the short man with blue eyes and a broad face happened upon a store, Providence Church Goods, with plaster religious figures in its window. Venturing inside, he discovered the shop owner was Ukrainian and — was it providence? — needed someone to paint church murals.

From that humble start, Mol forged a prolific art career in the city that became his home.

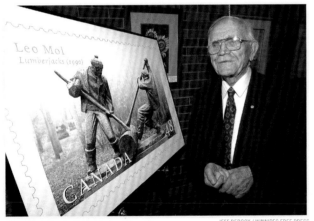

JEFF DEBOOY / WINNIPEG FREE PRESS

Mol was honoured in 2002 with a 48-cent stamp depicting his sculpture Lumberjacks.

Leo Mol on his 85th birthday, Jan. 14, 2000.

GREATNESS

During a Winnipeg-based career lasting more than 50 years, Ukrainian-born Leo Mol sculpted popes, cardinals, royalty, statesmen, community leaders, artists of the Group of Seven and many other notable figures.

He was chosen to create a bronze monument to Ukrainian poet Taras Shevchenko in Washington, D.C., followed by two more in Argentina and Brazil. In the year 2000, in a ceremony attended by Russian President Vladimir Putin, Mol gave a statue of Shevchenko to the city of St. Petersburg (formerly Leningrad), where he had studied art.

In 2002, the Mol sculpture Lumberjacks was featured on a Canadian postage stamp.

Mol's art dealer says the market for his works is strong and their value is growing. A version of the now-famous bronze of pilot Tom Lamb, the 40-cm tall one, has appreciated in value to $28,000 from $1,500. Some of Mol's life-size figures that started at $15,000 are now worth $80,000 to $90,000.

Mol, who continued sculpting until he was nearly 90, was appointed to the Order of Canada in 1989 and to the Order of Manitoba in 2000. He has received honorary doctorates from the universities of Manitoba, Winnipeg and Alberta, as well as many other honours. He is an elected member of the Royal Canadian Academy of Arts.

'This has really been the dream of my life, to have my work properly displayed'

— Leo Mol

Leo Mol Sculpture Garden in Assiniboine Park in 2003.

JEFF DE BOOY /WINNIPEG FREE PRESS

"He's probably one of the most determined people I've ever met," says Elise Swerhone, director of the 1993 documentary *Leo Mol: In Light and Shadow.* "Even at 80, he was still full of ideas. He had a whole slate of things that he wanted to accomplish."

Mol's work ethic is legendary.

"He was like a man on a mission," says David Loch, Mol's longtime dealer. "The creative juices were unbelievable."

Today, at 93, the master sculptor is in fading health, his creative years behind him. But his elegant works, which he always said could speak for themselves, are accessible to everyone in parks, public spaces and churches.

He had no children but left a legacy in bronze and stained glass. His sculpture of pioneer bush pilot Tom Lamb, which shows the parka-clad aviator reaching to spin a propeller, is an iconic image of Manitoban tenacity and spirit. Loch calls it Mol's masterpiece.

Mol kept a personal copy of almost every piece he created. In 1990, he donated his entire collection of more than 300 bronzes, paintings, terra cottas and other works — valued at $4 million — to the city of Winnipeg, on the condition the city create an appropriate setting.

The serene Leo Mol Sculpture Garden at Assiniboine Park, established in 1992 to display the bronzes among sheltering trees, winding paths and tranquil ponds, is North America's only such garden devoted to an individual artist.

The garden was completed in 2003, at a cost of $4 million. Its fundraising champion was philanthropist Hartley Richardson. The site includes an indoor gallery and the former one-room Birds Hill schoolhouse that served as Mol's rural studio.

"This has really been the dream of my life, to have my work properly displayed," the gentle-mannered sculptor said at the groundbreaking.

Mol took pride in his rigorous old-school training and had no use for abstract contemporary art or any artistic

Mol in his
basement studio in
November 1957.

WINNIPEG FREE PRESS ARCHIVES

"Leo was only interested in one thing: creating the work. He used to say, 'You need a Mercedes. I don't.'"

— David Loch, Leo Mol's longtime art dealer

WINNIPEG FREE PRESS ARCHIVES

Mol at work on sculptures in April 1977, above, and, below, in September 1979.

trend.

"I never want to be a fashion," he once said.

He revered the classical Greek and Roman sculptors and believed most ordinary people prefer art in a realistic style.

No one denied Mol's superb craftsmanship nor his skill at creating sensitive, lifelike, three-dimensional portraits. But the visual arts establishment, always preoccupied with boundary-pushing, had little time for Mol.

"He felt snubbed by the art community in Canada," recalls Swerhone.

"Sometimes I feel a little bit like an outcast," Mol said in an interview when the Winnipeg Art Gallery held a Mol retrospective in 1974. "(But) art is serving the community in a spiritual form... and I like to serve the silent majority."

Mol didn't regard art as a glamorous vocation; he compared himself to a bus driver who just "did his share." He was always interested in Canadian subjects, making ceramic figurines of curlers and square dancers in the 1950s or putting aboriginal figures into his stained-glass windows. His idea of relaxation was going to the Whiteshell to paint.

His wife became a teacher, and they settled in Norwood Flats. Mol amassed a large library and had an encyclopedic knowledge of great artists and their works.

After 13 years in Canada, Mol made his international breakthrough. He won a worldwide competition to create a towering bronze monument to Ukrainian poet-hero Taras Shevchenko for Embassy Row in Washington, D.C.

The four-metre statue's unveiling in 1964 attracted a crowd of more than 100,000.

After that, Mol secured more prestigious commissions. He had the honour of sculpting popes Paul VI and John Paul II from life and Pope John XXIII posthumously. He began to spend part of every year in

Mol in the studio surrounded by some of his most famous pieces.

PHOTO COPYRIGHT ANDREW ULICKI, MPA, WINNIPEG

PHIL HOSSACK / WINNIPEG FREE PRESS ARCHIVES

Mol and sculpture of former prime minister John Diefenbaker in March 1989.

WINNIPEG FREE PRESS ARCHIVES

Mol with his sculpture of Queen Elizabeth II in January 1970.

The bulk of Mol's work is sculpture, but he also painted.

WINNIPEG FREE PRESS ARCHIVES

Germany, where he had most of his bronzes cast at a foundry near Munich. A school there was named after him.

"Leo was really an international artist, but he never blew his own horn," says Loch.

He could have relocated to an art capital, but remained a committed Manitoban.

"He had this loyalty to Canada and Winnipeg which was unwavering," says Loch. "It was a city where he felt safe and was allowed to work."

Mol always stayed in modest accommodations in Europe and lived simply at home, Loch says. "Leo was only interested in one thing: creating the work. He used to say, 'You need a Mercedes. I don't.'"

In his portraits, Mol did more than simply render a likeness. He revealed complexity of character and, as *Free Press* critic Randal McIlroy wrote in 1989, did not deify his subjects.

"Whether the subject is Sir Winston Churchill, Taras Shevchenko or Pope John Paul II, the bronze result is noticeably, touchingly human — not a god, but a human being of noble aspiration and mortal frailty."

Mol is often described as a reserved, self-contained gentleman whose mind was always on his next sculpture. Friends say he was haunted by the trauma of his past.

"He buried himself in his work," says art collector John Crabb, who has known the artist since the 1960s.

For decades, Mol's pre-immigration life was shrouded in mystery. In interviews he falsely claimed to be an only child and to have trained in Vienna. Even now, little is known about his time in Berlin and Holland during the Second World War.

Swerhone's documentary revealed that Mol lived for nearly 50 years, from wartime until 1990, in fear that his family in the Soviet Union was being persecuted because of the path his life had taken. He was afraid to contact them for fear they would pay the price.

In 1990, his younger sister suddenly located him. He

Mol with one of his pieces in April 1989.

DAVE JOHNSON / WINNIPEG FREE PRESS ARCHIVES

learned that his father and brother had died in Stalinist camps, likely for their political views. His mother had died in exile.

The tragedy of Mol's story lends poignancy to his sculptures, especially works such as *Family Group and The Pioneer Family*. But to stroll through the Leo Mol Sculpture Garden is to hear a calm voice, whispering that the world can be orderly and compassionate.

"Mol may not invent new ways of seeing, but he reminds one that there is still room and need for grace, refinement and tenderness," wrote *Free Press* critic John W. Graham in 1977.

Mol is too frail now to visit his beloved garden. But he took great pleasure in knowing others would continue to appreciate its beauty.

"He would go there and just sit in the garden," says Swerhone, "and watch people looking at his work. If somebody recognized him and sat down next to him, he just loved that.

"(The garden) validated his entire life and his entire body of work. It was the recognition that he wanted."

MANITOBA-NESS

LEO Mol is Manitoba's best-known and most honoured sculptor.

Born Leonid Molodozhanyn in 1915 in the village of Polonne, Ukraine, he was taught to work with clay by his father, a potter.

Mol was a top student at the Leningrad Academy of Arts in the 1930s. When the Germans invaded Russia, he was conscripted and sent to Germany, but in 1945 managed to flee to Holland and continue his training. In 1948-49, Mol and his wife immigrated to Winnipeg.

Starting here as a ceramic artist and church painter, Mol gradually gained prominence as a skilled sculptor and stained-glass artist. By the 1960s, he was earning international commissions for bronzes.

To make his bronze casts, Mol used a revised version of the centuries-old "lost-wax" process — a rarity in Canada. The costly, time-consuming process involves sculpting a Plasticine model over an armature, then creating a plaster mould, inside which molten bronze ultimately replaces melted wax.

Mol is well-known for sculpting animals such as bears, graceful female nudes, Ukrainian subjects and busts or full-length likenesses of prominent personalities. He sculpted portrait-heads of many Winnipeggers, which helped pay his bills and keep his skills sharp for major commissions.

In the course of his career, he sculpted a number of the 50 finalists in the *Winnipeg Free Press* Greatest

Their Royal Highnesses Prince and Princess Michael of Kent open the final phase of the Leo Mol Sculpture Garden in Assiniboine Park in August 2003.

JEFF DEBOOY / WINNIPEG FREE PRESS ARCHIVES

1. When Mol was a new immigrant needing an income in the 1950s, he built a kiln and made Canadian-themed ceramic figurines such as robins, skaters, Inuit figures and square dancers. Managers at Eaton's and the Bay scorned the items, saying, "Who ever heard of Leo Mol?" But the more exclusive Birks store accepted the pieces. They sold extremely well and are now collectors' items. A ceramic robin that sold for $5 is now worth about $900. A $25 piece can now fetch $3,000.

2. Mol was so talented as a commercial ceramic artist that it could have been his ticket to New York, says dealer David Loch. A representative of the famed Rosenthal porcelain company saw Mol's figurines at Birks and refused to believe that a local artist with a kiln in his basement could make such exquisite work. When he saw that it was true, he offered Mol a job in New York, plus a house and a car. Mol said, "No thank you."

3. After former U.S. president Dwight Eisenhower unveiled Mol's high-profile Shevchenko monument in Washington, D.C., Mol was asked to sculpt a bust of Eisenhower. In 1965, Mol spent two weeks working on the portrait "from life" at Eisenhower's farm. The two became very friendly and the former statesman ended up helping Mol "muck around" in the kitchen with plaster. Mol later said that he never wanted his subjects to sit frozen like statues. "Eisenhower helped by talking, seeing visitors... and moving around," he said. "I prefer it this way — to have a person alive — instead of just sitting. This is boring."

4. In 1977, Mol went to Germany to cast a bust of sculptor Arno Breker, an approved artist of the Third Reich who had done portraits of Adolf Hitler. Mol said he had nothing but admiration for Breker's artistic ability, regardless of Breker's past Nazi Party ties. "It is what he left for us, the heritage, that is important, not his association," Mol said.

5. In 1985, Mol won the competition to create a statue of former prime minister John Diefenbaker for Parliament Hill. Four years later, he said that of all his major commissions, it meant the most to him. "To come to this country with absolutely nothing, other than my skills, and to find a way to apply those skills to such a major figure is quite an honour."

Manitoban contest, including Louis Riel, Terry Fox, Sir William Stephenson, Steve Juba and Tom Lamb.

His works around the city include the 2.7-metre Queen Elizabeth II in the courtyard of the Manitoba Centennial Centre and the sculpture of children climbing a tree in front of the Richardson Building.

He designed and executed more than 80 stained-glass windows for Manitoba churches. The most impressive include a magnificent Last Supper scene at Westworth United Church and 16 windows illustrating the history of Ukraine's people at the Sts. Vladimir and Olga Cathedral.

Institutions with Mol works in their collections include the Vatican Museum, National Portrait Gallery in Washington, D.C., Art Gallery of Ontario, McMichael Canadian Art Collection and Winnipeg Art Gallery. His pieces are in private and corporate collections throughout Canada, the U.S., England and Europe.

The Leo Mol Sculpture Garden in Assiniboine Park opened in 1992 as a permanent showcase for Mol's body of work. About 250,000 people visit the free attraction each year.

Former prime minister John Diefenbaker chats with Mol in December 1969.

SGT. TOMMY PRINCE

18

'Natural-born warrior'

Prince played hockey for the Scanterbury Eagles.

FAMILY SUBMITTED PHOTOS

Sgt. Tommy Prince in October 1952.

LONG before there was a Sgt. Tommy Prince, there was a Thomas George Prince.

There was a young boy from Brokenhead First Nation who was shipped off to residential school in the 1920s, separated from his parents and 10 brothers and sisters.

There was a boy who wanted to be an engineer, at a time when Canada had few, if any, aboriginal engineers.

Then after there was a Sgt. Tommy Prince, there was once again, a Thomas George Prince.

There was an activist for aboriginal dignity and human rights who went to Ottawa to deliver an impassioned and eloquent speech.

There was a man who twice saved people from drowning, and then simply walked away, not seeking credit or thanks.

There was a loving father.

There was an old soldier who suffered the sort of long-term damage only war can inflict.

And there was a society that twice sent Thomas George Prince off to war, pinned medals on him and then looked the other way when civilian life went sideways.

GREATNESS

Thomas George Prince, almost invariably referred to as Sgt. Tommy Prince, is Canada's most decorated aboriginal war veteran. In all, Prince was decorated nine times. He served with distinction in the Second World War and Korea.

Prince received the Military Medal from King George VI in a ceremony at Buckingham Palace, as well as the American Silver Star.

Prince's medals include: the Military Medal, 1939-45 Star, Italy Star, France and Germany Star, Defence Medal, Canadian Voluntary Service Medal with overseas bar, War Medal, Silver Star (U.S.), Presidential Citation Declaration, Diplome (France), Combat Infantry Badge, the Korea Medal, the United Nations Service Medal and the Canadian Volunteer Service Medal for Korea.

Among his honours: Sgt. Tommy Prince Street in Winnipeg; Sgt. Tommy Prince School on Brokenhead Ojibway Nation; The Tommy Prince Barracks at Canadian Forces Base, Petawawa, Ont.; The Tommy Prince Drill Hall at the Land Force Western Area Training Centre in Wainwright, Alta.; Government of Canada Sergeant Tommy Prince Army Training Initiative for aboriginal recruiting; The Tommy Prince Award: An Assembly of First Nations scholarship; The Tommy Prince Scholarship at Sault College, Sault Ste. Marie, Ontario; 553 Sgt. Tommy Prince PPCLI Cadet Corps, Winnipeg.

Prince with his nephew Clarence and niece Darlene.

FAMILY SUBMITTED PHOTO

Canada's most decorated aboriginal war veteran is rarely identified without his rank of sergeant, a rank he held in the Second World War and Korean War.

And while Manitobans and Canadians are slowly beginning to appreciate Sgt. Tommy Prince and what he did for this country — and understand what this country did to Thomas Prince — his war record alone does not define the man, says his nephew, Jim Bear of Brokenhead First Nation.

Like so many aboriginal children, Bear said, Prince was taken away from his family when he was very young and sent away to a residential school. Today, that Elkhorn school is a four-hour drive from Brokenhead — in the 1920s, it might as well have been across an ocean.

Prince dreamed of becoming an engineer, Bear said. But he became a soldier instead, volunteering at the outbreak of the Second World War. He'd grown up around firearms and quickly qualified as a sniper. "He was a natural-born warrior, and the military honed his skill," said Bear.

The stories are everywhere, in books, in *Historica Minutes*, in the annals of the Veterans Affairs Department, of Prince's war exploits in the fabled Devil's Brigade, an elite behind-the-lines commando unit of Canadian and American soldiers.

"He was quite the character. If they ever did a Hollywood movie of Tommy, they wouldn't have to make up anything. There was love, there was betrayal, there was tragedy, there was the residential school legacy," said Bear.

At the Anzio landing in Italy, Prince went behind enemy lines to call in artillery strikes on German Tiger tanks. He set up in a bombed-out farmhouse barely 200 metres from the German lines.

But when an errant shell cut his telephone wire, Prince put on some old clothes, took on the guise of an Italian farmer and strode outside to shake his fist at both the German and Allied positions — and fixed his

Prince, second from right, and other Canadian soldiers wait to be presented at Buckingham Palace in 1945.

CANADIAN ARMY PHOTO / MANITOBA PROVINCIAL ARCHIVES

phone line right under the gun barrels of the tanks.

And there's the story in occupied France about when Prince and a private were sent to scout enemy positions. Coming upon the Germans attacking a band of French partisans, the two members of the Devil's Brigade routed the Germans so devastatingly that the

rescued partisans later said they thought there'd been 50 of them.

After the war, Prince at first established himself as a respected leader of aboriginal communities, a forerunner of national aboriginal leaders Phil Fontaine and Ovide Mercredi, said Bear.

As head of the Manitoba Indian Association, Prince went to Ottawa in 1947 and spoke to the standing committee on Indian Affairs: "It was quite an eloquent speech — he made a speech to get rid of the Indian Act and to respect treaty rights," said Bear.

"He was a visionary. Back then, he was advocating to take the grievances over to England."

But it all started to go sideways for Prince. There had been adulation when Prince went to Buckingham Palace to have King George VI pin on the Military Medal, but back in Winnipeg, he was just another person looking for work.

Prince had opened a window-cleaning business before the war, but his employees drove it under while he was overseas, said Bear.

When Prince came home from the war, he'd hang out on Main Street and be challenged to fights. "The younger fellows would want to try him — he still had the skills."

Bear grew up idolizing his uncle but not for his military exploits. He never even heard those stories until a year or so before Prince died in 1977.

The man whose bravery left a great mark on the battlefields of Europe, then later in Korea, never talked about the wars.

"I was in school in Teulon in the early '60s, I used to come in and spend time with him," Bear recalled. "He was staying on Portage East... We used to go to wrestling matches with him at the arena."

Bear first learned of his uncle's heroism from Phil Fontaine when they were young chiefs together in the 1970s. History buff Fontaine told Bear about his uncle's war experiences.

'If they ever did a Hollywood movie of Tommy, they wouldn't have to make up anything. There was love, there was betrayal, there was tragedy, there was the residential school legacy'

— Nephew Jim Bear

Prince in 1976.

WINNIPEG TRIBUNE / UNIVERSITY OF MANITOBA ARCHIVES

FAMILY SUBMITTED PHOTO

By that time, Prince's life was beset by turmoil, by alcohol, by the mean streets of Winnipeg. He was struggling, but no one understood why. Post-traumatic stress disorder was unknown in those days, Bear said.

"He was always behind enemy lines," and saw and did things that scarred him.

Prince twice saved drowning victims in civilian life, once in Selkirk, once off Winnipeg's Alexander Docks, but there's no record of who they were or what became of them. "He didn't even give his name. He walked away, and someone recognized him as Tommy Prince."

It's Bear who's done more than anyone to keep Prince's memory alive, from recovering his missing war medals in an auction house in London, Ont., to the creation of a memorial in Winnipeg and the continuing campaign to have France posthumously award Prince the Croix de Guerre.

There's a documentary about Prince named *Fallen Hero*, a title Bear dislikes.

And yes, there's a Sgt. Tommy Prince Street in Winnipeg, a little side street in the North End.

"We were trying to get him out of the North End. We hoped to get it in a more prominent area," sighed Bear. "I just kept plugging away, trying to get more recognition for him."

Bear downplayed his effort to recover Prince's medals, now on display at the Manitoba Museum. "I don't know which is the proper story. Some say they were stolen, lost in a fire, pawned. If those medals could talk, they'd have quite a story to tell."

He'd like to see a formal museum erected for Prince, maybe in Brokenhead, maybe an expansion of the display at the Southeast Assembly of First Nations offices where Bear works.

Bear is the only close relative willing to talk at length about Prince.

Tommy Prince, Jr. says he's tired of being asked about his father; he turned down a request for a full interview. He would say his father did not receive the respect he deserved in his lifetime.

"He was a respectful and loving man. He loved his family. Nobody's ever done him right, from the army to the government to (the media). What did he get when he got back? He got sh-- from the army, from the government, from white people," said his son.

Wendell Sinclair, director of education for Sgt. Tommy Prince School on Brokenhead Ojibwa Nation, is related to Prince but also learned nothing growing up about Prince's war service.

"The older people knew but didn't talk about it," said Sinclair. "There's many. For a small community, we have a lot of veterans."

It's barely 20 years since the community chose to rename Scanterbury School, said Sinclair, a decision made at a time when only Brokenhead and military historians knew much about Prince's record.

"We make it a point to let the kids know about Sgt. Tommy Prince. In the gym, an artist has drawn a picture of Sgt. Tommy Prince," said Sinclair.

Tommy Prince is almost a hero lost to his people.

"It's so regrettable that you learn about him after the fact," said Assembly of Manitoba Chiefs Grand Chief Ron Evans. "I just wish something was done for him at that time.

"Something needs to be done for the trauma of war, how it affects people. Our kids need to know that. Not just First Nations, kids period — war is not something that should be fantasized. It can impact them the rest of their lives, which happened in Tommy's case," said Evans.

"First Nations should be proud that he was a decorated soldier — we need to celebrate those who represent us," Evans said.

"Each culture, each race have their heroes. We need ours, too."

MANITOBA-NESS

THOMAS George Prince was born Oct. 25, 1915, on Brokenhead Ojibwa Nation, one of 11 children to Henry and Annabella Prince.

As a very young child, Tommy Prince was sent to Elkhorn Residential School.

In 1940, at the age of 25, he joined the Royal Canadian Engineers. He later joined the Devil's Brigade, a crack team of Canadian and American commandos.

Prince was an entrepreneur who owned a Winnipeg window cleaning business before the war and after the war became a leader with the Manitoba Indian Association.

5 THINGS YOU DIDN'T KNOW

1. He was the great-great-grandson of Chief Peguis, the Ojibwa leader who brought literacy and farming skills to his people.

2. There is a Tommy Prince Street in both Winnipeg and Clandeboye.

3. Prince was characterized in the William Holden film The Devil's Brigade, though he was not afforded a major role.

4. Tommy Prince delivered an impassioned and eloquent address on treaty rights to Parliament's standing committee on Indian Affairs in 1947.

5. Prince rescued two people from drowning, one in Selkirk, the other off the Alexander Docks in Winnipeg.

Prince served in the Korean War, above.

Prince, right, joined a cadet corps, during the Great Depression, when he was still a student at Elkhorn Indian Resident School.

FAMILY SUBMITTED PHOTO

BY BRUCE OWEN

'The currents of life run deep, and we hardly know how they move us'

— Duff Roblin, from his 1999 autobiography Speaking For Myself

Currents of Duff Roblin's life run deep

IT was a few short days from his 87th birthday and his last major public appearance on behalf of every Canadian.

At a podium at Bény-sur-Mer in Normandy, France, former Manitoba premier Dufferin Roblin gave a speech many say was the most eloquent of his distinguished career. The occasion was the 60th anniversary of D-Day, the June 6, 1944, Allied invasion of Europe.

The Second World War shaped "Duff" and gave him the pluck and determination that guided him for the next half-century. In the course of those decades, he pulled Manitoba, sometimes in defiance, into the modern age. The lasting contributions Roblin made to the province — the Red River Floodway at the top of the list — have earned him his place as a Great Manitoban.

Roblin waves a greeting at press conference for floodway in 2008.

GREATNESS

As premier, Charles Dufferin Roblin led the province into the modern age from the shadow of the Second World War and Great Depression.
Some of his accomplishments:

June 1944 — Roblin comes ashore at Normandy, June 30.

December 1949 — Roblin is elected to the Manitoba legislature, sitting as an Independent Progressive Conservative MLA.

June 1954 — Roblin is elected leader of the Progressive Conservative Party.

June 1958 — Roblin's PCs win the election.

October 1962 — Work begins on Roblin's biggest project, the Red River Floodway, the project most identify with Roblin. But it is only one of his many contributions to the future of Manitoba. His government built rural high schools, three community colleges and enhanced education at the province's three universities. The Roblin government reintroduced French-language instruction in schools, modernized hospitals and expanded social spending.

1962 and 1966 — Roblin's PCs are re-elected with consecutive landslide elections.

October 1970 — Roblin is invested as Companion of the Order of Canada.

1978 — Roblin is appointed to the Senate by Prime Minister Pierre Trudeau.

July 2000 — Roblin is invested into the Order of Manitoba.

'The Conservatives had not been in government for about 25 years, really, not since Diefenbaker for any length of time. We did not have a lot of experience. I asked Duff to serve as government leader in the Senate. In cabinet he displayed all of the reasons Manitobans held him in such high regard. He was a calming influence on us all. He's a man of great wisdom. He has a thoughtful, careful approach to public policy. He was invaluable'

— Brian Mulroney,
Prime Minister of Canada
1984-1993

Premier Gary Doer, Roblin and PC Leader
Stuart Murray review names of fallen
from D-Day at legislature in 2004.

WINNIPEG FREE PRESS ARCHIVES

"There is hardly an area in public life not touched by Roblin and his government," retired University of Manitoba political studies professor Bill Neville said. "I don't think there's another premier in our history who's had the same impact."

Bény-sur-Mer is home to the Canadian War Cemetery and the 2,043 Canadian soldiers killed during the early days of the Normandy landing.

In his anniversary speech, Roblin spoke of the sacrifice made by the 2,043 Canadian soldiers killed during the early days of the Normandy landing. His speech was short — he worked from notes rather than text — yet it caught the significance of the moment and, in a way, defined what made Roblin and people of his generation tick: These soldiers died to make the world a better place and it's up to those who survived to ensure that happened.

"It was one of the most satisfying times of my life," the 91-year-old Roblin recently said of his trip to France.

"The war was undoubtedly a critical event in my life," Roblin wrote in his 1999 autobiography *Speaking For Myself.* "I entered it as a callow, rather self-centred 22-year-old, and I emerged from it much improved because war matures as very few other human activities can."

Within months of his return to Manitoba in 1946, Roblin entered the world of politics. Roblin said his main motivation in becoming a politician was to change how government did business. During the war years, a coalition government ran the province as there was no place for partisan politics with a war to win.

Once the war was over, though, the coalition government dragged on.

Roblin took it upon himself to change things. He was first elected to the legislature in 1949 to stir things up. Little did he know, he was going to get some unexpected help.

In 1950, the Red River spilled its banks into the city of Winnipeg, flooding 10,500 homes and costing more

Workers build a mud dike north of the Provencer Bridge in downtown Winnipeg during the 1950 flood. The St. Boniface Basilica is in the background. The flood led to the construction of Duff's Ditch.

THE CANADIAN PRESS ARCHIVES

than $100 million in repairs (in 1950 dollars).

"There was no sense of leadership in what the premier and cabinet were doing," Roblin said in his memoir. "We heard little about it, and we saw little of them."

The failure of the coalition to prepare and deal with the flood led to the Progressive Conservative party withdrawing from the coalition in October 1950. Then, the real work began. The PC party had to rebuild. It lacked fresh ideas to capture the attention of post-war Manitobans. It also did not have a solid leader in Errick Willis.

By the time the 1954 election rolled around, not much had changed. Roblin was not happy. When Willis was forced into a leadership contest, Roblin put his name on the ballot. And won.

"Why did I make the decision? For the same reason I was against the coalition: I wanted a better deal in Manitoba," he said in his autobiography.

Now he put his skills, much of what he learned during the war, to work. In 1958, he was elected premier.

His government's first challenge was pulling the province's education system from the one-room Prairie schoolhouse mindset of the 1930s to meet the needs of a growing province.

"Education is not a cost or a bill or expense but a wholesome investment in human life, growth and

Duff and Mary Roblin, May 28, 1968 at auditorium with supporters.

WINNIPEG TRIBUNE / UNIVERSITY OF MANITOBA ARCHIVES

'I just wanted to add one other comment, Mr. Speaker. The Honourable Duff Roblin was asked by the media, "What year did you enlist?" He said, "Well, I enlisted in 1941." And the reporter asked him, "Well, what made you enlist?" In typical Duff Roblin fashion, he looked at the reporter, he said, "There was a war going on. You might have heard about it." I thought it was classic Duff Roblin.'

— Stuart Murray (former leader of the official Opposition) in the legislature, June 1, 2004

Duff Roblin conducts a press conference at the Manitoba legislature during his term as premier.

Duff Roblin in 1957.

WINNIPEG FREE PRESS ARCHIVES

comprehension," Roblin wrote in 1999. "It is on such a foundation that successful societies are built."

This included creating three community colleges, strengthening the province's universities and re-introducing French as a teaching language in public schools.

Roblin is modest about what his government did for public education. In his usual humble way, Roblin said it was the work of others, not him, that paved the way.

"I got people who were smarter than me and put them to work," he said in an interview. "I was blessed with splendid colleagues."

One of those colleagues was Sterling Lyon, at age 31 the youngest member of Roblin's cabinet. Roblin appointed Lyon attorney general. Lyon went on to become premier in 1977.

"Yes, he was part of a team," Lyon said in an interview. "But he was the leader of the team."

There were other initiatives under Roblin's leadership, crop insurance for farmers, social allowance, increased access to medical care, new highways, northern development and clean water and sewer services for smaller towns.

"His policies were so progressive and so unusual that I really believe the Conservative party in the modern era will not see his likes again," said Ed Schreyer, the former New Democratic Party leader elected premier in 1969, two years after Roblin left office.

"It was a government where the progressive far outweighed the conservative," Schreyer said in an interview.

But what Roblin is most synonymous with is the Red River Floodway. He likes it that some people still refer to it as Duff's Ditch.

The building of the floodway around the east side of Winnipeg is well-documented, and in 1997 during the Flood of the Century it became obvious to every Manitoban that without it a large part of Winnipeg would have been submerged under the swollen Red River.

Fifty years ago that wasn't so clear to everyone. After the 1950 flood, two major reports outlined how Winnipeg could protect itself from another major flood. But nothing happened until Roblin took office.

In October 1962, work began on the floodway project, considered one of the largest projects of its kind, comparable to the Panama Canal almost 50 years earlier. The entire project cost $63 million, a huge price tag in 1962, and took five years to build.

Roblin later took two unsuccessful runs at Parliament and then left public life to return to private business. In 1978, he was appointed to the Senate by Prime Minister Pierre Trudeau and retired at 75 in 1992.

Since his trip to France in 2004, his schedule is more limited as old age catches up to him and wife Mary.

He goes to his office each day to review his investments and read newspapers, magazines and books. He does not get his news fix from the Internet.

"I'm an absolute technical idiot," he said, adding the best he can muster is sending a fax.

He lives in the same house in which he and Mary raised their family, son Andrew and daughter Jennifer.

"I'll not indulge myself in forecasting the future for me," he said in the quiet comfort of his living room. "I've had a very good run for a very long time. I'm grateful for that.

"I'm proud to say I put my best foot forward."

WINNIPEG TRIBUNE / UNIVERSITY OF MANITOBA ARCHIVES

Duff Roblin and his wife Mary in 1958.

WINNIPEG TRIBUNE / UNIVERSITY OF MANITOBA ARCHIVES

Duff Roblin, Queen Elizabeth and Prince Philip in 1959.

'His legacy is focused on the floodway, but the whole focus of his government was to be builders. He built public assets for the public good'

— Premier Gary Doer

THE RED RIVER FLOODWAY

A 47-kilometre ditch that runs around the east side of Winnipeg and funnels high water from the Red River to keep the city from flooding, as it did in 1950.

It was built between 1962 and 68 at a cost of $63 million. It was first used in 1969.

The floodway was nicknamed "Duff's Ditch" and "Duff's Folly" after Premier Duff Roblin who ordered its construction.

The floodway saved the city in 1997 in what is called the Flood of Century. Since its construction, it's saved about $10 billion in flood damage.

The floodway is now being widened to protect Winnipeg from a one-in-700-year flood. The final price tag is more than $665 million. Completion is expected in late 2010.

Duff Roblin poses at Duff's Ditch.

WINNIPEG FREE PRESS ARCHIVES

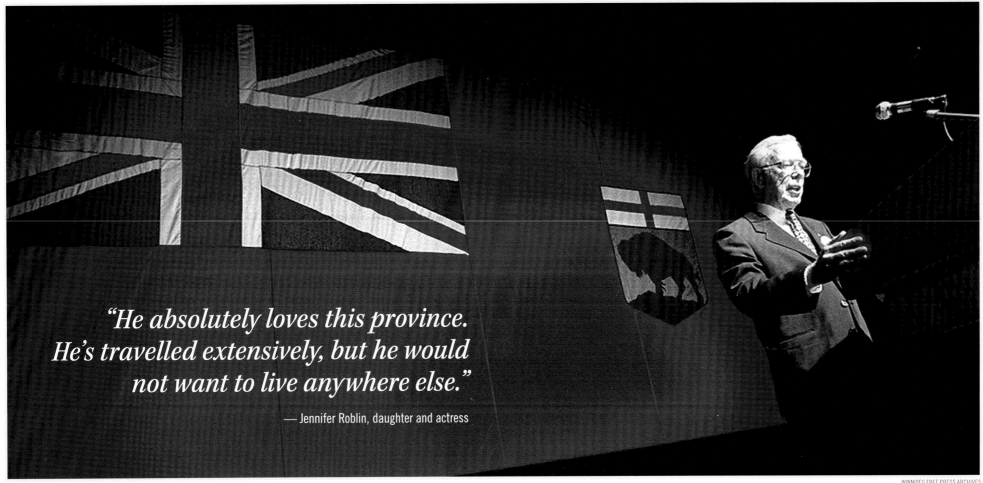

"He absolutely loves this province. He's travelled extensively, but he would not want to live anywhere else."

— Jennifer Roblin, daughter and actress

WINNIPEG FREE PRESS ARCHIVES

Former premier Duff Roblin addresses a Tory fundraiser in his honour in Winnipeg in 1997.

MANITOBA-NESS

DUFF Roblin was born in Winnipeg in 1917, the grandson of Sir Rodmond Roblin, who served as Manitoba premier from 1900 to 1915.

He served overseas with the Royal Canadian Air Force during the Second World War. Roblin was a logistical officer in a fighter group that closely followed ground forces, providing air support as the Allies fought towards Germany, and retired in 1946 as Wing Commander.

He was first elected as a member of the Manitoba legislature in 1949 and became leader of the provincial Conservatives in 1954. Four years later, Roblin led his party to success in the first of four Manitoba elections and was premier until 1967 when he resigned.

Roblin's government is now largely credited with bringing Manitoba into the modern age and resurrecting parliamentary governance with an active opposition, a system we now take for granted.

Roblin is mostly remembered for his leadership in building the Red River Floodway, a project criticized by many in the early 1960s as too expensive. The floodway is now credited with saving Winnipeg during the 1997 flood. Work is ongoing to increase its capacity in the event of a worse flood.

Overlooked in Roblin's premiership was his government's creation of a modern-day public education system, creating a regional government for Winnipeg, crop insurance for farmers, new highways to access the north and a social allowance program to help the province's most needy. There was also the creation of two new provincial parks, Grand Beach and Birds Hill — two of the most popular parks in the province today.

After his resignation as premier, he was a leadership

candidate for the federal Conservative party. He lost to Robert Stanfield.

Roblin was later dogged by criticism his government brought in a provincial sales tax. Roblin had said years earlier the idea of a tax was "as dead as a dodo."

His government was also criticized for its handling of the Churchill Forest Industries project, a project that saw millions of dollars paid out with nothing to show for it.

Roblin was appointed to the Senate by then-prime minister Pierre Trudeau in 1978 and later was leader of the government in the Senate under Prime Minister Brian Mulroney. He retired from the Senate at age 75 in 1992.

He has two children, five grandchildren and lives in the same River Heights house he and his wife Mary have shared since 1975.

WINNIPEG FREE PRESS ARCHIVES

Prime Minister Stephen Harper meets floodway father Roblin and Premier Gary Doer at the floodway gates during 2006 flood.

5 THINGS YOU DIDN'T KNOW

1. Duff Roblin is Canada's oldest living former premier. He turned 91 June 17.

2. His family's roots in North America trace to 1640 and a Venice-born crewman on a Dutch sailing ship that had landed in New Amsterdam, better known as New York.

3. Roblin's first government in 1958, a minority government, had nine cabinet ministers including Roblin as premier and provincial treasurer. Premier Gary Doer's government has 18, including Doer.

4. To relieve stress during long days, Roblin played the bagpipes in his office. "The cleaning staff soon got used to it," he quipped in his 1999 autobiography. He also was a regular cigar-smoker: "I found it a very handy device because when meeting delegations, it was useful to have something in my hand to look at and contemplate while I listened to the wisdom that was being offered. It somehow was a comforting thing to do. Not so much because I like cigars — only the first half of any cigar should be smoked, the second half should be thrown away immediately — but I found it to be a handy little gadget." Roblin doesn't play the bagpipes or smoke anymore.

5. Roblin still goes to the office at 9 a.m. each day. At 11:30 a.m., he goes for lunch at the Winnipeg Squash Racquet Club and returns to the office for a short period in the afternoon. He stopped playing squash in his late 70s.

WINNIPEG TRIBUNE UNIVERSITY OF MANITOBA ARCHIVES

'His contribution was absolutely in every corner of Manitoba society

— Jim Carr, president and CEO of the Business Council of Manitoba, former journalist and MLA. Carr assisted Roblin in writing Roblin's 1999 memoir.

Roblin poses for portrait in 2000 at release of his memoirs.

WINNIPEG FREE PRESS

NATIONAL POST

EDMONTON JOU

THE VANCOUVER SUN

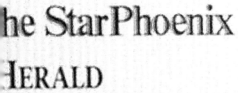
med broadcast.com

PRIME

te

CanWest

U
TV

Montreal The Gazette

he StarPhoenix

3
tv three

HERALD

CanWest Global
Communications Co

COLONIS

FM

rPost

sper

Israel Asper o.c., Q.C., L.L.D, Ph.D.
Executive Chairman
West Global Communications Corp

BY GEOFF KIRBYSON

Manitoba's mogul

H E was a lawyer, a politician, an entrepreneur, a music lover, a media mogul, a philanthropist and a visionary.

But perhaps above all, Izzy Asper was an unrepentant fan and booster of Manitoba.

The founder of Canwest Global Communications Corp., an international media empire that began with a single television station in North Dakota more than three decades ago, could have run his business anywhere on the planet but chose to base it in Winnipeg. He encouraged others to do the same and chastised those who left for what they perceived to be greener pastures.

Israel H. Asper also put his money where his mouth was, donating millions of dollars to educational and cultural endeavours, all with the goal of helping make Winnipeg the best city it could be.

Asper speaks at the Canadian Club in Toronto in May 1999.

GREATNESS

Called to the Manitoba bar in 1964.

Appointed Queen's Counsel in 1975.

Founder of Canwest Global Communications.

Leader of the provincial Liberal party 1970-75.

Established the Asper Foundation in 1993.

Inducted into the Canadian Association of Broadcasters Hall of Fame in 1995.

Became Officer of the Order of Canada in 1995.

Member of the Canadian Business Hall of Fame.

Inducted into the Order of Manitoba in 2000.

Received honorary doctor of law degree from the University of Manitoba in 1998.

Received honorary doctor of philosophy from the Hebrew University in Jerusalem in 1999.

Izzy Asper is all smiles at a press conference in July 2000.

Even though he led a fast-paced life and rarely was seen without a smoke or a drink — or both — in his hand, Manitobans were shocked to hear of his death in October 2003 at age 71. He and his wife, Babs, had recently moved into a highrise condo on Wellington Crescent after selling their longtime home, a bungalow on the same prestigious street.

WINNIPEG TRIBUNE / UNIVERSITY OF MANITOBA ARCHIVES

Asper in 1970.

His funeral was as close to a royal funeral as Winnipeggers will ever see. Mourners included a who's who of Canada's business and political elite: then-prime minister Jean Chretién; one of his predecessors, John Turner; Chretién's eventual successor, Paul Martin; Premier Gary Doer; then-mayor Glen Murray; Ted Rogers, CEO of Rogers Communications; Jim Shaw, CEO of Shaw Communications; Hartley Richardson of James Richardson & Sons; and Ray McFeetors, then-CEO of Great-West Lifeco, Manitoba's largest company.

Asper grew up in Minnedosa and Neepawa, the son of eastern European Jewish immigrants who were musician-entrepreneurs. He joked on more than one occasion that if he had followed through on his long-time dream to buy the *Neepawa Press* after graduating from law school, Minnedosa would have become the media capital of the world.

Once Asper entered the collective conscience of Manitobans in 1970 upon becoming leader of the provincial Liberal party, he never left. He sat in the house from 1972 until he stepped down in 1975. He was also a lifelong member of the federal Liberal party.

But before he left politics, he set himself up for his next career by buying television station KCND in Pembina, N.D. in 1974. A year later, the rebranded CKND was born, broadcasting out of a refurbished Safeway store in Asper's hometown. This tiny station was the seed that eventually grew into the biggest media company in the country, featuring national TV network Global Television, the *National Post*, major dailies in virtually every major city in Canada except Winnipeg — a point that gnawed at him — and a sprinkling of radio stations.

Canwest also had media properties in Ireland, Australia and New Zealand.

"He worked with purpose and focus, and he had a combination of personal charm and shrewd toughness. He thought big and he knew every detail. His reach was wide and deep and his passion immeasurable," said Jim Carr, president and CEO of the Business Council of Manitoba, a group of CEOs representing some of Manitoba's largest companies.

"He cut a huge swath. He thought globally but was rooted locally. He was nourished by his roots, but his influence spread worldwide."

Few colleagues knew Asper as well as Gerry Schwartz, who worked closely with him in two different careers. Now the CEO of Onex Corp., he started out in 1963 as an articling student at Asper & Co., a law firm that eventually became Pitblado LLP, one of the biggest in the province, through a myriad of mergers and acquisitions. Fourteen years later, they went into business together, co-founding Canwest.

"He's a brilliant businessman. He was a great lawyer. Everything he did, he did well," Schwartz said.

When told his descriptions of Asper varied between the past and present tenses, Schwartz offered no excuses.

"I think of him in the present tense. He's still a part of my life."

Schwartz said three things made Asper worthy of being among the Greatest Manitobans.

"He built one of the largest businesses ever built in Winnipeg. He insisted it be headquartered in

KEVIN FRAYER / THE CANADIAN PRESS ARCHIVES

'Energy, brains and guts'

— Jim Carr's explanation for Asper's business success;
Carr is president and CEO of the Business Council of Manitoba,
a group of CEOs representing some of Manitoba's largest companies

PHIL HOSSACK / WINNIPEG FREE PRESS ARCHIVES

Winnipeg, and he's been very generous to Winnipeg," he said.

Gail Asper, Izzy's daughter, said it's odd to think of her father as one of the greatest Manitobans of all time. Despite all his accomplishments, he was just "Dad" to her and her brothers, David and Leonard.

"He was a completely down-to-earth guy. He was very self-effacing. I remember when he was inducted into the Canadian Business Hall of Fame, he muttered, 'I guess they needed a Western business guy.' He never believed he was this great visionary."

Gail Asper said her father really was a man of the people and remembers driving home behind him not long before he died. They were both driving convertibles with the roofs down. But a ride that normally takes seven or eight minutes took nearly half an hour because at every red light or stop sign, people came up to chat with him.

"He loved having a convertible. He loved to be with people and to talk to people. It was funny watching him on the drive home, talking to people at every block. He was definitely a regular guy," she said.

Despite all that's been written over the decades about Asper during his life and since his death, there are still a few things that aren't common knowledge. For example, he was "addicted" to Oh Henry! bars, Gail said.

"They were always his favourite present on his birthdays."

And while he regularly travelled by private jet in his later years, Asper flew in more than his share of twin-engine six-seaters when he was in politics. Those trips terrified him, his daughter said. So to conquer his fear, he learned how to fly.

"Once he knew how it worked, he was much more at ease. He never had another problem with flying," she said.

A man of ideas, Asper didn't have a problem calling people in the middle of the night to share his thoughts, Carr recalled. During the Meech Lake affair in the late

Asper in his Canwest office in August 1998.

MARC GALLANT / WINNIPEG FREE PRESS ARCHIVES

1980s, Carr was on an all-party committee and thus had his finger on the pulse of the goings-on surrounding the proposed constitutional amendment.

"Izzy was intensely interested in the work of the committee and how it was going. He would call to chat about it at any time of the day or night," Carr said. "He was never very far from being awake."

In later years, Asper stepped away from his day-to-day activities at Canwest, handing over the reins to youngest son, Leonard. He was still involved, to a degree, as executive chairman but philanthropy became his major focus.

Asper received considerable attention for making headline-grabbing donations, such as giving $10 million to the University of Manitoba business school that now bears his name. Those media events were designed to encourage other people to get out their chequebooks, however.

What wasn't well-known was that countless cheques for smaller amounts regularly arrived unannounced at cultural and other organizations from the Asper Foundation, complete with a handwritten note from Izzy.

The depth and breadth of Asper's influence continues to be felt to this day. It will only increase once his dream of The Canadian Museum for Human Rights — a $265-million project currently being carried out by daughter Gail — opens in the next few years.

RUTH BONNEVILLE / WINNIPEG FREE PRESS ARCHIVES

Asper with the specialty doors for his Gershwin room in April 1999.

KEN GIGLIOTTI / WINNIPEG FREE PRESS ARCHIVES

With Premier Gary Doer at Canwest's 25th anniversary party in September 2003.

Artist's conception of the Canadian Museum for Human Rights, 2005.

MANITOBA-NESS

IZZY Asper was born Aug. 11, 1932, in Minnedosa. A lawyer, he was called to the Manitoba bar in 1964. He first came bursting into the living rooms of Manitobans in 1970 when he was elected leader of the provincial Liberal party, just months after it was decimated in a general election. He led the party for five years but was never able to win an election.

His first step in building his international media empire came with the purchase of a television station in North Dakota in 1974. A year later, he moved it to Winnipeg.

Throughout his career, he boosted Winnipeg and refused to move his business elsewhere despite global holdings.

In 2003, the University of Manitoba's business school was renamed the I.H. Asper School of Business after Asper donated $10 million.

Asper died at his Winnipeg condominium in October 2003.

5 THINGS YOU DIDN'T KNOW

1. He was addicted to Oh Henry! chocolate bars

2. He was once mugged in New York City and chased after the four assailants only to be hit by a car. The New York mayor sent him a new wallet.

3. He was a fervent fan of the Winnipeg Blue Bombers who had one rule in his upper-deck seats — nobody got up to get a drink, hotdog or go to the bathroom except at halftime.

4. He thought nothing of making phone calls in the middle of the night.

5. He bemoaned the lack of piazzas in Winnipeg.

DR. ALLAN RONALD

21

GREATNESS

Allan Ronald dedicated his life to studying infectious diseases and established training and HIV-treatment programs in Africa.

He has received many awards:

Dr. Hugh Saunderson Award for Excellence in Teaching, U of M, 1971.

Canadian Infectious Disease Society Award — first-ever recipient, 1983.

Officer, Order of Canada, 1994.

J.C. Graham Award, Royal College of Physicians and Surgeons of Canada, 2000 Fellow, Royal Society of Canada.

Frederic Newton Gisborne Starr Award, Canadian Medical Association, 2003.

Joseph E. Smadel Memorial Lecture Award, Infectious Disease Society of America, 2006.

BY DAN LETT

Infectious disease groundbreaker

FAMILY SUBMITTED PHOTO

Ronald at a patient's bedside in the early 1960s.

Allan Ronald in November 2000.

DR. Allan Ronald can remember the moment his life changed forever.

It was early 1981, and Ronald was in Nairobi heading a research study of an outbreak of chancroid — an extremely contagious sexually transmitted disease — among prostitutes in the vast slums of Kenya's largest city. He had studied and helped control a similar outbreak in Winnipeg where he served as head of medical microbiology at the University of Manitoba.

Ronald was eating dinner at the Nairobi Club Hotel with two of his colleagues on the chancroid project, Dr. Jim Curran, from the Centers for Disease Control in Atlanta, and Dr. Peter Piot, a researcher from the University of Washington in Seattle. Curran stunned his dinner companions when he announced he was heading back to the United States to help investigate the outbreak of a mysterious and deadly infectious disease.

'His energy, determination and scientific rigour have been an inspiration for so many. He has led the foundation of one of the most successful AIDS research programs in Africa, always paying attention to the need to support our African colleagues and institutions'

— Dr. Peter Piot, a former colleague of Ronald's who is now the head of UN AIDS, the United Nations' chief HIV agency

Ronald and Myrna married in 1962.

FAMILY SUBMITTED PHOTO

Ronald in February 1978.

WINNIPEG TRIBUNE / UNIVERSITY OF MANITOBA ARCHIVES

"I remember we each took turns expressing our opinions about what it could be. We didn't know what it was, but we knew pneumonia was the cause of death, and that it was resistant to any treatments we had and was creating a depressed immune system."

The team at the Atlanta centres Curran went to join eventually identified a new virus, HIV, and a disease that would become known as AIDS.

From that moment on, Ronald's work changed profoundly. As soon as investigators with Ronald's Nairobi project realized the same symptoms were showing up in the slums, HIV became the focus.

Over the next 25 years, the project Ronald established in Nairobi was to become world-famous for identifying a small group of HIV-resistant prostitutes who, many believe, may hold the key to an AIDS vaccine. Ronald also created one of the world's best medical microbiology programs at the U of M.

Simply put, his work has helped set the stage for some of the most advanced HIV research done anywhere on the planet, and he has trained some of the greatest minds working today on a cure for AIDS. In the process, he has made Winnipeg one of the world's top-five centres of excellence for research in infectious diseases.

Over his career, the awards and accolades he has received run for pages and pages. Ronald is a member of the Order of Canada and a recipient of a host of international medical honours. His students include the heads of some of the most important HIV-research institutes in the world, the deans of medical schools in Alberta and Saskatchewan and the head of infectious disease monitoring for Ontario.

However, the medical genius that spawned all this profound work came from the humblest of backgrounds.

Growing up on a farm north of Portage la Prairie, Ronald tried to live up to the Spartan example set by his father, David Emerson Ronald. A farmer and a naturally talented tradesman who built houses, David Ronald

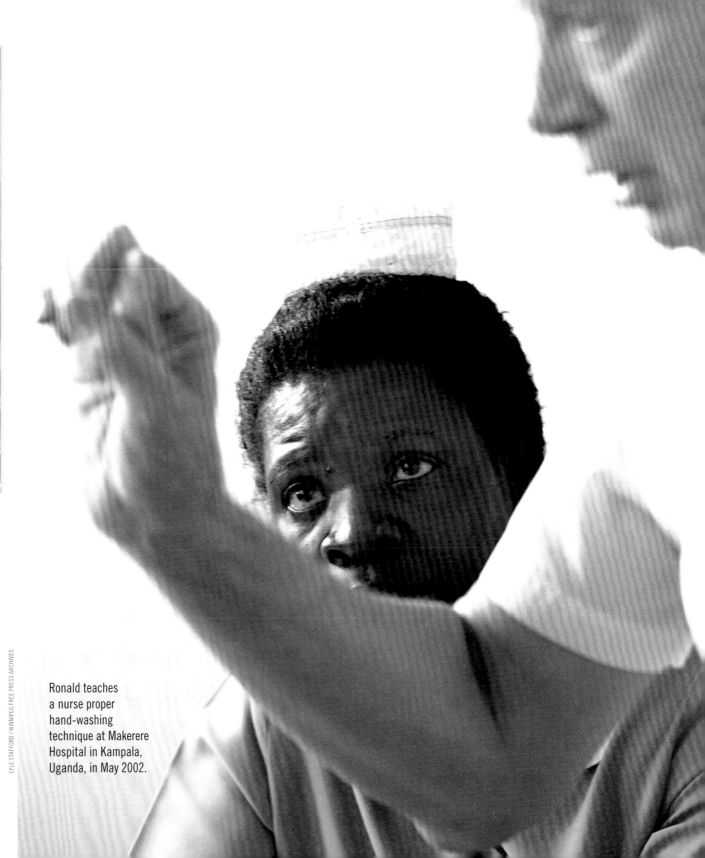

LYLE STAFFORD / WINNIPEG FREE PRESS ARCHIVES

Ronald at the Makerere Hospital in Kampala, Uganda in May 2002.

knew only hard work.

Ronald attended a one-room schoolhouse where he quickly demonstrated an aptitude for academics. School came so easy that teachers often called upon him to help other students.

After graduation from elementary school, high school in Portage la Prairie beckoned. In that environment, Ronald realized he wanted a life away from the farm.

"My father loved building things," Ronald says. "I was his only son, and unfortunately, I hated all the things he loved doing. He wanted me to learn all these things he could do well, and I struggled with them. I wanted to learn, to study."

LYLE STAFFORD / WINNIPEG FREE PRESS ARCHIVES

Ronald teaches a nurse proper hand-washing technique at Makerere Hospital in Kampala, Uganda, in May 2002.

In 1955, his appetite for education sharper than ever, Ronald convinced his father to let him attend the University of Manitoba. David Ronald assumed his son would study agriculture; his son had other ideas.

"I was actually in line to sign up for classes when I first told my father I wanted to enter pre-med," Ronald said. "I've always thought it was brave of my dad to let me go into medicine. It wasn't his choice, but he let me go."

That decision kicked off a career that's endured some 47 years and taken Ronald all over the world. After graduating from med school in Winnipeg, Ronald served a residency at Baltimore's University of Maryland Hospital, then fellowships in infectious diseases and medical microbiology at the University of Washington in Seattle.

It was during this time Ronald started a family of his own. He married Myrna Marchyshyn in 1962, his life partner who's been a constant companion for Ronald's globe-trotting work. Allan and Myrna have three daughters — Wendy, Sandra and Vickie.

The fellowships in the United States whetted Ronald's appetite to study infectious disease — and he felt an urge to do that work in Manitoba.

He returned to Winnipeg in 1968 and began to build support for the establishment of a world-class infectious disease program at the University of Manitoba. It seemed like an uphill battle.

"My goal was to change the capacity of the health-care system in Canada and throughout the world to address the challenges of infectious diseases. From a base in Winnipeg, I could create more momentum to change the way we addressed this. In some ways, it was actually quite foolish. Canada is a big place, and Winnipeg doesn't have a lot of leverage."

Ronald would eventually find his lever through his work in Africa.

The Nairobi clinic gave Ronald's students an opportunity to develop a unique model of public health delivery that combines life-saving treatment for some of the

'My goal was to change the capacity of the health-care system in Canada and throughout the world to address the challenges of infectious diseases'

LYLE STAFFORD / WINNIPEG FREE PRESS ARCHIVES

Ronald teaches nurses at Makerere Hospital in Kampala, Uganda about proper sanitation procedures in May 2002.

world's neediest people and groundbreaking research.

Those students and colleagues who worked with Ronald in the early days of research in Africa — including those who attended the dinner in 1981 when they first heard about HIV — fondly recall Ronald's steady hand and remarkable passion.

After helping identify HIV at the Centers for Disease Control, Dr. Jim Curran went on to become the dean of the Rollins School of Public Health at the Atlanta-based Emory University. Curran paid tribute to Ronald's

"extraordinary curiosity and entrepreneurial abilities" and the manner in which he inspires his students to become key members of research projects all over the world.

"The teams set up by Allan were groundbreakers in these early investigations, and Allan's own commitments grew and were sustained for nearly three decades," said Curran. "A great scientist, physician and man."

Dr. Peter Piot, now the head of UNAIDS, the United

Nations' principal HIV/AIDS agency, said he is proud to consider himself a graduate of the "Allan Ronald school of medicine."

"His energy, determination, and scientific rigour have been an inspiration for so many," said Piot. "He has led the foundation of one of the most successful AIDS research programs in Africa — always paying attention to the need to support in the first place our African colleagues and institutions."

Ronald's work has also paid dividends for his hometown. The array of top-flight scientists drawn to Winnipeg to work with Ronald set the groundwork for the decision to locate in Winnipeg the National Microbiology Laboratory and the Canadian Centre for Human and Animal Sciences, a facility often mentioned in the same breath as the Centers for Disease Control in Atlanta.

Ronald said he hopes his legacy will be measured not only by his research, but also by the number of doctors he trained. Particularly gratifying, he says, is the role he played in educating more than 90 African doctors to combat infectious diseases on their own continent.

"My role was to always expect more of people than they thought they could do. The idea of constantly trying to reach for things beyond your reach can be very annoying at times.

"But our patients expect us to give them the best treatment available in the world."

Sometimes that takes a simple form. Ronald recalls visiting his sister, a nurse in Zambia, more than a decade ago where he examined a young girl. He quickly treated her simple problem. Ronald said she was tremendously thankful.

Now, each time he visits Zambia, the same girl, now a grown woman, brings him a chicken as thanks.

"Those are not necessarily the big, award-winning things that people want to hear about. But they are the things you remember most about your life."

Ronald's high school graduation photo, 1955.

FAMILY SUBMITTED PHOTO

MANITOBA-NESS

ALLAN Ronald grew up on a farm and attended a one-room schoolhouse in Dale, just north of Portage la Prairie. Although his family wanted him to carry on the family farming tradition, Ronald developed an early appetite for education and was soon off to Winnipeg to attend pre-med courses at the University of Manitoba.

His lust for learning took him to Maryland and Washington states to study infectious diseases. But he yearned to continue his work in Winnipeg and set about establishing a world-class medical microbiology program in the city.

Although he travels the world helping underdeveloped countries battle HIV, he remains loyal to Manitoba and at age 70, still sees patients in Winnipeg.

5 THINGS YOU DIDN'T KNOW

1. At 70, Ronald remains an avid curler and curling fan.

2. Ronald's three daughters have given him 12 grandchildren, several of whom have travelled with their grandfather to Africa to see his work.

3. His infectious disease work in Uganda and Canada keeps him busy, yet he still volunteers as an on-call physician on summer weekends.

4. Ronald is famous among his peers for long, detailed memos and letters, but his worst subject in high school was composition and prose.

5. Ronald's work in Africa helped raise his profile among his colleagues, but it was not his first experience working in a developing country. Ronald volunteered once a year at a hospital in Zambia where his sister worked as a missionary nurse. He also worked briefly in Pakistan in the early 1960s.

MARC GALLANT / WINNIPEG FREE PRESS ARCHIVES

Ronald in November 2004.

Carol Shields,
November 1999.

BY MORLEY WALKER

Winnipeg's wordsmith

TO the English-speaking world, in the late '90s, writer Carol Shields was arguably Winnipeg's most famous living resident.

Bobby Hull had long fled, and so had his old hockey team, the Jets. Rock star Burton Cummings was missing in action. Film director Guy Maddin was still known only to a cult audience.

And our politicians, alas, seldom made a splash beyond our provincial borders.

But Shields, in her early 60s, stood tall as an international literary celebrity, thanks to the U.S. Pulitzer Prize awarded her in 1995 for her 1993 novel, *The Stone Diaries.*

CAROL SHIELDS

22

GREATNESS

Carol Shields received numerous awards and honours. Among them:

The 1976 Canadian Authors' Association Award for the Best Novel (Small Ceremonies)

The 1987 Arthur Ellis Award for Best Canadian Mystery (Swann: A Mystery)

The 1990 Marian Engel Award for her body of work to date.

The 1993 Booker Prize short list, the 1993 Governor General's Award, the 1995 the National Book Critics Circle Award and the 1995 Pulitzer Prize, all for The Stone Diaries.

The 1998 Orange Prize for Larry's Party.

A 1999 Guggenheim Fellowship.

The 2001 Charles Taylor Prize for Literary Non-Fiction for Jane Austen.

The annual Carol Shields Winnipeg Book Prize named in her honour in 1999.

The 2001 Order of Manitoba.

The Order of Canada in 1998 and elevated to companion of the Order in 2002.

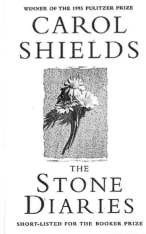

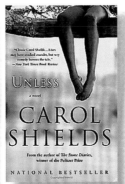
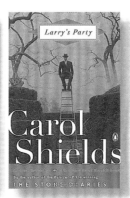

Charting the life of a quietly heroic Manitoba-born woman, Daisy Goodwill, the novel, Shields' eighth, also won the U.S. National Book Circle Award and the Governor General's Award in Canada. As well, it made the short list for Britain's prestigious Booker Prize.

In 1997, Shields' followup, *Larry's Party,* about an unassuming Winnipeg florist who becomes a successful garden-maze designer, received nominations for many of the top book prizes.

Among those it won was England's Orange Prize, given for the best novel by a woman.

With her bestselling novels' Manitoba settings, this American-born writer, who had moved to Winnipeg with her civil-engineering professor husband in 1980, shone quite the spotlight on our province.

FAMILY SUBMITTED PHOTO

Shields as a student at Hanover College in 1956.

Shields, too, was in demand. TV producers sent their crews here to interview her, and newspaper editors courted her to write articles and reviews.

A petite blond with a soft voice and bird-like mannerisms, she jetted around the world to glitzy awards ceremonies and gave speeches at high-profile events.

"She had a quality about her, like Meryl Streep, that made it impossible not to look at her," recalls her friend Blanche Howard, the Vancouver-based writer.

"She came across as everyone's most intimate friend. Everybody seemed to love her."

This was definitely the case in Winnipeg, where she carried on as though nothing had changed.

With her son and four daughters out of the family nest, she worked at her writing almost every day. She

FAMILY SUBMITT

Shields poses with the neighbours' dairy cows at her home at Monjouvent in the French region of Jura, circa 1986.

and her husband, Don, by this time dean of engineering at the University of Manitoba, took walks along Wellington Crescent near their condominium and stopped for coffee on Corydon Avenue.

They continued to summer in the second home they had bought years before in France.

In 1996, after winning the Pulitzer — she qualified for the top American prize because she maintained dual citizenship — she was appointed chancellor of the University of Winnipeg, where she earned a reputation

for giving unstintingly of her time.

"She was always coming into classrooms," says Neil Besner, an English professor and literary scholar who is now a vice-president at the U of W.

"You could not imagine a more active person."

Stories were legion among young writers about Shields critiquing their work at great length — and expecting nothing in return.

Organizations regularly called upon her to lend her name to their causes, and she seldom said no.

When an old friend contacted her out of the blue, wanting support during an illness, Shields was there for her, despite her busy schedule.

"She did things like this all the time," says her friend Moti Shojania, a University of Manitoba English instructor and chairwoman of the Winnipeg Arts Council.

"She was an inspiration to everyone who knew her."

Shields started writing when her children were young. She was already 40 and living in Ottawa in 1976 when she published her first novel, *Small Ceremonies*, about a female biographer who has her idea for a novel stolen by her male tutor.

The relationships between people, especially between men and women, supplied the glue that held most of Shields' books together, from her 1987 breakthrough *Swann: A Mystery*, her own favourite novel, to 1992's *Republic of Love*, which portrayed Winnipeg as a place of romance and myth.

Because her settings were domestic and middle-class and her characters brandished neither guns nor grand rhetoric, she was often slotted, in her early career by male reviewers, as a "woman's writer."

It took many years and many books for critics to grasp the persistent moral anger that motivated much of her writing.

"It is a manageable anger and artfully concealed by the mechanism of an arch, incontrovertible amiability," Shields wrote about her literary idol, the incomparable Jane Austen. But this description also applies to Shields: "Even her own family, her close circle of readers, may have missed the astringency of her observations."

In 1998, shortly after winning the Orange Prize, she felt a lump in her breast. The doctors diagnosed Stage 3 breast cancer. She was 63, and though she had written nine novels, three poetry collections, two volumes of short stories and four full-length plays, her renown was less than five years old.

Later, she told reporters that she wept for a month

JEFF DEBOOY / WINNIPEG FREE PRESS ARCHIVES

Shields, above, greets Richard Ouzounian at the premier of the musical Larry's Party at the St. Lawrence Centre for the Arts in Toronto in January 2001.

Shields and artist Eva Stubbs at the Winnipeg Citizens' Hall of Fame ceremony in September 2001.

WAYNE GLOWACKI / WINNIPEG FREE PRESS ARCHIVES

'The Stone Diaries is one of the great modern masterpieces. Larry's Party is one of the best books ever written about men. There's no lying in it'

— writer John Ralston Saul

'Jane Austen had a very exquisite touch in that she understood the finer details of life, and I think this was also evident in the writing of Carol Shields'

— writer Alistair MacLeod

RICHARD LAM / THE CANADIAN PRESS ARCHIVES

B.C. Lt.-Gov. Iona Campagnolo with Shields at Government House in Victoria following Shields' investiture as Companion to the Order of Canada in October, 2002.

while seeking solace from Don and their children. She underwent a mastectomy, radiation and round after round of chemotherapy. In the 4 1/2 years she battled cancer, she twice rallied from near death.

Miraculously, she continued to write. During those years she published another collection of short stories, *Dressing Up for the Carnival*, a short biography of Jane Austen and her 10th novel, *Unless*, which was short-listed for England's Booker Prize in 2002.

She also helped her friend Marjorie Anderson, a University of Manitoba professor, since retired, edit two anthologies of women's essays.

These books, the *Dropped Threads* series, touched a chord with Canadian women and sold almost as well as any of Shields' novels.

Don retired from the U of M in 2000, and as they had planned for three years, they moved to Victoria. They did this not as a slight to their adopted city. They simply wanted a climate more conducive to their daily walks.

"I'll always think of myself as a Winnipegger," Shields said in April 2002 while promoting *Unless*.

"I still keep up on the village gossip. Barely a week goes by where someone from Winnipeg doesn't come through. People know how to find us."

Cancer ended her life July 16, 2003, six weeks after her 68th birthday. The country, indeed the continent, mourned. Obituaries appeared on the front pages of Canadian newspapers and her death led TV newscasts.

The prime minister, the premier and the Governor General issued statements. Jean Chrétien called her "an extremely gifted author and educator." Gary Doer said her passing "left a tremendous void in Canadian culture." Adrienne Clarkson said "her sense of humanity and deft nod to the absurd will make her work live on."

So far it has. Her novels are taught in high schools and university classrooms. Book clubs continue to discuss her work.

McGill University Press in Montreal recently published a collection of scholarly essays about her work, co-edited by an academic from Ontario and one from France.

In September 2008, Shields' Canadian publisher, Random House, issued a 15th-anniversary commemorative edition of *The Stone Diaries*.

Next May, the University of Winnipeg will stage a three-day Festival of Voices, the inaugural Carol Shields Symposium on Women's Writing, which Anderson is co-organizing.

This coincides with the official opening of the Carol Shields Memorial Labyrinth at Kings Park in Fort Richmond.

And a movie version of *The Stone Diaries* is being planned by Toronto's Rhombus Media with Patricia Rozema hired as the director.

"There is an appetite for her work," says Besner. "And it's not just in Canada, but in the U.K. and the U.S."

But wherever people read Shields, she will be identified as a Manitoban first and foremost.

"She fell in love with Winnipeg right away," recalls Howard, who published a book of her correspondence with Shields.

"The city had the right ambience for her."

JEFF DEBOOY / WINNIPEG FREE PRESS ARCHIVES

MANITOBA-NESS

AMERICAN by birth, Carol Shields married and moved to Canada with her engineer husband in 1957 and after a time living in England, moved back to Canada, and became a Canadian citizen in 1971. The family moved to Winnipeg in 1980 and made it home for more than 20 years. Prairie themes run throughout her most well-known books. Her 1993 epic, *The Stone Diaries*, was set in Manitoba and is the only book ever to win the American Pulitzer Prize and the Canadian Governor General's Award. It was also nominated for Britain's Booker Prize.

'Her stature in this community was almost a life force. What she means to the world of literature outside Winnipeg validates the artistic journey for many of us who are writers'

— writer Martha Brooks

Shields after her investiture into the
Order of Manitoba in July 2001.

1. She had an older brother and sister, Robert and Barbara, who were fraternal twins.

2. She once appeared at a Prairie Theatre Exchange fundraiser playing the Ingrid Bergman character in Casablanca, though she had never seen the movie.

3. She once wrote a few poems and sent them to a literary magazine under a man's name to test her theory that male poets had an easier time getting their poems published. "Ian" received a reply soon after saying the magazine would publish them all and hoped to receive further submissions.
A problem arose when it came time for Carol to cash "Ian's" cheque.

4. In 1997 she established the Inez Sellgren Bursary, named after her mother, at the University of Winnipeg, to assist single parents in financial need entering university.

5. She left an unfinished novel, tentatively titled Segue, about a Chicago poet in wher 60s.

WAYNE GLOWACKI / WINNIPEG FREE PRESS ARCHIVES

A bust of Shields at Winnipeg's Citizens Hall of Fame wears a heart necklace that says, 'I love you Grandma' in July 2003.

ED SCHREYER

23

BY MARY AGNES WELCH

Controversial visionary

ALL this talk about Manitoba's hydro-electric power being the province's lucrative liquid gold, our green answer to Alberta's oil — Ed Schreyer thought of it first. About 40 years ago. Schreyer, Manitoba's premier during the heady 1970s, was remarkable for three reasons. He was uncommonly young at 33 when he formed the province's first NDP government. In a very short time, mostly in his first term, he created much of the province's modern social and economic infrastructure, everything from Autopac public automobile insurance to home care. And, he jump-started Manitoba Hydro's northern development, setting the company up to be the green energy leader it could one day be.

WINNIPEG TRIBUNE / UNIVERSITY OF MANITOBA ARCHIVES

Schreyer with wife Lily and daughters Lisa and Karmel in 1965.

Ed Schreyer in October 1999.

GREATNESS

Ed Schreyer dominated Manitoba politics when he was just a whippersnapper and defined the province's development in the 1970s. Here are some highlights.

1958 — Youngest Manitoban elected to the provincial legislature at age 22.

1965 — Moved to federal politics, winning the Springfield riding for the NDP.

1969 — Returned to Manitoba to lead the provincial party, elected Manitoba's first NDP premier but with a minority.

1973 — Re-elected with a majority.

1977 — Defeated by Tory Sterling Lyon.

1979 — Appointed Governor General by Prime Minister Pierre Trudeau.

1984 — Retired as Governor General, began a four-year term as the Canadian High Commissioner to Australia.

2006 — Ran unsuccessfully for the federal riding of Selkirk-Interlake.

'He's a man of integrity, very bright, committed, with a keen memory'

— Saul Cherniack, MLA and cabinet minister in Schreyer's government

WINNIPEG TRIBUNE / UNIVERSITY OF MANITOBA ARCHIVES

Schreyer and wife Lily say goodbye to Queen Elizabeth II and Prince Philip at the Winnipeg airport in July 1970.

Born on a small farm near Beausejour, Schreyer was first elected to the provincial legislature at 22, when most people have barely hit the workforce or are just slogging through their undergraduate degree.

Twenty years later, he had been to Ottawa as an MP, served nine years as premier, been defeated by the Tories and his political career was effectively over. At 43, when most political careers have not yet reached their zenith, Schreyer was appointed Governor General, normally the final chapter in a political life.

Even Schreyer hinted that he may have peaked too soon and would have preferred to have been a little older when he won the province's top job.

But in those two decades, Schreyer laid the foundation stones of the New Democrats in Manitoba, creating a coalition that included many Liberals and making the party, along with the Tories, one of the natural governing parties of the province.

Schreyer, a social democrat, believed in an activist government that could be used as an instrument of social and economic change. To that end, he created the country's first pharmacare and home-care programs, put in place an environmental assessment process to vet big projects, created Legal Aid Manitoba, the Manitoba Human Rights Commission, the ombudsman's office and the office of the rentalsman, the precursor to today's landlord and tenant agency.

That education property tax credit you get on your property tax bill? That was Schreyer.

Even Leaf Rapids, the award-winning centrally planned northern mining town came to be under Schreyer.

But his biggest battle came early, during the hot summer of 1970 that was also Manitoba's centennial. Schreyer risked his minority government and created a government-run car insurance company called Autopac — a move so controversial Schreyer and several in his cabinet frequently received death threats. The legislation passed by only one vote.

"It's got some points of operation that are annoying if not maddening," said Schreyer of Autopac, the Crown corporation many Manitobans still love to hate despite its low rates. "But it's still the best way to settle accident claims... in my not-so-humble opinion."

Almost as controversial was Unicity — the amalgamation of 13 urban municipalities into one big Winnipeg. "They were like squalling and scrapping siblings, each one trying to freewheel over the rest or outdo each other by slashing taxes," said Schreyer of the separate cities.

Binding the cities together helped curb urban sprawl, but the fractured history of Winnipeg still plagues its planning.

Today though, it was the development of hydro power in the north that defines Schreyer's legacy.

Schreyer points to three things that catapulted hydro ahead: the diversion of Churchill River waters into the Burntwood and Nelson rivers, the regulation of Lake Winnipeg's levels to maintain predictable flows on the Nelson and the construction of the Kettle and Long Spruce dams.

In the 1970s, critics called the hydro projects the "largest error in Manitoba history." And the flooding of traditional lands left a legacy of mistrust and anger among northern bands such as Cross Lake that still reverberates, despite millions of dollars in complicated compensation settlements.

But Schreyer's supporters say his government built the Crown Corporation into the cash cow it is today and positioned the province perfectly to combat global warming and end our reliance on oil.

"Thirty-five years ago, he began warning — to the extent of making a pest of himself — that oil was becoming scarcer and more expensive and that its increased utilization would cause global warming," Schreyer's longtime special assistant Herb Schultz wrote during the Greatest Manitoban debate.

"Everyone knows that now. He knew it then."

Schreyer with René Lévesque in 1978.

WINNIPEG TRIBUNE / UNIVERSITY OF MANITOBA ARCHIVES

Schreyer talks to the media after conceding to the Conservative candidate in Selkirk Interlake in January 2006.

PHIL HOSSACK / WINNIPEG FREE PRESS ARCHIVES

Critics said Schreyer ushered in an era of big government, that spending, staff and public debt increased exponentially, which they did. Critics on the other end of the spectrum said, as a social democrat, Schreyer failed to redistribute wealth in any meaningful way.

At the time — keep in mind, Schreyer's years as premier came at the tail end of a decade of social upheaval — Schreyer was considered a cautious pragmatist. But in retrospect, compared to the inching incrementalism of more modern governments, many of the things he did would require a steely political will Manitobans haven't seen in quite some time. Imagine a provincial government that merges Headingley and East St. Paul

with Winnipeg or creates a Crown telephone company.

Schultz, Schreyer's brother-in-law, writes that Schreyer was cool and confident as premier, rarely got angry and was low-key and unpretentious. As Schulz recounts, Schreyer's home number was listed in the phone book. Callers usually found themselves talking to Schreyer himself.

But Schreyer has also been described as somewhat pompous, with a propensity for flowery, Dickensian words like besmogged or solicitude when simpler words might do.

But he was also the party's centre, and his personal popularity buoyed the NDP, widely criticized at the

time as a ragtag bunch.

Schreyer lost the premier's chair in 1977 to Tory Sterling Lyon. Lacking the bloodlust needed to be Opposition leader, Schreyer was rescued from the role by an unlikely ally — Prime Minister Pierre Trudeau.

Schreyer was named Governor General, the youngest one in about 100 years, and served in the role for more than five years. Schreyer's wife Lily was almost as popular as he was, though he championed women's issues and the environment.

Retired from public life, Schreyer is among the most outspoken of the province's elder statesmen. He's been a loud advocate of the preservation of the Canadian

Wheat Board and advocated for more housing for the mentally ill, speaking candidly about his youngest son's battle with schizophrenia. He's also a pointed critic on energy issues — a big topic that brought him back in 2006 to the bully pulpit of political life to debate.

In a move that shocked many, he put his name on the ballot once more, this time in the federal riding of Selkirk-Interlake running for Jack Layton's NDP. He got soundly thumped by the Tories, but not before he packed community halls one more time.

Since then, he's been cheerfully critical of the Tories but equally stern with NDP Premier Gary Doer's handling of Manitoba Hydro, particularly the decision to build a transmission line down the west side of Lake Manitoba instead of the east side of Lake Winnipeg.

"I have every confidence that the rational choice will prevail," said Schreyer, with a characteristic flourish.

MANITOBA-NESS

ED Schreyer was born and raised in Beausejour, with the kind of Ukrainian and German heritage that defines Manitoba. He represented the province in Ottawa as an MP before returning to become the province's hotshot young premier in the 1970s. He was responsible for a lot of the things for which Manitoba is known — Autopac, great home care and northern hydro development. He was the first governor general from Manitoba, the youngest in almost 100 years. He has remained an outspoken critic on energy and environmental issues in the province.

WINNIPEG TRIBUNE / UNIVERSITY OF MANITOBA ARCHIVES

Schreyer in June 1969.

5 THINGS YOU DIDN'T KNOW

1. He donated two years of his pension to the Canadian Shield Foundation, an environmental group that funds wilderness research.

2. He won the 1969 election after just 18 days of campaigning. Schreyer won the leadership of the New Democratic Party on June 7, but Tory Premier Walter Weir called a snap election for June 25 while the leadership race was still ongoing. That left just more than two weeks for Schreyer to woo voters.

3. At 21, he was a talented baseball player, a second baseman, and was offered a contract with an American farm team, which he turned down.

4. While an MP, Schreyer rode the elevator to his attic office in the Centre Block most days with former prime minister John Diefenbaker, then the Opposition leader. Despite their political differences — Dief was a populist and a Tory — Diefenbaker became Schreyer's self-appointed mentor.

5. He has three honorary Indian names including Chief White Eagle and Chief Calf Chief.

WINNIPEG TRIBUNE / UNIVERSITY OF MANITOBA ARCHIVES

Schreyer at bat in 1979.

NARANJAN DHALLA

24

BY JEN SKERRITT

"IT looks like a book," Naranjan Dhalla said, waving around a laundry list of his medical accolades that more resembles an encyclopedia than a resumé.

"I grew up into a very famous scientist so there have been many articles written about me, all right. And I got so many awards, 150 awards."

The fixer

Dhalla is quick to point out he's a well-decorated pioneer of heart research. He's published more than 540 research papers and his awards include the Order of Canada and the Order of Manitoba. He's credited with pushing to make Winnipeg one of the country's centres of heart research, and he's been successful at recruiting some of the best research minds to Winnipeg.

Dhalla isn't shy when it comes to boasting of his accomplishments — although he proclaims he's a humble man — but his contribution to health care is not so easily measured as a researcher or a doctor who heals.

His gift is to be the lubricant that keeps the system running smoothly, the co-ordinator, the recruiter, the fundraiser, the motivator, the fixer.

JOE BRYKSA / WINNIPEG FREE PRESS ARCHIVES

Dhalla in 1998.

Naranjan Dhalla at the Institute of Cardiovascular Sciences at St. Boniface General Hospital Research Centre in August 2008.

GREATNESS

Naranjan Dhalla is a well-decorated researcher who has published hundreds of papers that have been cited more than 9,100 times. He is credited with recruiting some of the top minds in cardiac research to Winnipeg, and establishing the Institute of Cardiovascular Sciences.

Among his accomplishments:

Order of Manitoba (2002).

Canadian Medical Association Medal of Honour (2000).

Citizens Hall of Fame, Winnipeg, (2000).

Order of Canada (1997).

Order of the Buffalo Hunt, Manitoba (1996).

Dhalla chats with University of Manitoba chancellor Bill Norrie in March 2006.

PHIL HOSSACK / WINNIPEG FREE PRESS ARCHIVES

Dhalla, below, congratulates Stuart Murray, newly appointed president and CEO of St. Boniface Hospital and Research Foundation, with executive director of research Grant Pierce in September 2006.

MIKE APORIUS / WINNIPEG FREE PRESS ARCHIVES

A physiologist, not a medical doctor, Dhalla admits he's not a "test tube man." He hasn't done any hands-on lab work since 1968, claiming he isn't smart enough. But he speaks as a man who knows his true strength: brokering deals and connecting people.

The pursuit of greatness has informed Dhalla's life.

"I wanted to do things which were of some consequence because I knew if you do something of consequence then people will think you are important," Dhalla says.

He always believed he was destined to make his mark. Even his name, Naranjan, translates as one who can do no wrong.

The eldest of seven, Dhalla was born in 1936 and raised a Sikh in Ghanieke, a village near the India-Pakistan border. His father was the village moneylender, known as a *shahjee*. He had only a Grade 4 education, but as a *shahjee*, he lived like a king.

One thing that particularly displeased Dhalla's father was Dhalla. He frequently told the boy he wasn't smart enough, not as smart as his classmates and that he wouldn't achieve his dreams. The words of a harsh parent linger a long time, and that notion still echoes in Dhalla's mind to this day, he says.

Dhalla wanted to be a film director; surely, his gifts would have helped him achieve the greatness he craved in a business built on shmooz. But his plans were derailed when his parents decided he would marry. In a culture where arranged marriages are the norm, Dhalla's unhappiness didn't matter. He did marry, but the unhappiness continued, and he left to pursue studies in science, leaving his wife with his parents.

Dhalla had watched his father wheel and deal for years and learned skills that he found more useful than mere book smarts. He became known as "shah shan" or king of kings in university. He used his parents' money to befriend classmates who could help him move ahead, treating them to dinners and movies.

Those skills helped later when Dhalla was working

Dhalla in a lab at the St. Boniface Hospital Research Centre in June 2001.

PHIL HOSSACK / WINNIPEG FREE PRESS ARCHIVES

'You have to give him credit that this is something he wanted to do, and he pursued it with vigour. He is smart, he denies he is, but he really is'

— Paramjit Tappia, principal investigator of cardiac membrane biology at Institute of Cardiovascular Sciences.

Dhalla and his wife Ranjit.

FAMILY SUBMITTED PHOTO

in a New Delhi research lab, testing the effect of herbs on hypertension, a task he wasn't really up to, he said. Dhalla befriended another student, Pantulu, who did understand the work. Dhalla paid for Pantulu's movies and dinners, and in return, Pantulu taught Dhalla how to isolate the herbs' compounds.

That research was the basis of one of Dhalla's earliest published papers and helped him earn a scholarship at the University of Pennsylvania in 1961. He wanted to develop a cure for heart disease. But again, he faced the pull between work and family — again, work won. Dhalla said he abandoned his pregnant wife and two sons.

Sonny Dhalla is one of the sons Dhalla left behind. He can remember living in India without his dad until the 1970s, remembers his bitterness, but now he says he admires his father's work ethic.

"He married his work," said Sonny, a Brandon-based surgeon. "If someone is to be successful, you have to pay the price."

In America, a colleague told Dhalla he didn't have the appropriate education to find a cure for heart disease. The scientist told Dhalla there are two types of researchers: those who work with the test tubes and those who direct the people with the test tubes.

Dhalla set out to become one of those who directs the people with the test tubes. He visited universities across North America to study how officials had set up centres of heart research — an idea Dhalla brought to Winnipeg in 1969. He attended conferences and made friends with some of the most important scientists at the time.

By 1972, Dhalla was granted permission to organize a meeting of the International Study Group for Research in Cardiac Metabolism in Winnipeg.

Dhalla said he "dazzled" the more than 600 cardiologists and scientists at the event. But inside he felt very alone, and for the first time, felt longing for a more intimate connection.

"Here, I achieved the heights. I was going to be chairman, and there was not a single soul around me, who belongs to me, to appreciate that, what a greatness I have done," he said.

Soon after, friends helped him connect with Ranjit Bal, a woman in Ontario. The couple married the day they met.

Dhalla concedes his flagrant style of self-promotion riles some people.

"I used to be very arrogant up to 1975.... From '75 onward, I heard people say that I am the most humble person they ever met," he said.

His son said achieving a high level of success is bound to cause backlash.

"He's climbed the ladder to success, and some people must have gotten in the way. That's how you get to be successful," Sonny Dhalla said.

Paramjit Tappia, a colleague at St. Boniface Hospital Research Centre, said he believes some are envious of Dhalla's status and success, calling the man a visionary who treats everyone as his best buddy, whether they are or not.

Dhalla's reputation in the medical community was not helped when a colleague accused him of misappropriating research funds in 1981.

An RCMP criminal investigation and a U of M committee internal review did not find evidence to support charges. It was a dark period, Dhalla says, which may have damaged Winnipeg's chances of blossoming into a hub for heart health care and delayed the cardiac centre's start by five years.

His dream of curing heart disease still eludes him — and killed his eldest son at 46.

Dhalla sits, slouched in a chair in his corner office overlooking the Red River, pondering whether he has achieved the greatness he craves.

"What I wanted was to make a dent in curing heart disease, and I could not do that," he said. "I think that I have not done anything."

He says he never lived up to his name nor his dream. But then, he never thought people should like him anyway.

"Enemies are better than friends because at least once a day, they think about you. They are the people who make you popular," he said.

MANITOBA-NESS

DHALLA was lured to Winnipeg in the late 1960s, where he struck an interest in building Winnipeg's profile as an internationally recognized destination for heart research. He convinced the federal government to invest in medical infrastructure in Winnipeg and helped turn a small department within the St. Boniface General Hospital into the University of Manitoba's Institute of Cardiovascular Sciences, attracting specialists from around the world.

He has since trained more than 145 scientists and inspired students to combat heart disease. He chaired the World Congress on Heart Health in Winnipeg in 2001 and was honoured at the Global Conference on Heart Health and Disease, held in Winnipeg in 2006. He co-founded Medicure, a Winnipeg biotech firm with scientist Albert Friesen, that focuses on ischemic heart disease and hypertension.

Dhalla has maintained a strong connection with Winnipeg's Sikh community and helped promote, with the late Izzy Asper, the idea of acquiring a Gandhi statue for the Canadian Museum of Human Rights.

5 THINGS YOU DIDN'T KNOW

1. He initially wanted to be a film director and wrote his first manuscript in India before he was 18.

2. His eldest child, Samraj Dhalla, died of sudden heart failure in 2003.

3. Dhalla designed his own family crest.

4. He hasn't done any hands-on research in four decades.

5. Dhalla says Naranjan is Punjabi for "one who can do no wrong."

LLOYD AXWORTHY

25

BY LINDSEY WIEBE

Political giant

"**A**LWAYS look for that rare moment when a small sliver of light appears in the opposing line."

That advice from a football coach guided Norman Lloyd Axworthy well in his political career. But it was particularly helpful when he, as foreign affairs minister, was struggling through the complicated process that resulted in the Ottawa Treaty, the high-profile landmine ban supported by 158 countries.

The words were meant to help the former fullback with his game at Sisler High School, but Axworthy sees parallels in facing down political opposition over an effort that earned him a Nobel Peace Prize nomination.

After you see the light, "there is a chance to break into the open field and run like hell," the veteran politician recalled in his 2003 book, *Navigating a New World.* "Timing and opportunity are crucial.

"That is what happened to us in the campaign for a treaty to ban the use of anti-personnel landmines: We looked for the light, saw the opening, did some broken-field running and made a score."

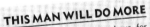

THIS MAN WILL DO MORE

"Politicians in this country have for too long been followers and not leaders. Leadership must provide more than competent administration — it means tackling the tough issues; speaking and acting in an independent, intelligent manner. Leadership means ideas, imagination, direction. The issue in this election is one of leadership."

— May 24, 1966

LLOYD AXWORTHY
LIBERAL FOR ST. JAMES

LLOYD AXWORTHY
Political Science Professor
at United College

Phone 774-0125   1654 Portage Ave.

Authorized by Lloyd Axworthy Election Committee.

WINNIPEG TRIBUNE UNIVERSITY OF MANITOBA ARCHIVES

A handbill from
Axworthy's 1966 campaign.

Lloyd Axworthy meets with Kofi Annan, then
secretary-general of the United Nations, in 1998.

GREATNESS

Served as foreign affairs minister
from 1996 to 2000.

Nominated for Nobel Peace Prize in 1997 for
co-ordinating Ottawa Treaty to ban landmines.

Received Senator Patrick J. Leahy
Humanitarian Award in 2000.

Received CARE International
Humanitarian Award in 2001.

Received Princeton University's James Madison
Medal for outstanding public service.

Invested into Order of Manitoba in 2001.

Helped develop the International Criminal Court,
founded in The Hague, Netherlands, in 2002.

Invested into Order of Canada in 2003.

Axworthy spent 27 years in politics, 21 as a federal MP. Internationally, he is known for his term as foreign affairs minister when he pushed through the landmine treaty, helped establish the International Criminal Court and shone a spotlight on the problem of child soldiers.

Locally, Axworthy was the Grit heavyweight who delivered the goods and the cash to Manitoba, credited with spurring downtown development, shaping The Forks and saving the Port of Churchill, among other achievements.

These days there's a sense of homecoming about the man who left politics to head a University of British Columbia policy think-tank in 2000, but returned to Winnipeg a few years later with wife Denise and son Stephen to become president of his alma mater, the University of Winnipeg.

"I didn't take to British Columbia. I didn't like mountains. I didn't like rainy winters," said Axworthy, seated on a sofa in his U of W office.

"This is home... I think I am rooted in this place."

Axworthy was born in 1939 in North Battleford, Sask., and grew up a North End boy in Winnipeg, a top student and athlete who liked drama and debating and modelled for Eaton's in his spare time.

He was politically precocious as a child. "I can remember him talking about political leaders that most of his peers, contemporaries, had never heard of," said former Winnipeg city councillor Bill Neville, a childhood friend of Axworthy's.

Axworthy is the oldest of four children: Tom, former principal secretary and speechwriter for former prime minister Pierre Trudeau; Trevor; and Bob, who still lives in Winnipeg.

Their father, Norman, served in the Second World War and missed the first six years of young Lloyd's life. Norman returned to eventually become an insurance salesman who helped on Axworthy's campaign trail. Mother Gwen, active with the Red Cross and later as a day-care worker, developed the strong United Church faith Axworthy cites as an influence today.

A formative encounter with Lester B. Pearson spurred Axworthy's already burgeoning interest in politics: The high school student was assigned to write about the soon-to-be-prime minister's speech in Winnipeg and found himself captivated by Pearson's message.

"It was a very significant experience for me, to listen to somebody who by their words made you think differently," he said.

Axworthy studied and later taught at the University of Winnipeg. He also directed the school's Institute of Urban Studies. He earned his MA and later his PhD from Princeton University.

In 1963, Axworthy married first wife Lynne, a relationship that ended after he entered federal politics.

Axworthy's first political triumph was being elected MLA for Fort Rouge after his academic career was underway. After two terms, he ran federally and won the Winnipeg-Fort Garry riding (today Winnipeg South Centre) in 1979, a seat he held for more than two decades.

DAVE JOHNSON / WINNIPEG FREE PRESS ARCHIVES

FAMILY SUPPLIED PHOTO

Axworthy meets with the Mayfair tenants group in February 1983.

Axworthy and Pierre Elliott Trudeau in the 1960s.

'He has been an absolute giant in Manitoba politics and perhaps the finest representative this province has ever sent to Ottawa'

— Winnipeg then-Grit MP John Harvard, shortly before Axworthy officially announced his retirement

PHIL HOSSACK / WINNIPEG FREE PRESS ARCHIVES

Axworthy campaigns with then-prime minister John Turner in August 1984.

Then-prime minister Jean Chrétien enjoys a laugh with Axworthy at his swearing-in as foreign affairs minister in 1996.

FAMILY SUPPLIED PHOTO

'He walked in there with a commitment of what he wanted to do. He stood for something. A lot of ministers become minister, and they fall in love with the limousine and the driver and the car and the trappings of office. That became quite secondary to Axworthy. He was never into that. He was into being able to articulate why he was there, and what he stood for'

— Donald Savoie, political scientist at University of Moncton

FAMILY SUPPLIED PHOTO

Axworthy early in his political career.

Axworthy's federal cabinet posts included transportation, employment and immigration and an unpopular stint in human resources when an overhaul of Canada's social programs left some supporters feeling Axworthy had betrayed his ideals.

He maintained his popularity in Manitoba by bringing millions of federal dollars to his home turf, boosting projects such as the Core Area Initiative, a multimillion-dollar project that transformed Winnipeg's downtown, and development of The Forks.

Axworthy developed what he calls his "great romance" with Denise Ommanney, his former press secretary and now wife of 24 years, during his early days in cabinet.

The relationship had a rocky start, recalls Ommanney

— both were married to other people when they met. The decision to leave those relationships caused a chill in Ottawa.

"We had this chance at happiness that might not come again," she said. "That's how I felt, anyway."

A former schoolmate described Axworthy as the student most likely to become prime minister, but his 1990 bid for the Liberal leadership fell through because he couldn't raise enough money.

In 1996, Axworthy received his long-coveted foreign affairs portfolio. Five years promoting peace-building and human security cemented his international standing. It was a busy time: In 1997 alone Axworthy visited nearly 40 countries, including a trip to Cuba that drew

American criticism. Other controversies flared during his time as foreign affairs minister, such as his support of the NATO bombing of Kosovo.

Axworthy did not take lightly his decision to leave politics in 2000 to head the new Liu Institute for Global Issues in B.C. He believes he could likely have held his seat a few more terms but wanted to devote more time to his wife and son Stephen, adopted soon after their marriage.

"I remember the discussion I had — which goes back a lot of years — with Pierre Trudeau, when I asked him when he thought it was the right time to leave," Axworthy told the *Free Press* in 2000. "And he said when your kids become teenagers because that is when they need you most. There have been a lot of years of his (Stephen's) growing up that I have not seen him, and this is a chance to change that."

The time apart took its toll: Growing up, Steve knew his father as someone who was often away, "gone off to save the world."

"There was a lot of personal resentment against Dad," said the now-23-year-old, who says their relationship is much stronger these days.

Ommanney admits she lobbied hard for her husband's political finale, believing it was better to go out on top: "It didn't seem like the perfect time to him, but it did to me," she said.

After three years with the UBC think-tank, during which Axworthy was nominated to the Order of Canada, an offer to head the University of Winnipeg lured him back to the Prairies.

In the past four years, he has reshaped the formerly cash-strapped institution, with the development of the Global College, a conversion of part of Spence Street into a pedestrian mall in the works and plans for a new science complex and student housing. Axworthy has renewed his contract with the school until 2014.

He isn't entirely comfortable speculating on why he was nominated as one of the Greatest Manitobans, but Axworthy concedes that politics aside, it might have something to do with returning home.

"I think people did appreciate that fact that I was making a kind of statement about who I was by that simple action, coming back," he said.

"And not just coming back to sit in my rocking chair, but coming back to be an active member of my community."

FAMILY SUPPLIED PHOTO

Axworthy was a student at the University of Winnipeg in the early 1960s.

MANITOBA-NESS

L LOYD Axworthy is Manitoba's Grit godfather. He was born in North Battleford, Sask., but he spent all of his 27 years in Canadian politics representing Manitoba and established a reputation as a political power broker for the province.

Axworthy grew up in Winnipeg and was educated at the University of Winnipeg.

His first political seat was as MLA for the Liberals in Fort Rouge; after two terms, he made a successful bid to be MP for Winnipeg-Fort Garry (today Winnipeg South Centre).

He became known as a Liberal heavyweight during his more than two decades in the seat because he secured a seemingly endless stream of funds for his city and province.

Axworthy lives with wife Denise Ommanney and son Stephen in Winnipeg, where he's president and vice-chancellor of the University of Winnipeg.

5 THINGS YOU DIDN'T KNOW

1. He planned to open a law office in Winnipeg before a professor encouraged him to apply for a Woodrow Wilson Fellowship, which led him to Princeton and a career in academia.

2. His weekend getaway for decades has been a cottage at Victoria Beach. "As soon as you hit the environs, the tension level goes down about 30 or 40 per cent," said Axworthy, who admits paperwork often follows him lakeside.

3. He was a teen model for Eaton's in high school — "desert boots, a cardigan sweater and a button-down shirt," he laughed.

4. He has a deep-rooted United Church faith that he still cites as integral to his identity.

5. He has an unusual connection to Timothy Leary. The 1960s counterculture hero was to play a show at the Royal Albert Arms, which Axworthy's brother Bob co-owned, in 1980. Leary had twice been denied entry to Canada because of drug charges in the United States, but Axworthy, then immigration minister, granted him permission to enter. The Conservatives raised an uproar. Axworthy was later cleared of wrongdoing, and today jokes he'd had little idea Leary was a "great psychedelic."

PHIL FONTAINE

26

GREATNESS

Native leader, politician, father, grandfather, mentor.

Was elected chief of Sagkeeng First Nation when he was just 27 years old, and brought about the first alcohol treatment centre on a reserve in Canada.

Three-term grand chief of Assembly of Manitoba Chiefs.

Three-term grand chief of Assembly of First Nations (*not consecutive. He won in 1997, was defeated in 2000, re-elected in 2003 and 2006).

Was one of the masterminds behind the symbolic rejection in the Manitoba legislature of the Meech Lake accord in 1990.

Helped negotiate the residential schools settlement with Ottawa, including the official apology in the House of Commons, delivered by Prime Minister Stephen Harper, June 11, 2008.

He has a BA in political studies from the University of Manitoba.

In 1996 he won the National Aboriginal Achievement Award for public service. He has received four honorary doctorates from the Royal Military College (1999), Brock University (2004), Lakehead University (2005) and the University of Windsor (2005) and was inducted into the Order of Manitoba in 2003.

BY MIA RABSON

Bridge builder

OTTAWA — He was a mastermind behind the defeat of the Meech Lake accord, a lead negotiator on the Kelowna accord and the man who pushed and pushed until the federal government finally admitted residential schools were a mistake and apologized.

And during that ceremonial apology in June, when the eyes of many Canadians were turned for the first time to the tragic era of this country's history, it was Phil Fontaine who stood in Parliament and became the first aboriginal leader in Canadian history to speak from the floor of the House of Commons and accept the apology on his people's behalf.

"Not bad for a guy from Sagkeeng," Fontaine half-jokes from his 11th-floor office in downtown Ottawa.

But the soft-spoken leader is so reluctant to talk about himself, the line, he admits, was borrowed from his son.

MARC GALLANT / WINNIPEG FREE PRESS ARCHIVES

Fontaine at an Assembly of Manitoba Chiefs meeting in 1992. To his left is Peguis Chief Louis Stevenson and further left is Black River Chief Frank Abraham.

National Chief Phil Fontaine on Parliament Hill in 2008.

Fontaine actually considered refusing to be interviewed for this profile and his discomfort when asked to ponder his achievements is palpable.

"I haven't invented anything, I'm not a rich guy, I'm not a heart surgeon," says Fontaine, as he lists a number of other accomplishments of Manitobans he thinks might be great, including philanthropists, academics and writers.

"Against all of that I'm pretty ordinary."

Ordinary if you think being elected as a band chief at age 27 is nothing to trumpet.

Ordinary if you think speaking publicly about being sexually abused as a child in a residential school isn't brave.

Ordinary if you think negotiating a $2-billion compensation agreement for residential school survivors is something to sneeze at.

Ajay Chopra, who has worked with Fontaine for almost a decade, said Fontaine is "the best human being I know."

Although critics believe Fontaine is cosiest with the Liberals, he has successfully worked with the current Conservative government in Ottawa as well, and it was the Conservatives, not the Liberals, who finally apologized for the tragedy of residential schools.

WAYNE GLOWACKI / WINNIPEG FREE PRESS ARCHIVES

Fontaine finds his late father in a group photograph of students at Fort Alexander Indian Residential School taken in 1917.

Phil Fontaine, second from right, with Joe Hudson, Albert Berens and Thelma Fontaine at Sagkeeng First Nation.

EMILY SUBMITTED PHOTO

Fontaine holds up that apology as a watershed moment for Canada and for First Nations in this country.

But it is not what comes to mind when he is asked what he feels are his greatest accomplishments.

Instead, he identifies getting local control for the education system in Sagkeeng when he was the chief, and opening the first alcohol treatment centre on an Indian reserve in Canada.

When asked if there is something about himself he doesn't think many people know, he stares at the floor in deep thought for a few moments then looks up and for one of the only times during the interview, looks the interviewer straight in the eye.

"I've been sober for 32 years," he says. "That is quite an achievement."

He is a runner and a hockey player who likes sports trivia and country music.

The ancient-looking stereo in one corner of his office is topped with piles of CDs.

Aside from the computer on his desk, there is little technology to be seen in his spacious office. The suggestion he procure an iPod for his vast music collection actually made him shudder.

"I am a Luddite," he says, without apology.

Instead of technology, he surrounds himself with native artwork and family photographs.

Fontaine says he is not a philanthropist, but Chopra points out Fontaine is generous despite a lack of overall wealth.

"He never walks by a panhandler without giving something," says Chopra. "He'll make me empty out my pockets (as well)."

Fontaine is hailed by those with whom he has worked on both sides of the table as a skilful negotiator.

Winnipeg lawyer Jack London, who has worked with Fontaine for more than two decades and considers the native leader a mentor, says Fontaine's style at the table is neither combative nor placid.

"History will find him to have been the bridge between the old (combative) relationship between government and First Nations and the new politics of reconciliation," says London.

"He is smart. He is tireless. He is courageous."

London says Fontaine's greatest strengths lie in his ability to quickly assess a situation and understand what he is being told, his confidence to surround himself with advisers he trusts and his wholehearted push to compromise, not confront.

Fontaine says his goal as a negotiator is to let everyone be heard, never seek to embarrass anyone at the table and never dismiss another's ideas or approaches entirely.

The residential schools settlement, says Fontaine, is an example of the success that can come from that approach.

He is, like many politicians, not entirely beloved. The nominations for Greatest Manitoban included comments from detractors but, says London, that represents a split in the aboriginal community about how to go about dealing with the federal government.

That split led to Fontaine's defeat after just one term as AFN chief, by other chiefs who were looking for a more

'He is a man who is dedicated to not only benefiting his people but to doing so in a way which is a benefit to the whole country'

— Jack London, lawyer for the AFN, former dean of the law school at the University of Manitoba

Fontaine with environmentalist David Suzuki in June 2007.

TOM HANSON / THE CANADIAN PRESS ARCHIVES

Fontaine talks with young players at a hockey school he organizes for native youth.

PHIL HOSSACK / WINNIPEG FREE PRESS ARCHIVES

aggressive, confrontational pushback against the federal government. Fontaine was found by some to be too cosy with the Liberal government, and certainly shortly after his defeat, then-prime minister Jean Chrétien appointed Fontaine to the Indian Claims Commission.

Fontaine was voted into the AFN again in 2003 and was re-elected in 2006. He said he has not yet entirely decided whether he will seek an unprecedented fourth term next summer when the AFN elections are held.

University of Winnipeg president Lloyd Axworthy worked with Fontaine numerous times when he was the senior cabinet minister from Manitoba during former prime minister Jean Chrétien's tenure in Ottawa.

Axworthy said there is no doubt Fontaine deserves to be included in a list of Great Manitobans.

"In a contemporary format, in a complex time, his leadership has really been outstanding," says Axworthy.

Fontaine was born in Sagkeeng, Man., in 1944. He is the youngest of 12 children, and his family went from middle-class to poverty-stricken after the death of his father when Fontaine was just six years old.

His mother, Agnes, was the first aboriginal woman elected as a band councillor in Canada when she was elected in Sagkeeng in 1952 when Fontaine was just eight years old.

But it wasn't until he was in his early 20s that Fontaine was drawn to politics himself while attending a workshop with First Nations students at the University of Manitoba in 1966.

"I was really impressed with these students," says Fontaine. "They seemed really determined. They were confident, educated and had a real sense of the world."

Six years later, Fontaine was elected chief of Sagkeeng. A decade later, he was elected grand chief of the Assembly of Manitoba Chiefs, a position he held for three terms.

It was during that tenure that he helped mastermind the plan for NDP MLA Elijah Harper to reject the Meech Lake accord in the Manitoba legislature by hold-

WAYNE GLOWACKI / WINNIPEG FREE PRESS ARCHIVES

Fontaine during the Meech Lake debate in June 1990.

ing up a single eagle feather and saying "no" to allowing the debate to proceed.

The accord, which was to have brought Quebec into the Canadian Constitution, would die after Manitoba and Newfoundland failed to ratify it.

His stint at the AMC also included negotiating the Aboriginal Policy Framework, which at the time was meant to be the pathway to self-government for Manitoba First Nations.

But after more than a decade of work, the agreement was quietly disbanded in 2007 without accomplishing a single one of its goals and Fontaine admits that troubles him greatly.

Fontaine and MLA Elijah Harper at a meeting during the Meech Lake debate in June 1990.

RUTH BONNEVILLE / WINNIPEG FREE PRESS ARCHIVES

George Hickes, Speaker of the Manitoba Legislative Assembly, congratulates Fontaine on his Order of Manitoba.

"That's probably one of my greatest disappointments," he says.

He wants to be remembered as someone who made a contribution to Canada. But he still isn't convinced he'll be remembered as a Great Manitoban.

"I'm not a complicated guy," said Fontaine.

At the end of the day, he says he is still just a kid from Sagkeeng.

MANITOBA-NESS

P HIL Fontaine was born in Fort Alexander, now Sagkeeng, on Sept. 20, 1944. He is the youngest of 12 children. His father died when he was six, and he spent a decade in residential schools. He holds a bachelor of arts in political studies from the University of Manitoba.

Before entering politics, he worked as a clerk in the Department of Highways for the provincial government but realized very quickly he aspired to be much more than a bureaucrat.

So he moved to Ottawa and lived on practically nothing while he honed his political skills with the Canadian Indian Youth Council and as a member of the Company of Young Canadians. The latter was a short-lived exercise of the federal government looking to encourage social, economic and community development in Canada.

He returned to his home in Sagkeeng and was the administrator of the band under his mentor, Chief Dave Courchene.

In 1972, he was elected chief of Sagkeeng, and held the position for two consecutive terms. He followed that with a stint as the regional Manitoba chief of the Assembly of First Nations.

In 1991, he was elected for the first of three consecutive terms as the grand chief of the Assembly of Manitoba Chiefs, and in 1997, he was elected to the Assembly of First Nations as grand chief.

He was defeated during a re-election bid in 2000 and spent a few years at the Indian Claims Commission, before being re-elected head of the AFN in 2003 and again in 2006.

In 2005, he helped negotiate the $5-billion Kelowna accord to bridge the standard-of-living gap between First Nations and the rest of Canada.

In 2006, he was at the table for the Indian Residential Schools Resolution, which had the federal government commit to compensate residential school survivors and establish a truth and reconciliation commission to research the schools' history and establish an archives.

In 2008, he was on the floor of the House of Commons when Prime Minister Stephen Harper apologized for the legacy of residential schools, a day Fontaine calls "achieving the impossible."

5 THINGS YOU DIDN'T KNOW

1. Fontaine has been sober for 32 years.

2. Fontaine once met with Nelson Mandela and considers the African leader one of his heroes.

3. Fontaine's mother, Agnes, was the first aboriginal woman in Canada to be elected to a band council.

4. Fontaine spent 10 years in a residential school, and in 1990, was one of the first to speak publicly about physical and sexual abuse he endured while a student at the schools.

5. Fontaine was the first aboriginal leader to address the Organization of American States and was also the first aboriginal government head to speak from the floor of the House of Commons when he accepted the apology for residential schools on June 11, 2008.

JEFF MCINTOSH / THE CANADIAN PRESS ARCHIVES

Fontaine speaks at a Calgary conference in March 2004, talking about his 10 years at residential school.

THE GUESS WHO

BY PAUL WILLIAMSON

GUESS what?

The more one digs into the history of The Guess Who, the more it resembles an archeological investigation of sorts. As each layer is uncovered, so, too is the history of rock music in Manitoba and in Canada.

Randy Bachman and Burton Cummings are household names, of course. But more than 40 members, some briefly, some for years, created and perpetuated the band's mysterious name and legendary songs.

It all started in 1960 when a talented Winnipeg singer and guitarist named Allan Kowbel formed a group called Al and the Silvertones. By 1962, Kowbel had changed his name to Chad Allan and the band was Chad Allan and the Reflections, later Chad Allan and the Expressions. Allan looked after vocals and guitar, with fellow Winnipeg boys Bob Ashley on the keyboards, Randy Bachman on guitar, Jim Kale on bass and Garry Peterson behind the drums.

'As big as The Beatles'

The Guess Who in the early days — Garry Peterson, Burton Cummings, Randy Bachman and Jim Kale — talk with band manager Bob Burns, also host of CJAY's popular Teen Dance Party, circa 1967.

GREATNESS

The Guess Who was the first Canadian rock band to get a No. 1 hit song in the United States with the controversial American Woman.

Their awards include:

Juno Awards — 1965, 1967, 1968, 1969, 1970, 1971, 1975.

Canadian Recording Arts & Sciences Hall of Fame 1987.

Canadian Walk of Fame 2001.

Canadian Music Industry Hall of Fame 2002.

Governor General's Performing Arts Award 2002.

Canadian Songwriters Hall of Fame, Cummings and Bachman, 2005.

In addition to American Woman, five of The Guess Who's songs cracked the Top 10 on the American charts.

These Eyes hit No. 6 in 1968.

Laughing hit No. 10 in 1969.

No Time hit No. 5 in 1969.

Share the Land hit No. 10 in 1970.

Clap for the Wolfman hit No. 6 in 1974.

Peterson, Cummings, Bachman and Kale show off their gold record for the single These Eyes. Dick Clark presented it to them on American Bandstand in August 1969.

Peterson, Bachman, Kale and Cummings, above, clown around with a fan's pennant at the Winnipeg airport as they leave for a tour of the U.K. in 1967.

The band's debut single, *Tribute to Buddy Holly*, was released on Canadian-American Records in 1962. Shortly after, Chad Allan and the Reflections signed with Quality Records and released several singles that received little attention and even less radio airplay. It took two years, grinding it out in the local music scene, but in 1965 the band scored its first big hit, a rocking rendition of Johnny Kidd & the Pirates' *Shakin' All Over*.

Looking to build an enigmatic buzz, Quality Records released the single in a plain white wrapper and credited it to Guess Who? The label surmised that disc jockeys and music fans would assume the Guess Who? identity was hiding famous performers working under a pseudonym. Maybe, just maybe, this mysterious song and the mysterious artists were members of The Beatles or members of some other British Invasion band. It was to get people talking, maybe generate some airplay.

Did the unknown promotion man's idea have anything to do with the song's success? We'll never know, but *Shakin' All Over* reached No. 1 in Canada, No. 22 in the United States and No. 27 in Australia.

Winnipeg was now home to one of the hottest bands in Canada. Even when Quality Records finally revealed that the band was actually Chad Allan & The Expressions, disc jockeys continued to call the group Guess Who? The question mark was soon dropped, and the name The Guess Who stuck.

The singles that preceded *Shakin' All Over* had good success in Canada, but received little airplay anywhere else. All that changed in 1965 when Bob Ashley left the band, and a fresh-faced 18-year-old kid from Winnipeg's North End named Burton Cummings stepped in. Cummings joined the band as keyboardist and co-lead vocalist with Chad Allan, who quit soon after, making Cummings the undisputed frontman.

Free Press writer Gene Telpner interviewed the band in December 1965, shortly after Cummings joined.

"I found the young men modest, humble about their success and still proud to call Winnipeg home," he wrote in his *Coffee Break* column. "Remember these names, because I predict they'll be every bit as big as The Beatles."

Telpner's prediction may have seemed far-fetched, but a few years later his fellow pundits were no doubt searching the newsroom for his crystal ball.

The magic arrived in 1969 by way of a heartfelt ballad titled *These Eyes*, a song that became the group's first TOP 10 U.S. hit. Cummings and guitarist Randy Bachman were the band's key composers, and the pair had moved away from the waning British invasion sound to an eclectic mix of heavy rock, blues and jazz.

By 1970, The Guess Who patented an edgy hard-rock sound and released the album *American Woman*. The title track was also the album's single, and *American Woman* quickly went on to become a No. 1 hit in the United States, beating The Beatles three weeks straight.

Randy Bachman left the band at the height of its popularity after playing one final show at the Fillmore East in New York on May 16, 1970. Bachman was replaced by two guitarists, fellow Winnipeggers Kurt Winter from the band Brother, and Greg Leskiw. Winter became the main songwriting collaborator with Cummings.

In 1972, The Guess Who released their highly acclaimed album *Live at the Paramount*, recorded at the Paramount Theatre in Seattle. The band followed with a tour later that year of Japan, New Zealand and Australia.

Leskiw left the band before the Paramount show in 1972 and was replaced by Don McDougall. Here's how McDougall remembers his initiation:

"It was a cold day in Winnipeg when I got the call. It was my first plane trip, and I met up with the guys in Phoenix. I thought that in winter it was cold everywhere. So I packed my bags and boarded the plane with my big parka, tuque and mukluks on."

Following a milk run that included several air-conditioned airports, McDougall arrived in Phoenix and spotted a limousine driver holding a sign bearing his name near the baggage carousel.

"The guy wanted to carry my bags, but I didn't know him so I told him to keep his hands off my gear," said McDougall.

He was impressed when the limo driver offered him an ice-cold beer. The other members of The Guess Who were all sitting around the pool at the hotel when he arrived.

"I walked into the courtyard in my parka, tuque and mukluks, headed straight for the diving board and jumped in the pool with all my clothes on. It was one of those moments where everyone wished they had a camera."

A few minutes later Burton Cummings handed him a Greyhound, (vodka and grapefruit juice), and he was officially a member of The Guess Who.

McDougall spent three days holed up in a hotel room learning all the songs, and on the fourth day, walked out on stage in front of more than 15,000 fans.

"I knew the band was big, but I had no idea they were that big," he offered in a recent interview. "I had never been to a concert that large before in my life, and there I was up on stage playing with the band."

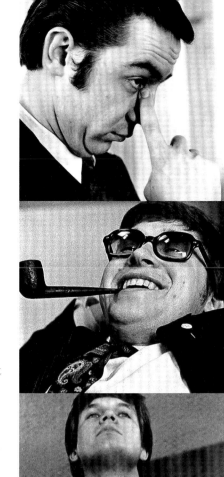

Publicity photos, shot February 1967, of Guess Who members, from top Kale, Peterson, Bachman.

WINNIPEG TRIBUNE / UNIVERSITY OF MANITOBA ARCHIVES

Cummings leads
The Guess Who
at a concert at the
Winnipeg Arena
in August 2001.

JOE BRYKSA / WINNIPEG FREE PRESS ARC

AARON HARRIS / THE CANADIAN PRESS ARCHIVES

KEN GIGLIOTTI / WINNIPEG FREE PRESS ARCHIVES

FRED CHARTRAND / THE CANADIAN PRESS ARCHIVES

hman and Cummings
orm at the Grey Cup
time show in Calgary in
ember 2000.

Jim Kale has fun on stage
during a Guess Who reunion in May 2000.

Bachman, Cummings, Donnie McDougall,
Peterson and Bill Wallace wear their Governor General
Performing Arts medals, November 2002.

MANITOBA-NESS

BURTON Cummings was a kid from the North End when he joined the band and quickly became the frontman.

More than 40 musicians have belonged to The Guess Who, but not all were from Manitoba. Some are known as Kale's Klones because they played in Kale's touring version of the group.

The band members: Chad Allan, Bob Ashley, Randy Bachman, Sonnie Bernardi, Bobby Bilan, Trevor Balicky, Kenny Carter, Charley Cooley, Burton Cummings, Ken Curry, Kurt Winter, Bruce Decker, Brent DeJarlais, Carl Dixon, Bob Fuhr, Jimmy Grabowski, Mike Hanford, Terry Hatty, David Inglis, Jim Kale, Greg Leskiw, Vance Masters, Allan McDougall, Donnie McDougall, Laurie MacKenzie, Mike McKenna, David Parasz, Garry Peterson, Terry Reid, Dale Russell, Brian Sellar, Bobby Sabellico, Ken "Spider" Sinnaeve, Derek Sharp, Leonard Shaw, Brian Tataryn, Domenic Troiano, Bill Wallace, Ralph Watts, Tom Whitnery.

5 THINGS YOU DIDN'T KNOW

1. It's been said American Woman was written after a U.S. Customs official treated the band badly at the border. Others say it was an impromptu lyric Cummings sang to Canadian women after a U.S. tour. The group denies it, but some still say the woman in the title is the Statue of Liberty.

2. In 1970, The Guess Who performed for Prince Charles at the White House. Pat Nixon asked them not to play American Woman because of its anti-American sentiment.

3. In 1977, Jim Kale discovered the name The Guess Who had never been registered. He promptly registered the name and maintains control of the band name to this day.

4. In 2001, the University of Brandon awarded doctorates to The Guess Who members.

5. In 2003, the band (including Bachman and Cummings) performed a well-received set before an audience of about 450,000 at the Molson Canadian Rocks for Toronto SARS benefit. The concert was the largest outdoor ticketed event in Canadian history.

Kale quit the band in 1972, and Bill Wallace, a former bandmate of Winter's, took over bass duties. Cummings, Wallace and Winter wrote the Guess Who's last big hit, *Clap For The Wolfman*, which reached No. 6 on the U.S. charts, and paid homage to famous disc jockey Wolfman Jack, whose trademark voice is in the song. McDougall and Winter left the band in 1974, and Domenic Troiano, the first non-Winnipegger, became the new lead guitarist and Cummings' chief songwriting collaborator.

That lineup never really repeated the success or sound the band had once achieved, and with little fanfare, The Guess Who broke up in 1975.

That didn't last long. In November 1977, the CBC approached the former band members about a reunion. Cummings and Bachman declined, but Kale, Peterson, Winter and McDougall responded. Kale continued on with The Guess Who throughout the late 1970s with Winter, McDougall and drummer Vance Masters. They released two studio albums, *Guess Who's Back in Canada* and *All This For a Song*, in 1979.

In 1983, Bachman, Cummings, Kale and Peterson reunited as The Guess Who to play a series of Canadian concerts and record the *Together Again* live album and video.

In May 1997, with Winnipeg facing a major flood, Bachman and Cummings reunited for a fundraising concert. Cummings, Bachman, Peterson and Kale also played together in Winnipeg in 1999 at the closing ceremonies of the Pan American Games. That show sparked a cross-Canada tour, on which the group was joined by previous band members McDougall and Wallace. The Running Back Thru Canada tour travelled to 27 cities and entertained more than 200,000 excited fans.

Bachman and Cummings have toured together since 2005.

Who knows if The Guess Who will ever reunite? But the band's amazing songs continue to remind music lovers around the world that for an important period in the history of rock 'n' roll, Winnipeg was ground zero in Canada.

NATHAN DENETTE / THE CANADIAN PRESS

Bachman, front, and Cummings in April 2006 just before kicking off their First Time Around tour.

The Guess Who, right, play at the first show of their Running Back Thru Canada tour in St. John's, NL, in May 2000. The CD cover, left, from the tour.

KEITH GOSSE / THE CANADIAN PRESS

ELIJAH HARPER

28

BY BRUCE OWEN

*But they that wait upon the Lord
shall renew their strength;
they shall mount up with wings as
eagles; they shall run and not be weary;
and they shall walk and not faint.*

— Isaiah 40:31

The strength of an eagle

Harper attends the Indian Residential School Survivors National Conference and Workshop in Winnipeg in April 2007.

KEN GIGLIOTTI / WINNIPEG FREE PRESS ARCHIVES

Elijah Harper holds one of two eagle feathers that brought him spiritual support during the Meech Lake debate, in this 2008 shot.

ELIJAH Harper's brother Darryl wasn't big on reading the Bible or going to church. That was back in June 1990. Darryl had come to Winnipeg from the family home of isolated Red Sucker Lake to run in the Manitoba Marathon. He brought with him a brown envelope.

Inside was an eagle feather Elijah's other brother Saul had found on a wilderness portage route near the spot where their grandparents once trapped.

Saul thought the eagle feather was a sign. He thought Elijah, then a provincial politician, should have it.

"He felt an urge for some reason to give it to me," Elijah said in an interview.

Darryl, the feather packed away, flew to Winnipeg and booked into the Balmoral Hotel on the edge of Winnipeg's downtown.

Once there he decided to go for a walk and soon found himself outside a gospel church. He went inside to hear the pastor's words.

GREATNESS

1978: elected chief of his community Red Sucker Lake in northern Manitoba.

1981: MLA for Rupertsland becoming the first Treaty Indian to sit in the Manitoba legislature.

1986: under then-premier Howard Pawley of the NDP, Harper is appointed to cabinet as minister without portfolio, responsible for Native Affairs.

1987: named minister of northern affairs — instrumental in setting up the Aboriginal Justice Inquiry that examined the treatment of native people by police and the courts.

June 1990: Harper blocks the Meech Lake accord in the Manitoba legislature by denying its quick passage. His "no" resonates across the country.

1990: Harper is voted as the Newsmaker of the Year in Canada by the Canadian Press, becomes Honorary Chief for Life by Red Sucker Lake First Nation and presented the Stanley Knowles Humanitarian Award.

1992: resigns as provincial MLA to run in federal election and wins a seat in Parliament in 1993.

1995: Harper hosts a Sacred Assembly in Hull, Que. Out of the talks come a declaration that June 21 is Canada's National Aboriginal Day.

April 10, 1996: Harper wins a National Aboriginal Achievement Award.

Jan. 19, 1999: Harper is appointed commissioner of the federal Indian Claims Commission.

"During the sermon someone in the room said out loud, 'There's somebody here carrying a brown envelope,'" Elijah remembers his brother telling him.

Darryl was spooked. He rushed back to his hotel room and for a reason he can't explain, started reading the Bible tucked in the table drawer.

"You should know Darryl isn't the type to go to church," Elijah said, "never mind read a Bible."

The verse he read almost immediately was Isaiah 40:31.

To him it was a divine sign. He took the feather to Elijah and told him what had happened.

And the rest, as they say, is history.

Harper holds an eagle feather and says no in the Manitoba Legislature to Meech Lake in June 1990.

Harper salutes supporters outside the Manitoba legislature after the Meech Lake accord dies.

Greeting supporters in November 1999.

WAYNE GLOWACKI / WINNIPEG FREE PRESS ARCHIVES

WINNIPEG FREE PRESS ARCHIVES

Harper, centre, Oscar Lathlin, left, and Phil Fontaine at an Assembly of Manitoba Chiefs meeting during the Meech Lake debate.

WAYNE GLOWACKI / WINNIPEG FREE PRESS ARCHIVES

WAYNE GLOWACKI / WINNIPEG FREE PRESS ARCHIVES

'Elijah had the courage to say no, and electrified the native communities in Canada and the States, who were excited that someone was standing up for the rights of aboriginal peoples. There was this quiet man, who did this quietly and made a global comment about what was going on with our people'

— Billy Merasty, Cree actor who played Harper in 2007 TV movie Elijah (CTV interview)

Within days Elijah Harper would defeat the Meech Lake accord and become a hero to First Nations people across Canada. He and those behind him, including current Assembly of First Nations National Chief Phil Fontaine, would put the concerns of aboriginal people at the top of the government agenda. No more would Canada's first peoples be excluded from the white corridors of power. No more would they be denied.

That feather — one of two Elijah was given in those stressful weeks — symbolized that. It still does.

"I don't deserve all of the credit," Harper said. "It was our people who did it. I just happened to be in the right place at the right time."

Harper, now 59, splits his residence between Ottawa and Red Sucker Lake, a small northern community about 700 kilometres northeast of Winnipeg near the Ontario boundary, where he was born in a log house belonging to his trapper parents

Forty-one years later, the stoic Harper held the fate of Canada in his hands. Or so Brian Mulroney, the prime minister at the time, had us believe.

The Meech Lake accord was a document intended to keep Quebec in Canada and bring each province under Canada's Constitution. To get Quebec to agree, Mulroney and the provinces negotiated special powers for Quebec: a recognition of Quebec as a "distinct society" and a constitutional veto.

The accord was then sent to the legislatures of the 10 provinces for approval. All of this had to happen before the June 23, 1990, deadline. If approval wasn't there, Quebec could secede.

In Manitoba, then-premier Gary Filmon had 12 days to get Meech Lake through the legislature. Filmon asked for the unanimous approval of MLAs to forego the necessary public consultation on Meech Lake, so that it could be approved by Manitoba before the deadline.

"No," was Harper's response.

All eyes focused on Manitoba where an Indian with a feather threatened to break up Canada. That same Indian also spoke for aboriginal people across the country. Through this one man, they were all heard. Loudly. They, too, wanted to be part of Canada's Constitution. They, too were distinct. More distinct than anyone — in government, anyway — gave them credit for.

"I felt nothing could stop me," the soft-spoken Cree Indian said. "There was no turning back. We were doing what was right."

"It was the beginning, in many aspects," added Lisa Meeches, who co-produced *Elijah*, a TV movie on Harper and his part in the Meech Lake crisis. "What's important is he didn't exclude anyone from the movement."

In Newfoundland, then-premier Clyde Wells watched on TV what Harper was doing in Manitoba. Seeing the accord was about to die, he cancelled a proposed vote on it in the Newfoundland legislature. Meech Lake was dead.

'What became impressive during those tense days was not the strength of Mr. Harper's resistance but the dignity and eloquence with which it was expressed. Whatever the constitutional results of Mr. Harper's stand, it drove home the point to all of Canada that aboriginal concerns had to be treated seriously'

— John Dafoe, retired Free Press editor, 1992

MANITOBA-NESS

ELIJAH Harper was born in 1949 in Red Sucker Lake, an isolated First Nations community about 710 kilometres northeast of Winnipeg. He was raised by his grandparents and at a young age was forced to attend residential schools.

Harper says it was his grandparents who instilled in him a need to be an advocate for his people.

The response in Quebec was predictable. In 1995 the province came to the very edge of separating from Canada. A referendum defeated Quebec secession by the narrowest of margins. In the following decade, talk of separation almost faded from Canada's national consciousness.

What hasn't disappeared is the plight of many of Canada's aboriginal people.

Elijah Harper said that was made painfully clear in June 2008 when Prime Minister Stephen Harper apologized to all aboriginal people for Canada's role in the federally financed, church-run residential school system — a system that saw young aboriginal children, including Elijah Harper — removed from their homes to be given a "proper" education. Many were sexually and physically abused.

"To me, that was a great moment in history," Harper said of the prime minister's apology. "It released the bondages and allowed us to begin to forgive. It will help our people heal."

At the time of Meech Lake, Harper was MLA for the huge northern riding of Rupertsland. He'd been a provincial politician for almost 10 years. The collapse of the accord threw him into the international spotlight. Almost overnight, he became the international spokesman for the treatment of Indians in Canada. His worldwide travel schedule earned him the dubious distinction of holding the worst attendance record in the legislature.

Two years later, the "MLA for The Hague" — the nickname Harper had earned by then — resigned from provincial politics when then-federal NDP leader Audrey McLaughlin asked him to run for Parliament.

While Harper took McLaughlin up on her offer, in the end he ran as a Liberal. He was elected in the federal riding of Churchill. He served as MP until 1997 when he was defeated by New Democrat Bev Desjarlais.

In Ottawa, Harper was a member of the Parliamentary Standing Committee on Aboriginal Affairs and played a role in establishing June 21 as National Aboriginal Day, a day that celebrates the culture and history of Canada's First Nations, Inuit and Métis people.

Most recently, Harper lobbied against plans by Premier Gary Doer's government to build a hydro transmission line down the west side of Manitoba. Doer has said a west-side line will protect a huge area of pristine forest on the east side from uncontrolled development.

Harper said the power line should be built down the shorter route on the east side of Lake Winnipeg. Not to build it there denies east-side First Nations communities a chance at economic development through new jobs and roads, he said, and an opportunity to address crippling social problems.

"Protecting the forest is one thing," Harper said. "It will be more costly for government in the future if we don't access this revenue ourselves. It's not right for us to live in these conditions.

"We want to take control of the situation. We're being excluded — that's what I've been fighting all my life."

His life in politics began in 1978 when he was elected chief of Red Sucker Lake. In the months that followed, he was introduced to provincial politics by Howard Pawley, then leader of the New Democratic Party, who became premier in 1981. That year Pawley encouraged Harper to run as MLA for the riding of

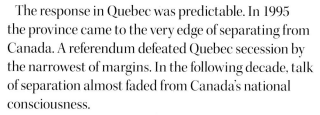

FAMILY PHOTO

Rupertsland. Thus Harper became the first Treaty Indian to sit in the Manitoba legislature.

He represented Manitoba's Churchill riding in Ottawa from 1993 to 1997.

Currently, he splits his time between residences in Ottawa and Red Sucker Lake. While retired from politics, he still leads a public life lobbying for the betterment of aboriginal people across Canada and throughout the world.

5 THINGS YOU DIDN'T KNOW

1. Harper is one of 13 children born to parents Ethel and Allan Harper, both trappers, in the remote northern community of Red Sucker Lake. He was the last one to be born in the family's log house. Two weeks after his birth, Elijah's parents bundled him up and went by dogsled to check their trapline.

2. It's commonly believed Harper had a single eagle feather when he blocked approval of the Meech Lake accord in the Manitoba legislature in June 1990. In fact, Harper had two, one found by his brother Saul near Red Sucker Lake and the other presented to him by native elder Paul Huntinghawk at a ceremony in Winnipeg.

3. Harper, 59, is restricted in his travels because he is on dialysis three times a week to contend with lost kidney function. He hopes he's a candidate for a transplant of a kidney donated by one of two of his children.

4. Harper is against the Doer government's plan to build a new hydro transmission line down the west side of the province. Harper says it should be built down the east side of Lake Winnipeg to open up the area for economic development and better the lives of First Nations communities.

5. Harper has a dry yet playful sense of humour. Example: Manitoba cabinet minister Gord Mackintosh, a former Harper adviser, remembers on June 22, 1990, the last day Harper said no to the Meech Lake accord, that he, Harper, and native leaders were walking away from the legislature to the Assembly of Manitoba Chiefs' downtown office.
"We were all kind of subdued and wondering, 'Now, what have we done? Is Quebec going to leave? Have we split the country?'
"Elijah quietly said, 'I don't know if I can continue in this line of work.'
"We all stopped in surprise and looked at him and asked, 'What will you do?'
"Then he smiled and said, 'Procedural adviser.'"

TOM HANSON / THE CANADIAN PRESS ARCHIVES

Harper holds one of his eagle feathers from the Meech Lake debate in this 2008 shot.

'He represents where we can be. He was the person who was the conduit of what we can be as aboriginal people. He has paid a very heavy price for that'

— Lisa Meeches, co-producer of 2007 TV movie Elijah

REV. HARRY LEHOTSKY

29

BY LINDOR REYNOLDS

The people's pastor

REV. Harry Lehotsky's first attempt at ministry was an utter failure.

The man who would one day change the face of inner-city Winnipeg started preaching on the streets of New York City, where he was born.

Though he had been raised in a supportive Christian family, Lehotsky began using drugs in high school and dabbling in dealing them.

His redemption came when he was 17.

He overdosed on PCP and was tossed from a moving car by people who didn't want a dead body on their hands. Lehotsky tumbled into a near-deserted street.

Two passing cops found him and raced him to hospital. The teenager vowed that night if he survived the overdose he'd spread God's word.

"He started going back to the people he'd sold drugs to," remembers his wife, Virginia. "He'd carry his Bible and try to convince them to stop using drugs."

She pauses and smiles. "It didn't go over very well."

MIKE DEAL / WINNIPEG FREE PRESS ARCHIVES

Lehotsky (left) with Gord Mackintosh, Manitoba's minister of justice and attorney general in 2006.

Harry Lehotsky inside the Ellice Cafe and Theatre, in 2005, which he helped to turn into the focal point of his neighbourhood.

GREATNESS

He came from humble beginnings in New York's Hell's Kitchen, but Rev. Harry Lehotsky went on to change the face of a Winnipeg inner-city neighbourhood.

He and his wife Virginia started New Life Ministries and through it worked to rid Winnipeg's West End of drug dealers, gangs and prostitutes.

His work was rewarded many times, only a few of them public:

In 2007, Lehotsky was posthumously awarded the Order of Canada.

Also in 2007, more than $270,000 was raised to wipe out remaining debts for three long-term projects Lehotsky started. They were Lazarus Housing, Nehemiah Housing (which fixes up and rents apartments) and the inner-city Ellice Cafe and Theatre. The money was donated in Lehotsky's memory.

The provincial government created a Rev. Harry Lehotsky Award for Community Activism.

The City of Winnipeg offers annual scholarships for inner-city youth in Lehotsky's name.

FAMILY SUBMITTED PHOTO

Harry and Virginia Lehotsky on their wedding day in 1982.

Lehotsky, (left) with Mona Wonnacott, Carlos Scott and Ralph Mueller, at a house Lehotsky's ministry bought to renovate.

PHIL HOSSACK / WINNIPEG FREE PRESS ARCHIVES

KEN GIGLIOTTI / WINNIPEG FREE PRESS ARCHIVES

Lehotsky poses at a Furby Street house his ministry hoped to make part of its affordable housing project.

But the young man who believed he had a debt to the Lord was undaunted. Harry Lehotsky eventually entered a Baptist seminary. Driven by a calling to work in an inner-city parish, he went through seminary postings in Boston, Chicago and Sioux Falls, where he met Virginia.

Nine months after their first date, they married.

The young couple's move to Winnipeg in 1983 was one Virginia Lehotsky undertook reluctantly. She didn't know anyone in Manitoba, and nothing could have prepared her for starting a church from scratch in a neighbourhood better known for drug dealers, gang members and prostitutes.

Their arrival in the city changed the course of their lives and helped transform Winnipeg's West End.

Before his death from pancreatic cancer in 2006, the 49-year-old Lehotsky had become a driving force in a movement to reclaim his community. He was as much a community activist as a preacher. He battled bureaucracies and made enemies, gave solace to the unloved and was relentless in his crusade for social justice.

"I thought I was going to meet a grizzled old navy veteran from the Bowery," says Rev. Larry Gregan, who knew of Lehotsky's reputation before they met. "I'd heard so much about him. But he was a boy!"

Gregan is now senior pastor at New Life Ministries, the church that began in the main floor of the Lehotskys' Ellice Avenue home. Those early days were

tough going. Some Sundays, only three chairs were pushed together into a prayer circle.

The family — which expanded to eldest son Matthew and twins Brandon and Jared — lived upstairs. Church meetings and services took up what is now a lovely kitchen, living room and dining room in the home where Virginia still lives.

The church eventually outgrew the house and moved into a permanent church building on Maryland Street.

Gregan says Lehotsky inspired his own mission.

"He came into the world with a certain inner drive and persistence," says Gregan. "There was a heaping helping of grace."

The pastor talks about Lehotsky's passion for bas-

Lehotsky worked to drive out the prostitutes and drugs from his neighbourhood.

KEN WONG fought to keep hosting a **massage parlour** in one of his Chinatown buildings...

MIKE APORIUS / WINNIPEG FREE PRESS ARCHIVES

Lehotsky stands at the door to an apartment building on Young Street that his work crew, above, was renovating.

MIKE DEAL / WINNIPEG FREE PRESS ARCHIVES

ketball as an example of his can-do attitude. As a boy, Lehotsky would go out on the New York streets and be beaten badly at the game.

"He'd go home, go into his parents' garage, close the door and practise madly," says Gregan. "He'd come back out, having figured out a few things. Now, he'd win sometimes."

Lehotsky first sprang to public attention in Winnipeg when he began to hold "prayer walks" through his new neighbourhood. After Bible study, he and his nascent flock would wander the streets, checking out boarded-up houses, pausing in front of drug houses and praying for solutions to the area's problems.

The walks brought New Life Ministries to the atten-

'The only thing Harry was afraid of was being afraid of something'

— Larry Gregan, senior pastor at New Life Ministries

'He loved the unloved'

— Virginia Lehotsky, widow of Harry Lehotsky

tion of drug dealers and other criminals. They also illustrated the desperate needs of the area to the young, dynamic minister.

Later, he encouraged area residents to copy down the licence plate numbers of johns' cars and posted them online.

Lazarus Housing was born in 1997. It was a project that saw 26 abandoned houses gutted, renovated and sold to low-income families. The Lehotskys' own house was the model as its transformation had been completed with volunteer labour and donated materials.

"The city planners called us the last-gasp housing, in the beginning," laughs Gregan.

Nehemiah Housing, an innovative not-for-profit property management company, began in 1998. It renovated and rented apartments, giving a wide variety of people safe, affordable places to live.

Other New Life Ministry initiatives included a free, private voice-mail system for West Enders who didn't

Lehotsky at the official unveiling of a mural on Maryland Street, a tribute to his work in the downtown area.

KEN GIGLIOTTI / WINNIPEG FREE PRESS ARCHIVES

have phones and the Ellice Street Cafe and Theatre, opened to give area residents a place to gather and get employment training.

Asked to describe her husband, Virginia Lehotsky reels off adjectives. Approachable. Caring. Sensitive. Capable, Ambitious. High-energy. Not easily overwhelmed.

She lowers her head.

"I knew that I was loved. That's what I remember most. That's what I miss most of all."

There were 2,000 people at Harry Lehotsky's November 2006 funeral.

In typical fashion, he had the last word.

In an emotional 30-minute video prepared in the weeks before his death, the rail-thin preacher gave an all-inclusive message of hope.

He began with a small smile and a joke.

"I admit this is a little bit weird," he said from the video screen. "It's not the last desperate act of a control freak. All I see this as is another way to speak to the people that I love, that have meant a lot to me and one more chance to say thank you and express the things again, reiterate some of the things we've talked about and lived for over so many years together."

First, he spoke directly to his wife.

"Virginia, 25 years ago almost now, coming to a place that was not your calling, it was my calling. That was a tough thing for you to do. I just kept pushing ahead.

"I just am so appreciative of the ways you were able to find a calling in the midst of someone else's calling."

And then to his sons, Matthew, Jared and Brandon:

"So much I've seen in you over the years and God has enabled me to see so much more. I remember from the earliest years when I'd sneak into your bedroom late at night and sometimes just kiss you on the forehead, sometimes just kneel by the bed not knowing what to say, other times just praying quietly by the side of the bed, for God to build everything into you, for us as parents, to make us good parents to you, and I pray that's

what we've been for you."

Lehotsky had words for his compatriots at New Life Ministries and for the people who worshipped with him, fought beside him and lived the dream of a safe inner-city neighbourhood.

"I can't imagine that I could have found a better place. God sure found the right place to put me and the right people to call into the building here with us. Together we have done some pretty amazing things."

"If you'd known me 30 years ago you'd say 'Man, is this kid messed-up. There's no way he's going to turn out good.' I thank God for what he made of my life.

"When it comes down to me, why me, why did I get cancer? Why not me? Am I something different than everyone else?"

He was different in so many ways large and small. But the beauty of Harry Lehotsky, the greatness in him, was he saw his life, his hard work and his enduring message of love and forgiveness as simply gifts from God.

And with that, he was free to be called home.

MIKE DEAL / WINNIPEG FREE PRESS ARCHIVES

Lehotsky greets a friend at a fundraising dinner in his honour in June 2006.

MANITOBA-NESS

ALTHOUGH he was born in New York and was fiercely proud of those origins, Rev. Harry Lehotsky spent most of his professional career in Winnipeg's West End. Part tireless community activist, part preacher, the dynamic Lehotsky formed New Life Ministries in 1983.

In the earliest days, church meetings were held on the main floor of the family's Ellice Avenue house while Harry, wife Virginia and their three children lived upstairs.

New Life Ministries vowed to be inclusive, welcoming everyone from drug users to sex-trade workers. At the same time, Lehotsky and his church worked to clean up the West End's streets, holding prayer walks, buying derelict buildings to renovate and sell and launching the Ellice Cafe and Theatre as a meeting place for isolated community residents.

5 THINGS YOU DIDN'T KNOW

1. Although he was only 5'9", Lehotsky loved basketball. He practised for hours as a teenager and coached a girls' team while he was in Bible college. He also coached his sons' teams.

2. He ran for the provincial Conservatives in 1999, losing to the NDP's MaryAnn Mihychuk.

3. For escape, he loved to read spy thrillers, especially the work of Robert Ludlum.

4. He spoke German fluently.

5. He regularly got up at 4:30 a.m. to go to work, showering in the church basement.

He inspired a nation

BY LARRY KUSCH

HE'S often named one of Canada's most inspirational icons, but Terry Fox's Grade 2 teacher recalls the future Canadian hero as "a very average kind of a boy" who sometimes got into mischief, but always owned up.

"I don't remember him being extremely over-intelligent and into books. He had a mischievous little smile and was always up to some little trick or other," said Jean Hanson, a.k.a. Miss Davidson when she taught Fox in 1965-66 at Wayoata School in Transcona.

"He was never sneaky or underhanded," she said. "He was just what I would call an all-around, average young boy at that age."

Terry Fox's future accomplishments were to be anything but average.

On April 12, 1980, three years after doctors located a malignant tumour in his right leg — which they then amputated 15 centimetres above the knee — he embarked on an ambitious cross-Canada run to raise money for cancer research and awareness of the disease.

Fox runs through Quebec City in June 1980 as part of his Marathon Of Hope.

A bronze statue of Terry Fox stands by the Peace Tower on Parliament Hill.

JACQUES NADEAU / THE CANADIAN PRESS ARCHIVES

TERRY FOX

30

GREATNESS

Fox's 1980 Marathon of Hope to raise money for cancer research and awareness of the disease inspired a nation and brought attention and support from around the world.

His accomplishments:

Ran 5,373 kilometres in 143 days, an average of 37.5 kilometres per day, with the aid of an artificial right leg.

His goal of raising $1 from every Canadian ($24.17 million) was accomplished by Feb. 1, 1981, five months after the premature end to his run outside Thunder Bay.

Awards and honours (a partial list):
Sept. 18, 1980 — Becomes youngest Companion of the Order of Canada.
Dec. 18, 1980 — Receives Lou Marsh Award for outstanding athletic accomplishment by Canadian sports editors.
July 17, 1981 — Mountain is named for Fox in the Rockies, 80 km west of Jasper.
Sept. 13, 1981 — Terry Fox Fitness Trail dedicated at Winnipeg's Assiniboine Park.
April 13, 1982 — Canada Post issues Terry Fox stamp, breaking with tradition of waiting 10 years until an honouree's death to do so.
June 26, 1982 — A 2.7-metre statue of Terry Fox is unveiled at Terry Fox Lookout, just off Terry Fox Courage Highway, west of Thunder Bay.

Continued on Page 199

Terry Fox shows his prosthetic leg to Prime Minister Pierre Trudeau in July 1980.

THE CANADIAN PRESS ARCHIVES

Fox runs through Ontario.

THE CANADIAN PRESS ARCHIVES

Fox's Marathon of Hope, aborted just west of Thunder Bay, when his cancer returned 143 days into the run, inspired and captivated the nation, raising more than $24 million. Since then, annual Terry Fox Runs in Canada and around the world have raised more than $400 million.

To Hanson, who remembers Fox as a conscientious student and "one of the nicest boys I ever had in class," there is an important lesson to be learned from this Greatest Manitoban's life. It's "that an average person can make a difference... that's what I keep in my heart about Terry."

TERRANCE Stanley Fox was born in Winnipeg on July 28, 1958. He was named after two uncles, one on each side of the family. Terry's father, Rolland, worked in various capacities for the Canadian National Railway, one of several successive generations of Foxes to be employed by the railway.

Terry's great-grandfather, William Adam Fox — whose ancestors came to North America from England in 1632 — put down roots in the Manitoba capital in 1913, when he became yardmaster of the Fort Rouge Yards. When Terry was a young child, his family lived near those yards, on Gertrude Avenue before moving to Transcona in the early '60s.

Rolland was one of eight children — four brothers and four sisters — and the family often picnicked at Assiniboine Park, on the west side of Winnipeg, where the large extended family had space to spread out. Terry's aunt, Nancy Wall, remembers that at one of those outings, the future marathoner, then a precocious child of about eight, badly injured his arm.

"There was a great amount of blood," Wall said, recalling the incident and the ride to Misericordia Hospital. "And you know, that boy never, ever cried. He just smiled — he must have been in a lot of pain, but he was just a happy kid." Wall, the eldest of Rolland Fox's siblings, said Terry reacted to his injury that day as if

he "wanted to put us at ease, not to cause us fright or problems."

The incident foreshadowed his stoic reaction to the pain he endured during the Marathon of Hope and in his brave battle with cancer.

ROBERT Frank, a Grade 12 pal and Fox's teammate on the Port Coquitlam High School basketball team, recalls Terry as a "good player" who was devoted to the sport.

"Terry was a little fanatical. He didn't come by his talent completely naturally. He worked at it really hard."

Terry and his family had moved to the British Columbia town east of Vancouver in 1966. Frank, now a supervisor with the British Columbia Liquor Board, recalled showing up at school with Fox, hours before classes began, to shoot hoops. The boys would also get a game going between classes or at lunch.

"We were always in the gym. We were gym rats," he said with a laugh.

Fox was painfully shy around girls, Frank recalls.

"Oh Lord, I had to work so hard to get his date for grad. It was insane," he said, chuckling again. "He was the shyest guy I ever met in my life. You could put him in a sport situation anywhere. He played soccer. He did a lot of things. But around girls, that was different."

The pair would go to the movies together and the occasional party. But after high school, they drifted apart. Frank went to school in Medicine Hat while Fox attended Simon Fraser University. When he learned that Fox had decided to embark on the Marathon of Hope, he thought his old buddy was "crazy" at first.

"Then it was just a real feeling of pride that he didn't just sit back and... (feel sorry for himself). He just got up and continued to live life and keep on going."

During 1983 — The Canadian Coast Guard dedicates its second most powerful ship to Fox's name.

Dec. 5, 1999 — Named second (to Pierre Trudeau) among the top 10 Canadian newsmakers of the 20th century.

Nov. 29, 2004 — Finishes second (to Tommy Douglas) in voting for The Greatest Canadian, a project launched by CBC television.

March 14, 2005 — Royal Canadian Mint unveils commemorative $1 Terry Fox coin.

His legacy:

To date more than $400 million has been raised for cancer research in Fox's name through the annual Terry Fox Run held across Canada and around the world.

Sept. 13, 1981 — The first Terry Fox Run attracts 300,000 participants in 760 communities in Canada and abroad.

Sept. 16, 2005 — More than 3 million students from more than 9,000 Canadian schools participate in the first Terry Fox National School Run Day, one of the largest events in the country's history.

By 2005, there were 14 schools and 15 roads in Canada named after Terry Fox.

Source: Terry Fox Foundation, Free Press archives

Terry Fox receives the Order of Canada from Govenor-General Edward Schreyer in September 1980

THE CANADIAN PRESS ARCHIVES

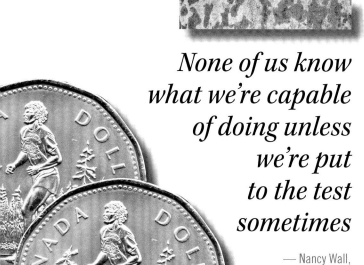

None of us know what we're capable of doing unless we're put to the test sometimes

— Nancy Wall,
Terry Fox's aunt

INITIALLY, Fox was devastated when told in late 1976, at age 18, that he had osteogenic sarcoma, a type of bone cancer. The survival rate at the time for the disease was only 50 to 75 per cent. But, according to a 1981 biography by Leslie Scrivener, Fox's old basketball coach planted the seeds for his historic run the day before his surgery when he dropped off a copy of *Runner's World*. The magazine carried a story about an above-the-knee amputee, Dick Traum, who had run in the New York marathon.

During his treatment, Fox had been moved and horrified by how cancer devastated those around him in hospital. A natural fighter who worked hard at everything he had ever done, Fox was wearing an artificial limb less than three weeks after his leg was amputated. Soon, he was playing wheelchair basketball, and later he took up running.

"In addition to the ordinary fatigue felt by two-legged runners, Terry had special problems," Scrivener wrote in her book *Terry Fox, His Story*. "His good leg suffered from the extra pounding he gave it. He developed blisters on his foot and cysts on his stump."

But his determination never flagged. By the time he began what he hoped would be a cross-Canada trek in the spring of 1980, he had logged 3,159 miles (5,082 kilometres) in training.

"**T**HE first few miles were the usual torture. My foot was blistered bad, but my stump wasn't too bad," Fox wrote in his diary on June 6, 1980, from Bristol, N.B.

"Today, I had tremendous support. Everybody honked and waved. People all over looked out of their homes and stores and cheered me on."

Fox, accompanied by younger brother Darrell and good friend Doug Alward in a van donated by Ford, received enthusiastic support in Atlantic Canada, a lukewarm response in Quebec and rock-star treatment in Ontario as the magnitude of his accomplishment started to sink in. Burned into the memory of anyone old enough to recall film footage of the time was his unusual gait — a double hop with his left leg followed by a long step with his artificial limb.

When he reached Toronto on July 11, 10,000 people greeted him in Nathan Phillips Square.

A Toronto newspaper had flown in the rest of the Fox family from British Columbia for a surprise reunion. "I still to this day remember the feeling of anticipation and excitement at seeing him," said his younger sister Judith, who was 15 at the time. The family went out to breakfast, and was amazed at how much food her now-celebrity brother could wolf down.

"It always was a joke that Terry would order everything on the left side and the right side of the menu," Judith said with a laugh.

ON Sept. 1, just outside Thunder Bay, Fox was forced to abandon his run after 5,373 km. He suffered from shortness of breath and a powerful pain in his chest. Tests detected cancer in his lungs.

There had been great anticipation among Fox's family in Winnipeg about his arrival in the Manitoba capital, and the reception he would receive in his original hometown. "All of us family, and I don't know how many others, were going to meet him on the road, coming into Winnipeg by the Perimeter (Highway)," his Aunt Nancy recalled. Instead, there was heartbreak.

Fox, back row second from left, in his Grade 2 class photo at Wayoata School in Transcona, school year 1965-66.

And by June 28 the following year, Fox had succumbed to his terrible disease, a month shy of his 23rd birthday.

Terry Fox, by then a symbol of courage and determination, inspired an annual run that in 2007 saw 150,771 participants in 856 communities across Canada raise just more than $20 million for cancer research.

Not bad for an "average" boy from Transcona.

But then as his Aunt Nancy says, "None of us knows what we're capable of doing unless we're put to the test sometimes."

MANITOBA-NESS

TERRANCE Stanley Fox, whose courageous run to raise funds for cancer research endeared him to millions of Canadians, was born in Winnipeg on July 28, 1958.

Terry's father, Rolland, worked for the Canadian National Railway — one of several successive generations of Foxes to be employed by the railway.

Terry's great-grandfather, William Adam Fox — whose ancestors came to North America from England in 1632 — put down roots in the Manitoba capital in 1913, when he became yardmaster of the Fort Rouge Yards. When Terry was a young child, his family lived near those yards on Gertrude Avenue before moving to Transcona in the early 1960s.

Betty Fox, Terry's mother, grew up in Melita. She has a brother who lives in Selkirk. A number of Terry's relatives on both sides of the family still live in Manitoba.

Terry attended Wayoata School in Transcona through Grade 2, before his family moved to British Columbia.

5 THINGS YOU DIDN'T KNOW

1. As a teenager Fox was painfully shy around girls, so shy that his pals had to line up his grad date.

2. Fox was named after his Uncle Terry, his dad's brother, now a retired salesman living in Lethbridge. The elder Fox's siblings teasingly call him "the original Terry Fox."

3. His sister Judith says Terry was "very funny," and his sense of humour "probably helped get him through a lot of his days." He and his brother Darrell, she says, would speak in funny voices and pretend they understood each other.

4. At Simon Fraser University, Fox chose kinesiology, the study of human movement, as a major. In his last year of high school, he received mostly As, except for a B in English.

5. Out on the road, Terry and his companions would mark the marathoner's progress by driving a stake into the ground at the end of the day, returning to that spot early the next morning to resume their journey.

Fox is silhouetted by a police escort as he resumes his Marathon of Hope through southern Ontario in July 1980.

PETER MARTINI / THE CANADIAN PRESS ARCHIVES

'She was definitely the woman of the Games'

— International Olympic Committee president Jacques Rogge speaking to reporters about Klassen just before the closing ceremonies in Turin, Feb. 25, 2006

MATT DUNHAM / THE ASSOCIATED PRESS ARCHIVES

BY PAUL WIECEK

'Woman of the Games

S HE is nothing less than Canada's greatest Olympian.

But as formidable as Cindy Klassen's accomplishments are — a Canadian record of six Olympic medals, including five in the 2006 Winter Games in Turin — so, too, is the unorthodox and unusually difficult path Klassen took to get to the medal podium so many times.

It is one thing, a remarkable thing to be sure, to win six Olympic medals — one gold, two silver, three bronze, in Klassen's case. But it is quite another thing, a nearly impossible thing, to achieve that kind of domination in a sport you took up at the relatively advanced age of 18.

And yet, that is precisely what Klassen did in speed skating, turning heads around the world in a sport she took up at a time many competitive teen athletes are winding up and, even then, only after abandoning national-calibre careers in three other sports.

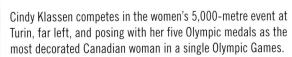

Cindy Klassen competes in the women's 5,000-metre event at Turin, far left, and posing with her five Olympic medals as the most decorated Canadian woman in a single Olympic Games.

MATT DUNHAM / THE ASSOCIATED PRESS ARCHIVES

GREATNESS

With six medals, Cindy Klassen is Canada's most decorated Olympian.

Bronze — 2002 Salt Lake City — 3,000 metres
Bronze — 2006 Turin — 3,000 metres
Bronze — 2006 Turin — 5,000 metres
Silver — 2006 Turin — 1,000 metres
Silver— 2006 Turin — Team pursuit
Gold — 2006 Turin — 1,500 metres

No Canadian prior to Klassen had ever won five medals in a single Olympic Games.

Klassen has also excelled at the World Speed Skating Championships. Here's a partial list of her accomplishments at that annual event:

Gold — 2003 Gothenburg — All around
Gold — 2005 Inzell — 1,500 metres
Gold — 2005 Inzell — 3,000 metres
Gold — 2006 Calgary — All around

JODY MOROZ / WINNIPEG FREE PRESS ARCHIVES

Klassen, seven years old, left, played defence for the 1986 Gateway Community Club.
Long track speed skater, above, on the provincial team in 1999.

FAMILY SUBMITTED PHOTO

Indeed, such is the remarkable tale of Klassen and such is her almost unparalleled versatility, that it is now mostly forgotten that long before Klassen was on the national speed skating team, she was on the national junior women's hockey team.

And the national women's in-line speed skating team. And the national women's lacrosse team.

Consider this: In addition to all her other records, Klassen also has the distinction of being one of just a tiny number of athletes anywhere in the world to have competed in the Commonwealth Games (lacrosse), the Pan Am Games (in-line skating) and the Winter Olympics (speed skating).

But it was Klassen's failure to get to a major Games in her fourth sport, hockey, that ultimately set the course of her remarkable life.

In a career full of what-ifs — What if Klassen had stuck with lacrosse? What if she'd been cut just a tiny bit deeper in a horrifying skating accident in 2003? — the biggest what-if of all is still this: What if Klassen had made the 1998 Canadian women's hockey team that won silver in Nagano instead of being one of the team's final cuts?

Even Klassen doesn't know the answer to that one.

"It's funny you'd ask because I've thought a lot about that," Klassen says. "I do wonder if I would still be play-

KEN GIGLIOTTI / WINNIPEG FREE PRESS ARCHIVES

Klassen displays her custom-made Olympic skates.

KEN GIGLIOTTI / WINNIPEG FREE PRESS ARCHIVES

Klassen promotes sports to kids in Churchill in July 2007.

ing hockey or what I would be doing now. Who knows? "It's hard to say. Maybe. It is kind of neat thinking how things might have been different in my life."

And, for that matter, the lives of everyone who sat transfixed for those two remarkable weeks in February 2006 as Klassen's exploits at Oval Lingotto in Turin made Winnipeg and Manitoba household words in homes from Shanghai to Sao Paolo, St. Petersburg to Saskatoon.

THERE was intense pressure on Cindy Klassen as she boarded a plane for Italy in February 2006.

She was already an Olympic medal-winner — she won bronze in Salt Lake City in 2002 — and she'd only gotten better in the intervening years. In 2003, she became the first Canadian in 27 years to win the overall title at the World Speed Skating Championships. Even three years out of Turin, there was already talk that Klassen might do something very special in Italy.

But then one morning in late October 2003, Klassen got the scare of her life. She fell going around a corner during a workout and slid into another skater, her arm catching the other skater's razor-sharp blade.

And then the world went black. A massive gash across

Klassen's right forearm had severed 12 tendons, some nerves and an artery. Blood pouring out of the huge wound, one of her coaches slapped the skater across the face repeatedly as he tried in vain to keep her conscious.

Klassen would remember later awakening, looking at all the concerned people standing over her and asking her coach: "Am I going to die?"

She not only didn't die, she thrived. Looking back on that time, three years later on the eve of Turin, Klassen told the *Free Press* the accident was a blessing that gave her time to reflect, rest and read her Bible.

Klassen is a Mennonite and she refers frequently to God in her interactions with reporters and the public.

She has said repeatedly that she believes her life is in the hands of God and all the things that have happened to her — good and bad — have been part of His broader plan for her.

And that includes her failure to make the 1998 national women's hockey team. It would have been the culmination of years of effort in the Winnipeg minor hockey system — including several years on elite boys' teams — and Klassen says to this day she believed she had made the national team that winter and was stunned when she was cut.

It was the first time Klassen could be said to have truly failed at something in sport, and it staggered her so deeply her story easily could have ended there, another promising athlete who got close but not close enough. But then her parents, Jake and Helga Klassen, intervened, encouraging their daughter to take up speed skating, if only to provide her a diversion from the disappointment.

Klassen has said she put on her first pair of clap skates very reluctantly. The unique skates that speed skaters use felt completely different from hockey skates, and she says she burned with embarrassment when children blew by her as she stumbled through her first few thousand laps at the Sargent Park speed skating oval in Winnipeg's West End.

And then there was the skin-tight clothing that goes hand in hand with speed skating but that Klassen — having spent so much time in the macho world of boys' hockey — found humiliating.

"All of my training for 13 years had been geared to hockey, and this was so different," Klassen would later tell a reporter. "There were still those weird outfits... For the better part of my first year in speed skating, I went against the grain and wore very baggy clothes."

It was an inauspicious start to what would become, less than a decade later, something historic.

Her coaches complained at first that she speed-skated like a hockey player. And even as she racked up the medals, one after another, in Turin, there were still times when, if you shut your eyes for a moment, you could picture Klassen skating up centre ice of some hockey rink in Winnipeg, a puck seemingly taped to her stick.

Her father once told a reporter that his daughter was born with a severe case of colic and spent her first three months howling through the night. The experience, Jake Klassen would say, steeled his daughter to the pain she'd have to endure en route to becoming the country's greatest Olympian.

And to becoming, now, one of Manitoba's greatest-ever citizens. Klassen is the only athlete in the collection of remarkable Manitobans you hold in your hand — a remarkable achievement coming out of a province that has produced the likes of Hockey Hall of Famers Terry Sawchuk and Billy Mosienko and fellow Olympian Clara Hughes.

"That's a huge honour," Klassen says. "But I'm surprised because there are so many Manitobans who've had such an impact on people's lives, not only in Canada but around the world. That's amazing."

Klassen says she's humbled by her selection as, effectively, the province's greatest athlete and she says she ventures that she might not have been a greatest anything if she hadn't first been a Manitoban.

"Manitoba is just a great province to grow up as an athlete," she says. "And this is funny, but I think one of the reasons is the harsh climate. In speed skating for sure, where we're outside all the time, we really have to tough it out. So when we do compete, we're pretty fierce competitors."

How very Manitoban of this, one of the greatest Manitobans, to say so.

Klassen was Canada's female athlete of the year in 2006.

Klassen drops the puck at the MTS Centre in March 2006.

Klassen is awarded an honorary degree from the University of Manitoba in October 2006.

1. That bison you see with Klassen in those MTS commercials is really there. "It's really neat. They're massive and they're really soft," says Klassen. "Doing the commercials, that's the first time I've actually been up close to a bison. They're incredible animals. It's fun."

2. Klassen credits her earlier experience in team sports such as lacrosse and hockey with making her the speed skater she's become. "I think that everything I did before this helped me get to where I am today," she says. "I think playing team sports was really important. Speed skating, even though it's an individual sport, has a lot of team elements. We train together and we're all teammates, and we all push each other to do the best we can."

3. Klassen laughed during the 2006 Winter Olympics when she was asked where she'd display her six Olympic medals when she got home. "Maybe in a closet," she said.

4. As a hockey player growing up in Winnipeg, Klassen used to make fun of the skin-tight suits speed skaters wear.

5. Klassen's first introduction to sport came at age two when her father made a wooden hockey stick for her.

BORIS MINKEVICH / WINNIPEG FREE PRESS ARCHIVES

Klassen, above, holds the sign for a street named in her honour in 2006. Klassen, right, on her tricycle at two years old.

MANITOBA-NESS

CINDY Klassen was born in Winnipeg, learned to skate in Winnipeg — first as a hockey player and later as a speed skater — and she continues to spend much of her summers living in Manitoba, while training in Calgary the rest of the year.

Klassen credits the bitterly cold training sessions she endured as a teenager on the outdoor oval at Sargent Park for toughening her up and giving her the fortitude to fight through the gruelling pain that comes with skating long-distance races.

She is a descendant of Mennonite immigrants and she remains close to her family, who continue to reside in Winnipeg. In 2008, Klassen abruptly cancelled her skating season to fly home to Winnipeg to be with her sister, Lisa, who had been badly injured in a car accident.

The skater maintains a large public profile in Manitoba and is frequently seen on TV and on billboards in her role as a spokeswoman for MTS. The endorsement deal is worth an estimated $1 million to Klassen and is believed to be the most lucrative ever for a Canadian amateur athlete.

Klassen, already Canada's most decorated Olympian, is again considered a leading medal hope for the nation at the 2010 Vancouver Winter Games.

FAMILY SUBMITTED PHOTO

You are the One

BY DARREN GUDMUNDSON

You are the one.

You work in the sunshine and play in the rain.

When it's 40 below, you persevere, don't complain.

The summer brings mosquitoes, you wince as they bite.

But you enjoy the good weather before the long night.

You welcome others from around the world.

You share, you donate, you contribute, you engage.

Though you may leave this land of endless sky,
you take with you the pride, the joy, the sense of belonging — of knowing,
that through your contributions Manitobans will keep growing.

You are the Greatest Manitoban of all, for you know the accomplishments
of others can only be achieved by the contributions you have made
to this community we call Manitoba.

BIBLIOGRAPHY

We gleaned the stories in this book from human memories, archives, oral histories and the printed page.
If you enjoyed them, here are books you might also enjoy.

LLOYD AXWORTHY

Navigating a New World
by Lloyd Axworthy, Knopf Canada, 2003

Axworthy Then and Now
by Noelle Boughton, Winnipeg Magazine, published by the Winnipeg Sun, May 1984

Lloyd Axworthy
by Bruce Wallace, Maclean's, Dec. 1, 1997

DR. BRUCE CHOWN AND DR. JOHN BOWMAN

Winnipeg Free Press archives

A Vision Fulfilled: The Story of the Children's Hospital of Winnipeg
by Harry Medovy, Peguis Publishers Ltd., 1979

NARANJAN DHALLA

CV Network, Vol 5 – No 3.

Winnipeg Free Press archives

India Abroad magazine, June 2008

Manitoba Court of Queen's Bench, 1988, CI88-01-29267 Curriculum Vitae, Naranjan Dhalla

TOMMY DOUGLAS

Sources: Archives of Manitoba, The Canadian Press, Tommy Douglas Research Institute, Winnipeg Free Press archives, Brandon University Alumni News

TERRY FOX

Terry Fox: His Story
by Leslie Scrivener, McClelland & Stewart, Toronto, 1981

The Terry Fox Foundation website

Henderson's Winnipeg City Directory 1958-1965

THE GUESS WHO

Winnipeg Free Press archives

American Woman: The Story of The Guess Who
by John Einarson, Quarry Press, 1995 The Millennium in Manitoba, by the Winnipeg Free Press

ELIJAH HARPER

Elijah: No Ordinary Hero
by Pauline Comeau, Douglas & McIntyre, 1993

A Deal Undone: The Making and Breaking of the Meech Lake Accord
by Andrew Cohen, Douglas and McIntyre, 1990

STEVE JUBA

Winnipeg Free Press archives (Free Press and Winnipeg Tribune articles)

Juba
Michael Czuboka, Communigraphics, 1986

CINDY KLASSEN

Skater Cindy Klassen: Speed Queen
by Ken MacQueen, Maclean's, March 1, 2006.

Cindy Klassen Speeding for His Sake
Shirley Byers, www.canadianchristianity.com, undated.

Cindy Klassen returns home to visit injured sister, www.ctvwinnipeg.ca, Feb. 8, 2008.

STANLEY KNOWLES

The Man from Winnipeg North Centre
Susan Mann Trofimenkoff, Western Producer Prairie Books, 1982

TOM LAMB

Tom Lamb's Memoirs
100 pages, family document, unpublished, written 1960s

Tom Lamb and His Backwoods Empire
by Harold Hilliard, Star Weekly magazine, October, 1952

The Last Great Frontiersman: The Remarkable Adventures of Tom Lamb
by Leland Stowe, Stoddart, 1982

First Family of Flight
by Bill Redekop, Winnipeg Free Press, March 09, 2008

Muskrat Resettlement Project
by Jerome Beatty, The American Mercury magazine, New York, December 1940

NELLIE MCCLUNG

Canadian Women: A History
by Alison Prentice, Paula Bourne, Gail Cuthbert Brandt, Beth Light, Wendy Mitchinson, Naomi Black, Harcourt Brace & Company Canada, 1988

The Canadians: Nellie McClung
by Mary Lile Benham, Fitzhenry & Whiteside Limited, 2000

Nellie McClung: Voice for the Voiceless
by Margaret Macpherson, XYZ Publishing, 2003

Nellie McClung: The Complete Autobiography
Edited by Veronica Strong-Boag and Michelle Lynn Rosa, Broadview Press Ltd., 2003 (Clearing in the West originally printed 1935 and The Stream Runs Fast in 1945)

Our Nell
By Candace Savage, Goodread Biographies, 1979

Firing the Heather
by Mary Hallett & Marilyn Davis, Fifth House Ltd., 1993

MARSHALL MCLUHAN

Speaking of Winnipeg
Marshall McLuhan interview by Danny Finkleman, edited by John Parr, Queenston House, 1974.

Marshall McLuhan: Escape into Understanding
by W. Terrence Gordon, Stoddart, 1997

Marshall McLuhan: Wise Guy
by Judith Fitzgerald, XYZ Publishing 2001

Marshall McLuhan: The Medium and the Messenger
by Philip Marchand, Vintage Canada 1989.

The Playboy Interview: Marshall McLuhan
Playboy Magazine (March 1969 ©, 1994 by Playboy)

LEO MOL

Leo Mol Sculpture Garden
by Paul Duval, Leo Mol Sculpture Garden Trust, 1993

PEGUIS

Peguis, A Noble Friend
by Donna G. Sutherland, Chief Peguis Heritage Park, 2003

Illegal Surrender of St. Peter's Reserve
Report by T.A.R.R. Centre of Manitoba Inc., 1983

Public Archives of Canada. St. Peters Indian Reserve
Report of the Commissioner Hon. Chief Justice Howell, 1906

JAMES A. RICHARDSON

The Story of a Pioneering Spirit, Celebrating 150 Years
James Richardson & Sons, Limited, 2007

LOUIS RIEL

Louis Riel v. Canada,
by J.M. Bumsted, 2001

The Birth of Western Canada: A History of the Riel Rebellions,
by George Stanley

The False Traitor: Louis Riel in Canadian Culture
by Albert Braz Myth, 2003

Louis Riel: A Comic Strip Biography
by Chester Brown, 2003

DUFF ROBLIN

Speaking For Myself: Politics and Other Pursuits
by Duff Roblin, Great Plains Publishers, 1999

DUFF ROBLIN

Speaking For Myself: Politics and Other Pursuits
by Duff Roblin, Great Plains Publishers, 1999

ANNE ROSS

Clinic with a Heart: The Story of Mount Carmel Clinic
by Anne G. Ross, Rinella Printers Ltd., 1998

Pregnant and Alone
by Anne Ross, McClelland and Stewart, 1978

ED SCHREYER

A View from the Ledge: An Insider's Look at the Schreyer Years
by Herb Schulz, 2005
The Government of Edward Schreyer: Democratic Socialism in Manitoba
by James McAllister, 1984

CAROL SHIELDS

A Memoir of Friendship: The Letters Between Carol Shields and Blanche Howard
edited by Blanche Howard and Allison Howard, Viking Canada, 2007

Jane Austen: A Life
by Carol Shields, Penguin Books, 2001

Random Illuminations: Conversations with Carol Shields
by Eleanor Wachtel, Goose Lane, 2007

FRANK SKINNER

Horticultural Horizons: Plant Breeding and Introduction at Dropmore, Manitoba
by Frank Leith Skinner, M.B.E. LL.d, F.R.M.S. Published by the Manitoba Department of Agriculture and Conservation, 1967

Dr. Frank Leith Skinner
booklet published by Manitoba Department of Cultural Affairs and Historical Resources, 1981

The Plant Genius of Dr. Frank Skinner
by Wilbert Ronald, Alberta Gardener, Centennial Issue Vol. 4, Issue 3, 2005

Dictionary of Manitoba Biography
by J. M. Bumsted. Published by University of Manitoba Press, 1999

The Encyclopedia of Manitoba
Ingeborg Boyens, managing editor, Great Plains Publications, 2007

SIR WILLIAM STEPHENSON

The True Intrepid: Sir William Stephenson And The Unknown Agents
by Bill Macdonald, Raincoast Books, 2001

J.S. WOODSWORTH

The Historical Woodsworth And Contemporary Politics
scholarly article by Allen Mills, U of W politics professor

Winnipeg Free Press Archives

Canadian Encyclopedia (Historica) online edition

Time Links historical website

Manitoba Historical Society website

They, too, were Great Manitobans

BIG BEAR
Aboriginal leader, pioneer, negotiator

FAST FACTS:

Chief of the Plains Cree First Nation during the latter half of the 1800s.

Also known as Chief Mistashimaskwa.

Employed mostly non-violent means in pursuit of justice for aboriginals from the Canadian government.

His conviction for the Frog Lake Massacre is widely regarded as a miscarriage of justice.

He was released early from Stony Mountain Penitentiary due to failing health and died soon after.

MARGARET LAURENCE
Author, social activist

FAST FACTS:

Born in Neepawa, she studied at Winnipeg's United College.

Her most famous book, *The Stone Angel*, is set in a small Manitoba town and draws deeply on her Prairie roots.

She won a Governor General's Award in 1967 and was later made a Companion of the Order of Canada.

In her later years, she spoke out on social issues, including nuclear disarmament.

BALDUR ROSMUND STEFANSSON
Scientist, Father of Canola

FAST FACTS:

While working at the University of Manitoba, he led the development of a variety of rapeseed that could be transformed into the edible oil now known as canola.

He has many honours, including an Officer of the Order of Canada, the Icelandic Order of the Falcon and induction into the Canadian Agricultural Hall of Fame.

FRANK H. GUNSTON
Developed the artificial knee

FAST FACTS:

Gunston, with an engineering degree and a medical degree, used both disciplines to develop the first artificial human knee in 1968.

He refused to patent the idea because he wanted it to be as widely available as possible.

He went on to develop other joint replacements.

In 1989, he received the $100,000 Manning Principal Award as one of Canada's top innovators.

GABRIELLE ROY
Author

FAST FACTS:

She won three Governor General Awards for her writing.

She was born, raised and worked in St. Boniface before moving away at 28.

While her career as a writer did not begin in earnest until she left, Prairie themes and the world of the immigrants she met while living in Winnipeg dominated her work.

She was one of the first Canadian authors to be recognized internationally and is a Companion of the Order of Canada.

E. CORA HIND
Agricultural expert, newspaper pioneer

FAST FACTS:

Western Canada's first female journalist.

Agricultural editor for the *Winnipeg Free Press* from 1901-37.

Her yield estimates for Canada's wheat were so accurate, they influenced world markets.

In 1909, she missed by only 0.5 per cent on a 118,719,000-bushel crop.

Upon her death in 1942, Mackenzie King proclaimed her "one of the greatest of Canadian women."

Terrorized editors.

ETIENNE GABOURY
Architect

FAST FACTS:

A descendent of Louis Riel.

Born in Swan Lake into a family of 11 children.

Studied at the University of Manitoba and won a bursary to the famous Ecole Des Beaux Arts in Paris.

Designed more than 300 buildings around the world.

His Winnipeg works include the Royal Canadian Mint, Eglise du Precieux-Sang, the St. Boniface Cathedral and the Provencher Bridge.

HAROLD BUCHWALD
Prominent lawyer, activist, volunteer

FAST FACTS:

Co-founded law firm Pitblado.

Headed provincial law society.

Tax reform advocate.

Presided over many boards, including the Health Sciences Centre Foundation, the Canadian Consumer Council and the Winnipeg Symphony Orchestra.

Member of the Order of Canada.

JOHN WESLEY DAFOE
Newspaper editor

FAST FACTS:

Widely regarded as one of the most influential Canadian journalists in history.

Edited the *Manitoba/Winnipeg Free Press* from 1901 until his death in 1944.

His editorials were considered must-reads in Ottawa and throughout the Commonwealth at a time when the *Free Press* was considered one of the world's premier newspapers.

Predicted the start of the Second World War in 1939.

ARNOLD SPOHR
Ballet dancer, choreographer and artistic director of the Royal Winnipeg Ballet

FAST FACTS:

Danced with the Winnipeg Ballet 1945-54, becoming a principal dancer.

Served as executive director of the Royal Winnipeg Ballet 1958-88 and is widely credited with helping form its reputation as one of Canada's most acclaimed performing arts groups.

Promoted in 2003 to Companion of the Order of Canada, the highest rank.

JOHN HIRSCH
Founder, Manitoba Theatre Centre

FAST FACTS:

Born in Hungary, came to Winnipeg as a refugee after the Second World War.

Founded MTC in 1958 and was its first artistic director.

Later became artistic director of the Stratford Festival and head of TV drama for CBC.

His stage productions in New York and Los Angeles received many awards, including the New York Drama Critics' Circle Award, the Obie Award and the Outer Circle Critics Award.